Kingbird
Highway

The Story of a Natural Obsession
That Got a Little Out of Hand

Kenn Kaufman

A Mariner Book

HOUGHTON MIFFLIN COMPANY

Boston   New York

First Mariner Books edition 2000

Visit our Web site: www.hmco.com/trade.

Library of Congress Cataloging-in-Publication Data

Kaufman, Kenn.
Kingbird highway : the story of a natural obsession that got
a little out of hand / Kenn Kaufman.
p. cm.
ISBN 0-395-77398-9
ISBN 0-618-06235-1 (pbk.)
1. Bird watching — United States — Anecdotes.   2. Bird watching —
Mexico — Anecdotes.   3. Adventure and adventurers — United States —
Biography.   4. Adventure and adventurers — Mexico — Biography.
5. Kaufman, Kenn — Journeys — United States.   6. Kaufman, Kenn —
Journeys — Mexico.   7. United States — Description and travel.
8. Mexico — Description and travel.   I. Title.
QL682.K38   1997
598'.07'23473—dc21   97-581   CIP

Book design and ornaments by Anne Chalmers.
Type is Sabon, an Adobe Postscript Type.

Printed in the United States of America

QUM 10 9 8 7 6 5 4 3 2 1

Kingbird Highway

Ted Parker was not destined to slow down, ever.
He was like a runaway train,
except that he was running on tracks that
he had planned out for himself, and he knew
exactly where he was going.

Table of Contents

Capitalizing of Birds' Names

BECAUSE so many kinds of birds are mentioned in this book, we have followed standard scientific practice of capitalizing the names of species. Ornithologists and serious birders find that such capitalizing brings clarity in discussing the nearly 10,000 species of birds in the world. For example, there are dozens of kinds of blue jays around the globe, but the Blue Jay is a particular species that lives mainly in eastern North America. Any trogon might be described as elegant, but the Elegant Trogon is a specific type. In a similar vein, we can write of "western ducks" and mean all the ducks of the West, but the capitalization of "Western Tanager" signals that we are discussing one particular species. Readers who are unfamiliar with birding may find all these capital letters jarring at first, but we hope that they will be able to glide over them smoothly after a few chapters.

Preface

PEOPLE always called us "birdwatchers." But if we had been, there would be no story to tell.

Nothing could have been simpler than "birdwatching." An activity by that name would have required nothing more than one person, alone, watching birds, any birds. The birds rarely would have watched the person in return: perfectly independent, birds had no reason to care about humans. So the watching would have been one-way, and the matter would have ended there, with no ramifications.

But in the early 1970s, we were not birdwatching. We were *birding,* and that made all the difference. We were out to seek, to discover, to chase, to learn, to find as many different kinds of birds as possible — and, in friendly competition, to try to find more of them than the next birder. We became a *community* of birders, with the complications that human societies always have; and although it was the birds that had brought us together, our story became a human story after all.

People have always looked at birds, but the hobby and sport of birding really developed in the twentieth century. It developed gradually, for the most part, with only a few landmark events, like the invention (in the 1930s) of the modern field guide for recognizing birds. But there was one brief period when birding went through revolutionary changes. Improvements in communication and in travel made it possible for people to seek birds from coast to coast, and birding changed from a mild local pastime to a continent-wide craze. It is only now, looking back from a distance of two decades, that we can see how far-reaching and thorough the changes were. Birding for the 1990s — indeed, birding for the twenty-first century — was born in the brief period from 1970 to 1975.

This is a story about that time. I was fortunate enough to be traveling throughout North America, in pursuit of birds, during that formative era. It was a good time to be on the road, a good time to be very young, a good time to learn and travel and grow while we played this great new game called birding.

Kingbird Highway

Not Quite the West

I WENT OUT on the road, to chase my dream, at the age of nine.

That was what I used to tell the girls I met while I was bumming rides around North America in the 1970s; and, of course, they didn't believe me any more than you do. But the truth is that the seeds for all my later travels were planted on my ninth birthday. That was the day the family moved, the day the last thing was packed and we drove away from the house in Indiana for the last time.

That day's drive still comes to mind with surprising clarity: the tree-lined streets of South Bend falling away behind us, the country opening up, the Illinois state line coming up as a milestone to be remarked upon. My father pointing things out and explaining things: the construction of the bridges, the uses of the farm machinery, the history behind the "Land of Lincoln" signs. My mother, so good with words, making up little poems and word games to amuse the kids in the back seat.

Always the quiet and introverted one, I was quieter than usual that day, sitting in the back and staring out the window. My parents noticed and said once again they were sorry we had had to move on my birthday. But they need not have worried. Already a rebel in the quietest way, I had decided for myself that holidays or special days meant nothing if they were dictated by the calendar. Any day might be a special one — you just had to get outside and see if it was.

This was an incredibly special day because of where we were: out on the highway, with the tires drumming hypnotically on the pavement, and with new possibilities everywhere just beyond the wide horizon. That day I was first aware of feeling a significant difference from my parents and my brothers. They were thinking about our destination, mostly, or about the place we were leaving behind. I was focused on the road itself, on the feeling of going somewhere, anywhere, just going. As the sun moved down the western sky directly ahead of us, it seemed to draw us along. A crazy sense came over me that we should just follow the sun and keep pace with it, around and around the earth, and the day would never end.

And as long as the day was unending I would be staring out the car windows with all the intensity of a nine-year-old boy, scanning the fences, the wires, the open fields, the distant treetops, and the sky, because I had a purpose, a mission, a passion: I was watching for birds.

A curiosity about nature — or about picture books on nature — had come to me out of nowhere in earliest childhood. By the time I was six, having concluded that there were no tigers or comets or dinosaurs in our humdrum Indiana neighborhood, I had turned to birds as the best thing available. After that I had never looked back. My interest became a driving force, fueled by books from the local branch library, encouraged by parents who promoted any genuine learning and so had refused for years to have a television in the house.

The other boys in my neighborhood idolized baseball players or movie cowboys, but my hero was the great bird expert, Roger Tory Peterson. I had checked his books out from the library and read them over and over again. I had studied all of his paintings, especially of the birds I could not find in the South Bend suburbs. When my parents started to talk about moving, my first thought was "New birds!"

Poring over Peterson's bird guides every night, I had figured out something that seemed important: every bird had its place. None was "free as a bird." A few kinds were found all over the continent, but they were the exceptions. Many birds were regional, found only in the South, for example, or only in the West. Some were limited to only a few small areas. Still others were rare visitors to North America. But no two species seemed to have quite the same range on the map, and no two places had quite the same birdlife. It followed that the way to see more kinds of birds was to go to more different places.

So when my father started casting around for employment possibilities in other states, I pestered him constantly for the latest news on the job front. Every time a new place was mentioned, I would look up everything I could find about the birding potential there.

There was brief discussion of a job in Seattle. I read about ancient mossy forests along the fog-shrouded coast, and about little seabirds called auklets and murrelets on the waters of Puget Sound. Then my parents also read some things about the area, and rainy Seattle was out: they were looking for a warm, *dry* climate. The job search, and my basic bird research, shifted to locales that were farther south and farther inland.

A job in Utah was considered, and I read about Sage Grouse strutting on sagebrush flats, and about flocks of shorebirds in the marshes of Bear River. Possibilities in California came up, and I read about sickle-billed California Thrashers skulking in the chaparral, and about the last of the California Condors sailing over wilderness crags. New Mexico held some promise for a while, and I read about Roadrunners dueling with rattlesnakes in the cactus gardens, about Western Tanagers flashing through the mountain pine forests like burnt gold, and about Prairie Falcons keeping lonely vigils on the plains.

Because they wanted a dry climate, my parents never really looked at anything in the eastern states — so my early reading focused on birds of the West. Years later I would realize that the East had some of the best birding on the continent; but as a bird-crazed kid of eight years old I was convinced that the West was the place to be.

And then the best job offer came from Wichita, Kansas. Farther west than Indiana, Kansas was not far enough over to have birdlife typical of the West. But that was where we moved.

At first the birds of suburban Kansas seemed pretty similar to those of suburban Indiana: mostly sparrows and starlings. But spring was coming, so I thought things might improve.

They did. One day when I was walking home from school I saw a bird the size of a robin, but patterned in pale yellow and gray, perched on a wire near my house. Running home, I grabbed my field guide (stubbornly, I used Peterson's *western* bird guide, even though Wichita was in the region covered by the eastern book) and rushed back to find the bird still there. Squinting first at the bird and then at the field guide pictures, I figured out what it was: a Western Kingbird. *Western* Kingbird! I was ecstatic. Maybe I was in the West after all. In that instant, the Western Kingbird became my favorite bird.

More kingbirds arrived over the following weeks. There were few large trees in our neighborhood, but the kingbirds built their nests against the crossarms of telephone poles and perched on the wires to survey the surroundings. They seemed utterly fearless. If a larger bird, such as a crow or a kestrel, came anywhere near their nest, the kingbirds would dart out at once with staccato sputtering cries, harassing or even attacking the bigger bird to drive it away.

During that summer and the next, I found many kingbird nests. I spent hours watching them and taking notes. I admired the aggressive exploits of the adult birds as they drove away predators or rivals, tried to see what kinds of insects they brought to feed their young, and watched the actions of the young birds when they left the nest and learned to fly.

I was not allowed too far from the nest myself then, so I couldn't find very many different kinds of birds. Those I did find, I spent a lot of time on: watching, drawing sketches, taking notes. But gradually I ranged farther afield, on foot and by bicycle. As I found more kinds of birds, and as I entered my teens, a new restlessness took over.

It began with knowing my birds well enough to know them at a distance: a Western Kingbird on a distant wire, a Lark Sparrow calling its metallic *chip* as it flew overhead, an Orchard Oriole singing its jumble of notes a block away. Soon I could predict where I would see them: the Warbling Vireos would be in willows along the canal, the Swainson's Hawks would be sailing over fields along Meridian Avenue, the Solitary Sandpipers would be lurking along the bank downriver from Herman Hill. With a

Western Kingbird

little planning, I could head out on my bike and see dozens of birds in one day — and the more I saw, the more I wanted to see.

One day I saw fifty different species, and I thought that was an unbeatable record for my little area; but then I hit sixty, and then seventy-five. Finally — at the height of spring migration, when flocks were passing through on their way north — I was able to break one hundred in a day.

For a lone kid on a bike in Kansas to see and hear a hundred kinds of birds in one day was, I felt, a real accomplishment. Even though it was just a game, it was a game based on knowledge; and the more I knew, the more I wanted to learn.

And the more I learned, the more I became dissatisfied with just seeing the birds in my neighborhood. I knew that North America had more than seven hundred species of birds, and I knew I could spend a lifetime birding in Kansas and not see more than half of them. Every bird had its place. If I wanted to see Snail Kites or Green Kingfishers or Painted Redstarts, I would have to go to where they lived. They were never going to come to me.

State law dictated that I had to stay in school until I was sixteen. As my sixteenth birthday approached, I began to dream of how much I could learn about birds by leaving school as soon as it was legal and heading out of the state. The fact that I would miss two and a half years of high school didn't bother me.

But it bothered some people. I made the mistake of mentioning my idea, offhandedly, to one of my teachers, and the next thing I knew I was in the school counselor's office.

"Why is this a big deal?" I wanted to know. "Tommy Wells dropped out a couple of months ago, and nobody said a word."

"Wells?" The counselor frowned. "Your friend Mr. Wells was not really applying himself to his studies or his grades. Now, your situation is different."

"I didn't say he was my friend. I hardly knew him. But did anyone try to keep him from dropping out?"

"Think about how that sounds," said the counselor. "Think about the word 'dropout.' Giving up. Dropping out. Do you want to be a loser? I've looked at your record . . . with your grades, and your honors classes, you'd have no trouble getting into college. And the student council at Truesdell last year — wouldn't you be ashamed of yourself if you went from student council president to dropout?"

"So you're saying Tommy didn't have good grades, so it's okay to let him drop out. That's backwards. If his grades were bad, maybe he needs a diploma more than I do."

"He was failing school."

"Or school was failing him," I shot back, and then was sorry I had said it. "Have you really looked at my record? I was the first student council prez to get kicked out of class for causing trouble. I was only elected because the rebels voted for me. Look, uh, Sir, I don't cause trouble when I'm studying things I want to learn. But I'm wasting my time in these classes."

By now he was angry and perplexed. "Do you want to waste your life instead? If you want to do anything in life, you have to at least finish high school! You're no different from everyone else!"

My silent response was: Listen, Jack, *everyone* is different from everyone else, and we ought to be celebrating that instead of squashing it. But out loud I just said that I was bored and needed more challenge. They bent the rules to put me into what was usually a senior honors class. There I flirted with the older girls, argued about literature with everyone, and got an A in the course. When the semester was over, I left school.

During June and July of that year — 1970, the year I turned sixteen — I worked as the nature instructor at a summer camp. In August, with money saved from that job, I hit the road.

There was a day at the end of August that held a special symbolism for me. Not that I did anything unusual that day: like the days before and after, I spent it looking at birds. That day was significant because I knew that, back at home, kids my age were going back to school.

They had the clang of locker doors in the halls of South High in

Wichita, Kansas. I had a nameless mountainside in Arizona, with sunlight streaming down among the pines, and Mexican songbirds moving through the high branches. My former classmates were moving toward their education, no doubt, just as I was moving toward mine, but now I was traveling a road that no one had charted out for me . . . and my adventure was beginning.

Finding the Road

IT WAS MY ninth birthday, with the family car rolling down the highway, when I saw them for the first time. I think I was silent and watchful as we passed the first one, and maybe the second and third. But eventually I had to ask. "Why are those men standing by the road holding their thumbs up?"

My parents always answered our questions with great care. At the time, we didn't know enough to appreciate it; my brothers and I probably assumed that everyone in the world was open-minded, fair, nonjudgmental. Mom or Dad would have replied: What those men were doing was called "hitchhiking." They were hoping to get rides.

With a curious kid, of course, one good answer leads to more questions. If these guys wanted to go somewhere, why didn't they drive cars? Why were all these people driving by and not giving them rides? For that matter, why weren't *we* stopping to give anyone a ride?

Again, the answers were careful and fair. Automobiles are expensive. A lot of people don't have them. There are plenty of reasons why a person might not be able to afford a car — maybe a run of bad luck, maybe lost a job; maybe just footloose and not wanting to work right now. Nothing wrong with that.

Ah, and why weren't we picking them up. Well. These hitch-hikers were probably all perfectly nice . . . but you never know. One in a thousand might be dangerous, might be escaped from prison. A man with his wife and kids in the car could not take the risk of picking up that one dangerous thumber.

At that I lapsed into silence, but I remember trying to see the expressions on the faces as we passed the occasional hitch-hiker. Were they dangerous, after all? Was there something wild, something from outside my comfortable world, in those faces? It seemed doubtful — after all, they were just standing there, doing nothing, going nowhere. Then I thought that they might be like the hawks we saw stationed at the tops of roadside trees: silent and immobile as statues, but they might fly at any moment, might be gone, might never pass this way again.

Seven and a half years later I was on the road myself, but not as one of the hitchhikers. Not at first. My parents had made that clear. Those thumbers out there might arrive at their destinations, or they might disappear forever in the wilderness of the road — but if it was unwise to pick them up, it was far more unwise to follow their dangerous example.

Sure, I said, without paying close attention. I was glad to have parental permission, but I had no idea just how lucky I was to be allowed to travel alone at the age of sixteen.

My father knew something about young independence. He had lost his parents young, and he had traveled the world young, lying about his age so he could get into the army before he was eighteen — maybe the only lie that this gentle ironman told in his life. My mother's experience had been more traditional, but she had the fiercely independent viewpoints of an artist; she had al-ways encouraged her sons to pursue their own interests, not to worry about conformity. Still, it was years later that I found out how my parents had agonized over the decision to let me go, and how friends and relatives had criticized them for letting me follow my own star. All I knew was that my permission to travel was tied to stern instructions: Stay in touch with us. Remember the things you've been taught about responsibility. Travel by public transportation; don't do any hitchhiking.

So I began my first big solo trip on a Greyhound bus. That was fine at first, for getting across the country in big jumps, but the buses simply did not go everywhere I wanted to go.

Fine. I would walk. If I wanted to take the road to the top of Mount Lemmon, for example, I would just walk there — it was only forty-five miles from Tucson. But if I were walking and some passing driver stopped to offer me a ride, I couldn't see any reason to turn it down.

It was an easy progression after that — from accepting casual rides on back roads, to thumbing across town, to setting off on premeditated long hitchhiking trips across great distances. I never really planned to break the rules, but my mind was preoccupied with other things.

My mind was preoccupied with birds, mainly. Southeastern Arizona was a wonderland for birds, as the books had told me. Now the pictures in the books came to life, both the birds and the landscapes they lived in.

Here in Arizona, great cactus gardens were arrayed across the rocky slopes. Grasslands swept away toward the horizon, with isolated mountain ranges rising high above the plain. On the upper ridges of these mountains, the air was cool, and forests of pine and fir clothed the peaks, supporting exotic Mexican mountain birds that crossed the border only in this region. Camping in the canyons, I would awaken every morning to the sounds of unknown birds and hurry to find them. And in those weeks I found more than birds. I found challenges to overcome, time alone for thinking, and enough mild hazards to make me alert. I found a level of independence known by very few sixteen-year-olds of my generation.

After more than a month in Arizona I hitched on into southern California, intending to travel and bird up the Pacific coast until my money ran out. But on the coast, I ran up against the law.

It was a technicality: at that time, it was illegal for minors to be in California without adult supervision. The police locked me up for a couple of days in a juvenile detention home, while they arranged to put me on a plane back to Kansas, paying for the ticket with the last of my own money. I was sick with anger and disappointment and disgust but I buried the worst of it deep inside me, in a tight core of resentment against all authority. On the surface I could not show my pain — not while I was sitting there surrounded by genuine hoodlums, many of whom no doubt were headed for a life of crime and jail time, not birdwatching. So I shrugged and said, "This is the West. We expect things to be tough out here."

This is the West. It was a good line, and I would be using it a lot in the years that followed.

So I found myself back in Wichita, which wasn't quite the West. But by then I had found, also, how easy it would be to get back on the road.

All I had to do was to get a little money together. So I would sell a pint of my blood plasma, for five dollars, twice a week. I would go to a temporary-employment company where, if I were among the first in line at six in the morning, I could usually get a day's work for minimum wage. As soon as I had fifty dollars, I could hit the road again.

This pattern was repeated many times during the next couple of years. I could easily go birding for a month on fifty bucks. All my travel was by hitchhiking. I never slept in motels — literally never; I slept outside, regardless of the weather. For food, I tried to get by on a dollar a day. Going to grocery stores, I would buy cans of vegetable soup, cans of hominy, perishables marked down for quick sale. Later I discovered that dry cat food was palatable, barely; a box of Little Friskies, stuffed in my backpack, could keep me going for days.

In those days I was always lucky. Sometimes I was out in very bad weather. Sometimes the drivers who picked me up were dangerously drunk. Sometimes, with my long, unkempt hair, I attracted the ire of the local rednecks. But I was always lucky enough to come out unscathed. It was all luck, too. It was not skill or savvy or world-wise smarts, because I did not have those things; all I had was dumb luck. I was learning, though. My sole intention was to learn about birds, but on the way I also learned some things about the world.

On each trip, when the money ran out, I would thumb back to Kansas. I could get to my parents' house in Wichita from anywhere in the Lower 48 within three or four days — and it didn't hurt to go hungry for that long. Then I would start saving and planning for my next birding destination.

But the economy in Wichita was going through a slump. Boeing Aircraft, one of the biggest employers there, had lost some major contracts, and they were trimming their work force. With the passing months the local job market grew tighter and tighter, businesses struggled or failed, and morale dropped with each round of layoffs at Boeing. Finally they laid off the best they had, and my father faced unemployment.

At the temporary-employment office, I was competing with more men for fewer opportunities each day. There were more and more days when I would come back empty-handed, having wasted a precious thirty cents on a bus ride downtown, followed by a long walk home. It was getting harder every time to raise my modest traveling capital.

There were many things about Kansas that I admired, or even loved: thunderstorms and sunsets over wide horizons; the sweep of bird migration through my area every spring and fall; the diversity of nature, with a mix of elements from both East and West (including my favorites, the Western Kingbirds); and especially the quiet strength and integrity of the people. I might have used Wichita forever as a base from which to make my birding trips. But I could see no future there. It was time to strike out on my own for good, to chase the dream I had been forming since my ninth birthday.

Out of the things I had read, out of the things I had learned on the road, a plan was developing. A birding plan. The timing of my plan turned out to be both bad and good: bad, because the birding world was changing; good, because it was changing much faster than I could have realized. North American birding was entering a revolution, and I was destined to get caught up right in the middle of it.

A Record for the Breaking

THE bible of my early teen years had been a book called *Wild America*. Coauthored by my hero, Roger Tory Peterson, and his British friend James Fisher, it chronicled a long trip they had made around North America, visiting all the great natural places. That book became my daily passport to the wilderness. After another afternoon of looking for birds around our Kansas suburbs I would come home and read a chapter of *Wild America*, and the book would carry me away to the Everglades, or Crater Lake, or the Blue Ridge, or the Alaskan tundra. I would dream about how one day I would travel to all these places, too, and see the birds that lived there.

Peterson and Fisher were interested in all of nature, and in *Wild America* they wrote of everything from rocks and ferns to snakes and bears. But they were birdmen first. Wherever they traveled they sought out as many birds as they could, watching them, photographing them, filming them, recording their voices, writing detailed notes about them . . . and, of course, keeping a list of every species they saw.

This list-keeping clearly was not of central importance to either Peterson or Fisher. It was a harmless diversion from more serious kinds of bird study. But for me, as a teenager, it sounded like a lot of fun. Part of the attraction was the way that listing totally contradicted the general public image of birdwatching as a passive pastime. Keeping a list was a way of keeping score. The list could turn birdwatching into birding, an active game, even a competitive sport.

My own entry into listing began with keeping a life list. I knew, from reading Peterson's other books, that most birders kept such a lifetime tally, so I began keeping track of each new bird I encountered in my bicycle forays around the neighborhood. But before long I discovered the fun of "Big Days," trying to see how many species I could find in one day.

Such one-day attempts certainly were nothing new. Before the turn of the century, Lynds Jones and others had been doing Big Days on the Lake Erie shore in Ohio, running up one-day lists of 100 as early as 1898. Lynds Jones was president of the Wilson Ornithological Society for several years, and his Big Day totals reflected a knowledge of birds that few people had at that time. By the 1930s, bird experts like Charles Urner in New Jersey, Ludlow Griscom in Massachusetts, and Milton Trautman in Ohio were all doing ambitious Big Days, getting totals well over 100.

In those early days, most birders did not travel much, but one who did was a businessman named Guy Emerson. When he could, he timed his business trips for the best birding seasons in each area. Emerson was among the first birders to keep serious track of his annual lists for each year. His careful scheduling of travel had paid off best in 1939, when his business/birding trips around North America had produced a Big Year of 497 species. That record stood until 1952, when a young birder named Bob Smart broke it with a list of 510 species.

It was in 1953 that Peterson and Fisher made their great trek around the continent. Although James Fisher went back to England by midsummer, Roger Tory Peterson continued birding in North America. In a quiet footnote in *Wild America* he reported that his North American list for that year had totaled 572 species.

In 1953, that was an astounding list. The total number of species that normally lived in the United States and Canada was said to be about 650 — and it was flatly assumed that no one would ever see all of these in a lifetime. That anyone should see the great majority of them in a single year seemed almost unbelievable.

More incredibly, Roger Peterson's new record of 572 stood for only a short time. In 1955, a young Englishman named G. Stuart Keith came to the States to see our birds; in 1956, following the Peterson/Fisher route and doggedly tracking down a few rare birds on side trips, he managed to scrape up a year's total of 598 species. And there the matter rested for a decade and a half. It seemed impossible that anyone could crack that barrier and see 600 of North America's birds in just one year.

At the time, perhaps, it *was* impossible. But during the years that followed, something happened: birding changed.

An information revolution was taking place in birding, the second one of the century. The first had come in 1934, when Roger Tory Peterson had published his first *Field Guide to the Birds,* the book that took bird recognition out of the domain of the specialist and made it possible for everyone. With the *Field Guide* in hand, the birder could take to the field with a new confidence: if he were lucky enough to find some uncommon bird such as a Henslow's Sparrow, he would know what it was.

The second revolution was a natural extension of the first. The birder was prepared to recognize that Henslow's Sparrow, and now he wanted to know *where* to find it. Such information was first provided in the early 1950s, with the publication of Olin Sewall Pettingill's *Guide to Bird Finding.* In two thick volumes (eastern and western editions), with one chapter for each state, Pettingill described hundreds of good birding spots and listed some of the notable birds to be found at each. By checking the cross-references in the index, a birder could find specific places to seek practically any bird.

Stuart Keith used the Pettingill guides when he broke Roger Peterson's Big Year record in 1956. Many other birders also relied on their trusty Pettingills wherever they traveled in North America. But as with any revolution in information, having more facts only made people want still more. For example, the Pettingill guides said that Elegant Trogons could be found in the Santa Rita Mountains; but birders who went there wanted to know exactly *where* in those mountains the wily trogons lurked. With more birders traveling in the 1960s, there was a demand for a new kind of bird-finding guide.

The demand was answered by Jim Lane, a birder with wide experience and a willingness to share what he knew. Friends would ask Lane where he had found the trogons, and he would tell them — in detail. His directions were not on the order of, "Go to Madera Canyon and start looking." No, he would say, "Drive to the parking lot 1.1 miles past the lodge, then walk 200 yards up the streambed, and look in the tall sycamores." Lane compiled such details in a pamphlet called *A Birder's Guide to Southeastern Arizona,* which he published himself in 1965. The booklet was an immediate hit, so Lane started compiling others, covering southern California, the Texas coast, and other hot spots. With each addition to the series, traveling birders could find birds more quickly and more easily.

There were more and more birders in the field in the late 1960s, making more and more new discoveries. Texans discovered that the Ringed Kingfisher, a Mexican species, could be seen regularly at Falcon Dam. Floridians found that the Black Noddy was a routine visitor to the islands of the Tortugas. Arizonans located a population of Five-striped Sparrows north of the Mexican border. The number of "findable" bird species went up with every new discovery. And then there were rare visitors. Some rarities stayed for days, even weeks, and birders could travel to see a Black-tailed Godwit in New Jersey or a Yellow-billed Loon in California — *if* they happened to find out about them quickly enough. Informal hot lines were established among friends; and in some regions of high birding activity, taped messages were updated weekly for anyone who wanted to phone in for news of rare birds.

No continent-wide organization of birders existed then. There were scores of local bird clubs, often local chapters of the Audubon Society. But the National Audubon leadership always had been oriented more toward bird conservation than birding. During the 1960s, with the surge of interest in the environment, Audubon was recasting itself as a broad-based environmental group, pushing birds further into the background.

The closest thing to a continent-wide group of birders was one that existed mostly in name: the "600 Club." It had begun in 1961 after Stuart Keith had wondered, in print, whether anyone (besides himself and Roger Tory Peterson) had seen more than 600 bird species in North America. A few others had, and those who wrote to Stuart Keith were welcomed to the club. Beyond that, there was no organization. But at least the 600 Clubbers knew about each other now.

By 1968, North America had hundreds of birders who were working on their bird lists, spending lots of time in the field, traveling long distances to see new birds. One of the most energetic of these birders was James A. Tucker. Jim Tucker had been birding all his life, almost literally: he could remember birds he had seen at the age of three. His family had moved often while he was young, giving him the chance to learn new birds at every stop. He made friends with birders from a number of states. And he discovered for himself the fun of keeping bird lists of all kinds.

Competition was never the main point in those days: at the most, Jim was keeping lists for little competitions against himself. And the fun increased when he got one of his college friends, Benton Basham, involved. Jim and Benton would strive to see which of them could find more species of birds in a month, or over a weekend, or over the lunch hour. It was all great fun. But after college they went off to separate states.

In Florida in the mid-1960s, Tucker compiled bird records for

Audubon Field Notes, and he became president of his local Audubon chapter. For a while, he had enough outlets for his interest in birding and birders. But in 1968, he moved to Austin, Texas. Once again, his birding pals were far away. To bridge the isolation he felt, Jim Tucker printed up a little newsletter and sent it off to a dozen friends in December 1968. *The Birdwatcher's Digest,* he called it, and he jokingly numbered it "Volume 0, Number 0."

But his friends did not take it as a joke. They wanted this kind of communication, and moreover, they thought that the active birders needed their own little club. So, when Volume 1, Number 1 of the rechristened *Birding* came from Jim Tucker's desk at the beginning of 1969, the American Birding Association was born.

I heard about the American Birding Association in early 1970, while I was still fifteen. A tiny paragraph in the newsletter of the Kansas Ornithological Society gave notice of this new club. Writ-

Rose-throated Becard

ing away for membership, I had my eyes opened to a whole new world.

These people in the ABA were active, intense birders. They knew things that were not in any of my books. Rose-throated Becard? I'd heard the name, but it was a rare bird, hardly more than a rumor north of the Mexican border. Wrong: ABA could describe the precise tree where it nested in Arizona. Cape Sable Sparrow? It was so rare that even Roger Tory Peterson had never seen one. But ABA could give exact road directions to a Florida marsh where this bird was a sure thing. Astounding. The "bird-finding inserts" in *Birding* were a fabulous gold mine for me, and when I began to travel I carried those sheets of information in my backpack, as precious to me as my binoculars.

Reading over this bird-finding material from the ABA, I could not help noticing that these active birders were all intense list-chasers as well. Every issue of *Birding* in those early days contained reports of list totals of one kind or another: life lists, state or province lists, state year lists, Big Day lists, and so on. And many of the reported totals seemed remarkable to me.

I had thought that seeing 600 species in North America must be the result of a lifetime's effort by the most dedicated bird experts. At one time, that would have been true. But by 1970 there were many birders with lists well over 600; one guy, Joe Taylor from New York State, was pushing seriously toward 700. "Serious" was the wrong word, though: all of these intense, hard-core listers appeared to be having a great time.

It seemed that the way to be accepted into this crowd of fun-loving experts would be to work up my life list, my state lists, whatever, and then send in my totals to *Birding* magazine. So as I began to travel, I began to tally up lists like never before. I was still eager to learn things about each bird, but more and more I was thinking about what each new species would do for my list totals.

In one of the first issues of *Birding* I had received in 1970, an editorial by Jim Tucker had offered predictions for the decade of the seventies. Many listing milestones would be achieved before 1980, Jim wrote, and many old barriers would be shattered. Before the decade was over, someone would succeed in finding 700 species in North America. Most likely that would be Joe Taylor, who was already into the high 680s. Sometime in that decade, someone would reach the point of having seen half the known bird species in the world. That quite possibly would be Stuart Keith, who was now birding Planet Earth as intensely as he had covered North America in the 1950s. And sometime in the seventies, someone would edge past Stuart's old Big Year record from 1956 and find more than 600 species in North America in just one year. However, Tucker made no prediction as to who might be the record-breaker on this last milestone. Since it was a matter of one intense year, rather than a gradual accumulation, the field was wide open. Anyone might do it.

That fact revolved slowly in my mind as I traveled around the continent, learning the birding areas and the birds. As the calendar ran down the final days of 1971, I began to ask: Why not me? Why not try to be the first to do a Big Year of 600 species?

The idea drew me like a magnet. With the new bird-finding guides and the communication of the ABA, locating specific birds was now far easier than it had been in the 1950s. Hitchhiking could take me anywhere — I knew that now. A month into the new year I would be turning eighteen, so I wouldn't run afoul of the unsupervised-minor law in California again. And I had no other commitments except my commitment to myself, to learn as much as possible about birds. In January 1972, I packed my things and set out to break the 600 barrier.

I hitched south, filled with purpose, from the cold of a Kansas January to the gentle warmth of the Texas coast. My luck held: birds were everywhere. Heading south along the coast from Houston, I found terns and egrets and flocks of wild geese; stopping in at the Aransas refuge, I saw the famous Whooping Cranes on their traditional wintering ground. Nothing, it seemed, could hold me back from my goal.

But I should have known — when the gods seem to smile, they may in fact be laughing. Barely a month into the new year I was stopped cold by an incredible piece of news. The record already had been broken.

It had happened just the preceding year, 1971, and the new record was a whopping 626.

But what amazed me most was not the record itself, but the news of who had pulled it off. It was not, as I might have supposed, some well-known older birder. It was not some wealthy hobbyist with time for unlimited travel. The new record-holder was a kid about my age, a student from Pennsylvania just starting college in Arizona, a kid named Ted Parker.

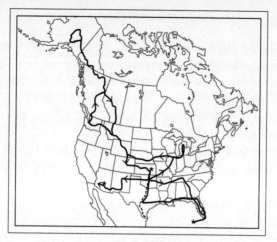

The Tucson Five

IT'S NOT an easy thing to admit: as soon as I heard the news, I gave up.

A Big Year of 600 birds had sounded attainable, just barely ... but 626 loomed as an impossible figure to beat, especially by hitchhiking. So I quit.

After wandering around the Southwest for a while I went back to Wichita, where the economy still had not improved. There I almost got involved in starting a rock band; I almost got involved with various girls; I worked on identifying the local plants and insects and paid less attention to the spring bird migration than I had in twelve years.

But events in June would put me back into the thick of birding. I heard about a chance to take a chartered boat trip from Key West, Florida, out to the Dry Tortugas, site of a big tropical tern colony. So I paid $35 for a ticket — a lot of money for me then — and in early June I picked up my binoculars and backpack and hitchhiked down to Florida.

Reaching the dock in Key West several hours before the boat

was to depart, I took off my backpack and sat down to wait. Royal Terns were passing occasionally. My sketchbook was out and I was trying to draw the wing patterns of the terns when a voice right behind me said, "Hey! You must be a birder! Are you here for the Dry Tortugas trip?"

The kid looked to be my age — he *was* my age, eighteen, he said. Joel Greenberg was the name, and he was an active birder from Chicago. He did not look like anyone's stereotype of a birder: the round spectacles and slim build might fit, but not the long, wild hair that stuck out in all directions. I liked the kid immediately.

Joel's father Sam looked more like the birders I had seen, but that was an illusion; he wasn't going on the boat trip. "I just drove him down here," said Sam, patiently. "I'm gonna relax here on the Keys while you crazies go out there for the birds. I've already seen more birds than any other nonbirdwatcher in Chicago. Go on, you kids have a good time." He left, and Joel and I sat down to talk about birding.

Joel's imagination was as wild as his hair. He made a connection between the tour company, Bird Bonanzas (sponsor of our trip), and the TV western show *Bonanza*, and went on to suggest a rival tour operation called "Bird Gunsmoke." The next thing I knew he was inventing a birdwatching motorcycle gang, "Hell's Birders." His brain never stopped working overtime, and the bizarre ideas never stopped coming.

But he knew a lot about birds, and about birders as well. When I mentioned my aborted Big Year attempt, and the record set by this mysterious Ted Parker, Joel snapped to attention.

"Hey, I know Ted! I met him last summer, when all the godwits were at Brigantine. My dad drove me out there."

"What's he like?"

"You mean my dad, or Ted Parker?"

"Come on."

"Ted's sort of like a superior being," said Joel. "Like, he plays football and basketball, on top of being a great birder."

"*Is* he a great birder?"

"Is he ever! He could name all the shorebirds a mile away. He could name all the little birds flying overhead. Everybody was waiting for *him* to find the Black-tailed Godwit."

I'm going to hate this guy, I thought.

Joel saw my expression. "The funny thing is, he's a nice guy anyway. At least, he's nice until he's focusing on a bird, and then he forgets you're there. And he likes to shake people up. We were all standing around talking, and not looking at birds, and Ted suddenly yells 'EURASIAN CURLEW!' Everybody was grabbing their scopes and looking where Ted was pointing, and he was cracking up laughing. But five minutes later he did it again, with a different bird, and everybody believed him again."

"So he's a superior being," I said. "Is he superior enough to have figured out where the girl birders are?" [Yes, it was a dumb question, but I was just eighteen then.]

"Yeah," said Joel. "In outer space. In a laundromat in Albania. What are you, nuts? There aren't any girl birders."

The timing couldn't have been better. "Okay," I said. ". . . then who are those two, behind you?"

The expression on Joel's face, the I'm-not-going-to-fall-for-that-one look, drained away as he heard voices behind him. He whirled around.

They had all the field marks of birders: serious binoculars, scruffy field clothes, even a Peterson bird guide peeking out of a day pack. They were good-looking, too — not in the plastic Hollywood sense, but with the healthy good looks of active young women who spend time outdoors.

Joel, who had just been denying their existence, recovered quickly. "Hey, I know one of them! The tall one is Rose Ann Rowlett. I don't know who her friend is." And he hurried over to greet them.

Rose Ann and her friend Peli were active in the Texas birding community, and they knew all the hotshot Texas birders and great Texas birds. We spent a long time talking with them. A couple of things were confusing me though: "What's the origin of the name 'Peli'? Is it short for 'Pellinore'? And if *her* name is Rose Ann, how come you keep calling her 'Grebe'?"

"So you don't know about the bird names!" said Rose Ann. "It's a Texas tradition. Edgar Kincaid started it — he calls himself the 'World's Oldest Cassowary,' and he's given bird names to lots of us. 'Peli' is short for 'Pelican.' People used to think her name was Suzanne Winckler, but Edgar re-identified her. 'A wonderful bird is the pelican . . .'"

"So I'm the Brown Pelican," Peli interrupted. "Rosie is the Western Grebe, if she isn't the Upland Plover instead."

"Okay," said Joel, "so what am I? How about a Fiery-tailed Awlbill? I saw that name in some book."

"Edgar gives the names," Rose Ann smiled, "or sometimes they're decided by the whole birding group. But they have to be appropriate. Victor Emanuel is the Hooded Warbler, and if you knew him you'd understand why — he's hyperactive but profound. Ben Feltner is the Brown Jay, because he's big and rambunctious and outgoing. Roger Tory Peterson is the King Penguin. The names have to be chosen with care."

More birders were arriving, and Joel introduced me to Dr. Harold Axtell, a quiet, precise, friendly man who knew an incredible amount about North American birds. "Ask him something," Joel urged me. "Go ahead, ask him how to identify a Baird's Sandpiper." To humor Joel, I did ask. Fifteen minutes later, Axtell was still describing Baird's Sandpiper to us, giving minor points we had never imagined, detailing the field marks that would make Baird's distinctive at any season.

Dr. Axtell, like Ted Parker, had done a Big Year the previous year, listing 608 species. His wife Rachel had reached 602. They had both broken the old record, but their attempts had been overshadowed by Ted's list of 626. Axtell said he didn't mind, though. They had kept their lists for fun, and fun it had been, record or no record.

When the boat left the dock late that evening, there were forty birders aboard — intense, active birders, from all over the continent. Most of my previous birding had been solitary, but here it became a social activity. As a group we enjoyed the great tern colony of the Tortugas — the boisterous Sooty Terns and their somber cousins, the Brown Noddies. As a group we studied the gulls and watched the frigatebirds.

That boat trip in 1972 changed my outlook on birding in one important way. Previously, despite the contacts offered by my reading of *American Birds* and *Birding,* I'd never realized that birders made up a *community*. But they did — now I could see that. By the time the boat returned to Key West I had made friends with birders from all over North America, people with knowledge to spare and information to share.

From Florida I hitched to Texas, and Pelican took me out to see Golden-cheeked Warblers and Black-capped Vireos. I thumbed up to Chicago, where Joel Greenberg showed me Henslow's Sparrows. From there I went on north into Michigan to see the rare Kirtland's Warbler; then, inspired by success, I took the crazy notion to hitchhike up the AlCan highway to Alaska. Several adventurous weeks and many northern birds later, I arrived back at my parents' house in Wichita, tired and flat broke, but filled with new knowledge about birds.

But there was no time to rest: Joel Greenberg was on the phone, calling from Tucson. "I'm at U of A," he said. "Guess what? I was registering at the dorm and they asked did I know anyone here and I said yeah, just one guy, so now I've got Ted Parker as a roommate! And there are a couple of other guys in the next dorm who are hot birders. You have to get down here."

So I did.

It took me only a day and a half to hitchhike from Wichita to Tucson. I got dropped off at the off-ramp at South Stone and walked and thumbed into the middle of town, to the University of Arizona campus.

Joel soon introduced me to the other birders: Mark Robbins, a tall and excitable freshman from Missouri; Dave Hayward, from southern Illinois, as introspective as Mark was outgoing; and, of course, Ted Parker. Though I was an out-of-towner, I was accepted into the group (which Joel dubbed "The Tucson Five") because I shared the requisite craze for birding. Whenever classes or homework didn't interfere for the other guys, we would pile into Mark's big station wagon and hit the road, with the radio turned up high, Mark pushing the buttons to try to find something by Neil Young. (Mark, Ted, and I had been fans of the iconoclastic Young since his days with the rock group Buffalo Springfield. Joel had nearly ruined my reputation in advance by telling the guys that I admired Neil Diamond instead. "I *think* it's Neil Diamond. It's Neil *Somebody*. Did he do a song called 'Buffalo Girl'?") And over the sound of the radio, the birding conversations would go on nonstop.

Joel and I had invented a mythical bird, Rowlett's Owlet, named for Rose Ann. It was the ultimate owl. While most owls were difficult to see or hear, this one was genuinely impossible: transparent and silent. When we babbled on about the Rowlett's Owlet concept, Dave would listen gravely, but then he would offer the most outrageous suggestions of all. Ted asked sensible scientific questions: "If it's silent, how will it communicate with potential rivals or mates? Will it use chemical cues, like some insects do?" Mark shrugged off the whole business — "You guys are nutcakes" — and kept punching the radio.

When we got to our destination, however, it all came down to serious pursuit. We were here to bird. We would split up to scour the area, trying to find every single bird there.

The guys were all highly skilled, and their company challenged me to sharpen my approach. Mark Robbins was notably adept at finding specific target birds, and when he found such a desired species, the rest of us would know immediately. If we were looking for, say, a Five-striped Sparrow, after ten or fifteen minutes, we usually would hear Mark's voice: "*TED! It's the Stripe-fried . . . the Frive-stye . . . the Fripe . . . the Stive . . . the . . .*" echoing through the canyon, and the rest of us would dash over to see the bird.

But although all of us had our moments of glory, there was never any doubt about who was the leader. When it came to choosing a destination, or deciding how to work an area, or picking out the most obscure callnote, or identifying the most difficult bird, or finding the most unexpected rarity, we relied on Parker.

When Joel had first introduced us, out on the sidewalk in front of Graham Hall, I had not been particularly impressed. *So this is the great Ted Parker,* I thought. He looked like what he was: a student, just a year older than me, getting started on another year of college.

But gradually, after many days in the field and many hours of conversation, I came to realize that Joel had been right. Ted really *was* a superior being.

"Yeah," said Mark Robbins.

He was leaning back, one lanky arm draped casually over the steering wheel, as the station wagon roared down the interstate. "I know what you mean. The dude is something else. Amazing."

Joel leaned forward from the back seat, the passing headlights illuminating the fringes of his wild hair. "Binoculars of the gods," he intoned. "Have alien birdwatchers from outer space invaded Planet Earth?"

"Maybe," I said. "I get the impression that Ted doesn't look at birds the same way I do. I'm still looking at field marks, little details for identifying a bird. Ted seems to see all that without even trying, and mostly he's looking at the whole bird and how it fits into its environment. He sees the total picture, not just the pieces."

From a dark corner of the back seat, Dave Hayward broke his customary silence. "I've been reading some material on Eastern religions," he said. "Ted — especially the way you describe him — seems close to the Zen definition of a Master. He begins at the center of his subject, not at the edges."

"Well, he's headed for the southern edges now." While the four of us were headed to southern California for the weekend, Ted had gone to Mexico with a couple of biology grad students. "You know," I continued, "he was listening to that Davis tape of Mexican bird songs a few days ago. But Ted wasn't even paying attention to the birdcalls in the foreground, the labeled ones. He was listening to the other birds, the faint calls in the background, figuring out what *they* were. In Mexico! He'd never even been there until a year ago."

"Well, the guy has an amazing ear," Mark admitted.

"Two of them," said Joel. "I counted. But, yeah, great hearing. I bet if there were a Rowlett's Owlet out there by the highway, not calling, Ted would be able to not hear it way before the rest of us."

Mark ignored this. "His hearing is good and his eyesight is good, but that doesn't begin to explain it."

"Intense concentration," Dave said, quietly. "Focus. When he's in the field, he's concentrating on birds."

"Yeah, you know, that's part of it," Mark said. "If you watch sports — I know *you* don't, Kenn, but if you did — every once in a while there's an athlete who's just twice as good as anyone else in his sport. You can analyze it to death, and you still can't explain why. But you do get the impression that this guy *cares* about the game more than anyone else."

It was true: there was something uncanny about Parker's single-minded drive. Out in the field he was not daydreaming, or thinking about girls, or wondering about next week's big exam, which he was probably going to skip anyway. He was completely focused on birds. Not that he had a one-track mind — if pressed into discussion on other topics, he had complex ideas about nearly everything. It was just that he had disciplined himself to zero in on his chosen subject. His focus brought to mind the word "integrity," or even "purity," but I could not figure out a good way to say that.

With the lingering silence, our conversation trailed off into the night. Through the car window I watched the dark Arizona desert flowing past, and the occasional outpost town. We were heading for the Salton Sea, in the hot Imperial Valley of southern California, and then planning to check some coastal birding spots. After that the guys would be going back to Tucson, while I birded my way up the coast.

Up to that point I had been largely avoiding California since my run-in with the law two years earlier. Even now I was tempted to just hang around Arizona, to go birding with the Tucson Five, to learn from the amazing Parker. But California, from what I had heard, had some of the best birding on the continent. It was rumored to have some of the best birders as well. Sooner or later, I would have to go and see if the rumors were true.

California Influence

"OH, they're sharp in southern California," Ted Parker had told me. "If you don't believe it, just ask them."

But I didn't have to ask. Southern California birders were famously active, intense, racing around the state searching for rare birds and actually finding them. They could identify even the most confusing birds, because they knew field marks that were not in the books. They were sharply competitive — against each other and against everybody else.

Everyone in southern California looked up to Guy McCaskie. Even Roger Tory Peterson had called him "that genius." Guy McCaskie was not a professional ornithologist — he worked a full-time job and had no more time for birding than anyone else — but he was the leader, the discoverer, the predictor, the final bird authority in southern California.

I had read much of McCaskie's writing in *American Birds* and other journals. Discovering a vagrant bird, far from its normal range, he would report and analyze the record. Discerning that some species might occur, overlooked, in southern California, he would predict where it should turn up, and likely as not he would be the one to discover it there. Finding inaccuracies in the old records, he would bring them to light. If a bird was very difficult to identify, he would work out the definitive field marks. And rather than keep information for himself, he would publish it for others to use. It all went into print, and even birding kids from Kansas knew who Guy McCaskie was.

Older and more placid birdwatchers in southern California were still not sure what to make of this new style. But it had a strong attraction for energetic youngsters. Following McCaskie's lead, a number of L.A. kids like Jon Dunn, Kimball Garrett, and Richard Webster were starting to make birding shock waves of their own. Competition was intense. Maybe because of this, in the fall of 1972, I passed through southern California rather quickly and headed up to the northern part of the state.

As I thumbed north along the coast, I tried to remember what I had heard about northern California. People talked as if the northern and southern halves were two different states. Evidently their birding cultures were quite different. The northern California birders, from what I had heard, were just as skillful but far less competitive. They welcomed beginners; they were glad to share their knowledge with anyone who might find birds interesting. Time spent birding was like a continuous party outdoors, and at the end of the day it was likely to be followed by another party indoors. Such was the fanciful impression I had, built up from half-remembered fragments of things I had been told.

Someone had even told me that the northern Californians had a leader, a great birder who was an opposite-number to McCaskie in the south, whose personality pervaded the birding scene. But try as I might, I could not remember his name.

Black and broken rocks came down to the end of land. To my right, the shoreline faded into the fog, feeling its way toward the gardenways and wharves of Pacific Grove and Monterey. To the left, the shore jutted out a hundred yards and then ended, cutting off the view from that quarter: Point Pinos. Out of the gray mist, waves came rolling, shattering on the rocks and sending white spray into the air.

Far out over the gray water, appearing dimly through the fog, flew hundreds of seabirds. They passed in lines, their flocks gathering and dispersing, massing and moving on. All of these dark birds flew in the same peculiar way: gliding and scaling on stiff wings, low over the waves, showing a flash of white under the wings as they tilted away. Sooty Shearwaters, visiting from their nesting islands thousands of miles away in the Southern Hemisphere, they were performing their great cyclic migration around the perimeter of the Pacific. Elsewhere holding to the open ocean, here they had been brought within sight of land by the deep cold waters of Monterey Bay.

Closer to shore, near the lines of floating kelp, gulls were flying. Occasionally the angular form of a Parasitic Jaeger would knife among them, to single out some gull, chase it, and force it to drop or disgorge its catch. Jaegers lived by harassment and theft. The gulls protested, but their cries were lost in the noise of the surf.

It was September, and I was out near the end of Point Pinos, with this great pelagic theater spread out before me. Binoculars trained toward the invisible horizon, I sat among the jumbled rocks, tasting brine, feeling fine curtains of spray, watching the endless flight of these ocean wanderers. Hours must have passed, but I did not notice. At length, when I turned to look behind me, I saw — standing at the top of the sea cliff — what appeared to be a pirate.

He was a big, stocky bear of a man, with black hair, a bristly black mane of a beard, and ominous ledges of eyebrows. He stood, arms folded, gazing out across Monterey Bay. At any moment, it appeared, he was going to command Neptune to rise up from the sea and speak with him.

But he didn't. Instead, he started down the rocks toward me. I noticed then that a dark-haired, pretty girl was following the pirate, looking down toward her feet as she stepped from one rock to the next, as if she might be searching for flowers among the stones. Reaching my slab of rock, the pirate raised his hand in greeting: "Hi! What have you been seeing?"

Maybe he was asking about birds, and maybe not, but it made no difference in my answer. "Everything," I said. "Man, it's all out there. I've never seen anything like this."

Planting his feet firmly on the rock, the pirate pulled a well-used binocular out of his sweatshirt and began scanning the waves. From behind the glasses, he said, "You're the kid from Kansas, right? Bill Reese said you might be out here. I'm Rich, and this is Georgianne."

Just in case this Rich character knew something about the birds here, I asked him about jaegers. Three species were possible, but all I'd seen had looked like Parasitic Jaegers. Rich nodded. "Sounds about right," he said. "The Parasitic is the easy one to see from shore. There are a lot of Pomarines around, but they like to stay farther out on the bay. The Long-tail — that's tough. You're having a great day if you see a Long-tailed Jaeger, even from a boat." Returning to his scanning of the bay, he asked if I had seen any shearwaters besides the abundant Sooties.

"Yeah," I said, enthusiastically. "I saw a Buller's Shearwater. I'm sure of it." Rich raised one eyebrow, but didn't contradict me.

A few minutes later, Rich started talking about how to identify distant, flying shearwaters. His point may have been to explain to me, diplomatically, that I had seen not the Buller's but rather the more common Pink-footed Shearwater. I hardly noticed I was being corrected, though, because I got so caught up in listening. This guy knew *all* the shearwaters, even rare ones like Flesh-footed and Short-tailed, and he could describe them vividly. He spoke of everything from general impressions to specific details, motioning with his hands to indicate the particular flight-action of each species.

It was fascinating to hear. In fact, he seemed to be fascinated by it himself. It had to have taken him years to amass this store of knowledge; but he spoke as if he had just learned it all that very day and was now eager to share it with all his friends.

Listening, I suddenly realized who the man was. This was the legendary leader of the northern California birders, Rich Stall-cup, the Pirate of Point Pinos.

That afternoon I went out birding around the Monterey Penin-sula with Rich and Georgianne. Near the mouth of the Carmel River, we found a Baird's Sandpiper — a familiar enough bird in Kansas, but apparently scarce here in California. Rich was im-mensely pleased. He had half expected to find a Baird's here, but it was his first one of the year. Idly, I asked if he kept a year list.

Rich grinned. He was keeping one this year, he said, just for birds seen within California. Baird's Sandpiper brought his total for 1972 up to 406 species.

"Doesn't that put you in good shape for breaking the record?" I asked. "I mean, isn't the California one-year record 417 species — McCaskie, a couple of years ago?"

Rich seemed surprised that I knew this bit of California list-ing trivia (I'd read it in *Birding* a few weeks earlier), but he gave me the whole story. He had not set out to work on a record; he had just been doing as he always did, birding intensively all over the state. But in late summer he'd been talking with a young southern California birder, Richard Webster, and the topic had turned to year listing. Webster boasted of the unusual species he had seen already during 1972, adding that he expected to break McCaskie's record.

That conversation had set the wheels turning in Rich Stallcup's mind. He had seen most of the same rarities that Webster had. Counting up, he found that his list for the year was already close to 400. So the contest was on, and now Rich was traveling around the state on a shoestring budget, looking for rare birds, evading some federal agents who (for some vague reason) wanted to talk to him, and generally making a Great Adventure out of it.

The next morning I was again out on Point Pinos, watching the jaegers and shearwaters, when Rich and Georgianne came racing up in Georgianne's Volkswagen to tell me that Rich had just found a Magnolia Warbler. I had seen plenty of Magnolia Warblers in the East, but here it was a rare stray, a year bird for Rich.

After a brief search, we located the warbler again. The little bird was flitting high in a cypress, flashing the white spots in its tail. To me it was a familiar bird, but seen through the eyes of the Californians it took on a new importance, even a new magic.

"I think this is it," I told the driver. "Yeah: Arcata–Sunny Brae exit. This is where he told me to get off." Thanking the driver, I got out of the car and stood under a street light, studying the little sketch map that Rich Stallcup had drawn for me.

I found the exit on the map. Maybe a mile south, just beyond the railroad tracks that paralleled the highway closely on the west side, a little square represented the Jacoby Creek Country Club. "Don't expect a regular country club, though," Rich had said. "That's just a name . . . what's really there is a red wooden house sitting up on stilts, out in the marsh. Gary Friedrichsen's the caretaker — he'll put you up. Ron LeValley ought to be hanging around there, and probably some other birders too. They're all good people. They can show you around."

At one in the morning, my mind was about as clear as the fog drifting in off Humboldt Bay. Walking south along the shoulder of the highway, I eventually spotted the roadbed for the railroad off to the right. Wading across a ditch knee-deep in cold water, I continued to walk south along the tracks. Ahead in the night, two dark objects loomed out of the marsh. The larger one, when I drew close enough to make out the shape, was only a billboard. The closer one was some dwelling, perched on stilts: obviously, the Jacoby Creek Country Club.

But it was in sad shape. Even in the dark I could see holes gaping in its roof and walls. The only access was via a broken-down catwalk, half its boards fallen into the mud. The shack surely was abandoned. Alone on the tracks, peering dejectedly at the pathetic structure, I thought: So much for the camaraderie of birders in northern California. Gary Friedrichsen must have moved out (who wouldn't have?), and Stallcup just had not gotten the word yet.

Too tired to hitch any more rides that night, I spread out my poncho on the marsh grass and went to sleep.

Daylight confirmed my first impression: the shack directly across from me was obviously deserted. But light also brought a revelation: there was another house on the marsh, a few hundred yards farther south. The billboard had blocked my view in that direction the night before. This one, as I approached, looked much more promising. It had glass (and even curtains) in the windows, and a driveway ran to it, crossing the railroad tracks. It was red, too. Confident now, I walked to the door.

When I knocked, I heard movement inside. Good, I thought, Friedrichsen's at home. Rich and Georgianne had described him as a big jovial guy, with a ready laugh and a flaming red beard. I waited for the man to open the door . . .

But when the door swung open, there stood a beautiful young blond woman.

Laura Osborne and her husband, Tim, had been living at Gary's place for a while, so she was used to finding people with backpacks and binoculars standing at the front door. In other words, she was considerably less surprised than I was. She invited me in for a cup of coffee (I must have looked as if I needed it) and told me that the local guys were out birding. Tim, Gary, and a couple of other birders — Ron LeValley and Stan Harris — had left before dawn for an intensive day in the field. "But maybe I can track them down," she said. After a couple of minutes on the telephone, she had good news: "I called Mrs. Harris. The guys are going to be stopping by there, by Stan's place, at lunchtime. So you can join up with them then . . . I'll take you over."

With my faith in northern California restored, I went out to bird the "back yard" of the red house — the great marsh extending down to the edge of Humboldt Bay — until about noon, when Laura drove me over to the Harrises'.

The guys arrived in a rush, enthusiastic after a successful half-day, stopping in to feast on hamburgers and to marshall their energies for the hours that remained. They were making a Big Day of it, trying to break their own past records for Humboldt County. Although they had never heard of me, they immediately invited me to join them for the afternoon.

They had started the day in the eastern part of the county, up in the mountains, so we spent the afternoon near the coast. Along the bay, at a place with many Western Sandpipers and other shorebirds, we were pleased to pick out one Baird's Sandpiper and one Pectoral Sandpiper — both good finds here. While we were watching them, a sudden ripple of panic raced across the flats, and every sandpiper took to the air in a tight flock that twisted and darted and wheeled in unison. A large dark falcon flashed across the sky right behind them. Racing to a nearby ridge for a better view, we were just in time to see the falcon — it was a Peregrine — pull up above the fleeing shorebirds and then drop like a bomb through the center of the tightly packed flock, plucking one bird on the way down.

Later, at the mouth of Humboldt Bay, we clambered out to the end of the stone jetty to scan the ocean. The waves were so high that it was hard to see very far out, but every so often a Sooty Shearwater would appear, tilting and gliding by, coming into view for a few seconds and then disappearing. Eventually a couple of Parasitic Jaegers came past.

These two species, the common near-shore pelagics, were the only seabirds that the guys expected to pick up. However, there were many others out there, a little farther from land. Seeing a few seabirds from shore was fine, they said, but there was nothing like getting out there on a boat and seeing lots of them up close. An organized birding boat trip was coming up in October, and they urged me to sign up for it. "You won't regret it," said Gary. "It's the farthest thing you can imagine from birding in Kansas."

The pelagic trip sounded too good to pass up. I gave my last five dollars to Stan Harris, to reserve a place on the boat, and then headed north. Other hitchhikers had told me I could get work picking apples in central Washington; so I spent five days in the orchards of the golden Yakima Valley, making enough money to sustain my modest lifestyle through the fall. From there I hitched down to the Washington coast, hoping to find a Sharp-tailed Sandpiper, but my time ran out and I headed down toward Humboldt Bay again.

I got to the red house on the marsh about noon on the day before the pelagic. When I arrived, no one was home except Ron LeValley, who had stopped in between birding forays. Ron was in high spirits because he had found a Rose-breasted Grosbeak that morning (an eastern bird, displaced here), and because so many of his friends were coming from out of town for the boat trip.

Rich Stallcup and Georgianne Manolis turned up promptly. Georgianne had brought along her birding family: brother Tim, an artist; brother Bill, a cheerful nomad; and mother Anne, an energetic little woman who was like a second mother to all the younger birders in northern California. We all went out birding around Humboldt Bay, and at each stop we continued to run into more and more birders.

Toward evening the tribe gathered at the red house on the marsh. It was not a quiet gathering — at least thirty people were crammed into the front room, drinking wine and carrying on a dozen separate conversations about birds — but the scene was warm and friendly.

The feeling in the red house mirrored what I had seen out in the field with the northern Californians. A sense of wonder at the natural world was always apparent. Walking through the woods with them in search of birds, I had noticed how they might suddenly stop to examine a wildflower, or pause to turn over a log, looking for salamanders — always returning the log carefully to its original position. These gentle naturalists were striving constantly to learn more about birds and nature, and to improve their field skills, but they did not seem driven by competition as so many birders were.

I was beginning to see why Rich Stallcup was the guru for this community. It wasn't just that he *knew* so much about birds. It wasn't just that he shared this knowledge so freely. More than mere facts, what Rich radiated to all those around him was the sense that birds were magical, and that searching after birds and watching them was a Great Adventure.

The pelagic trip the next day was a Great Adventure itself. Rich had let me in on his safeguard against seasickness: if you took a few swigs of hearty Burgundy before the boat even pulled away from the dock, *mal de mer* couldn't touch you.

Lines and legions of shearwaters flew past the boat, Sooty Shearwaters by the thousands, with lesser numbers of Pink-footed Shearwaters. A few of the small Buller's Shearwaters appeared, flying fast, tilting up high on one wingtip at each glide, like paper airplanes caught in a sidewind. Northern Fulmars circled near, and Cassin's Auklets buzzed away across the waves. And those great long-winged mariners, albatrosses, appeared in numbers. Scores of the big Black-footed Albatrosses came past, some gliding by within yards of the boat.

A dark bird went powering by, white flashes in its wings, and a shout went up from the bow: "Skua! It's a skua!" But Rich Stallcup shook his head. "No. It didn't *feel* like a skua."

Pressed for an explanation, Rich described aspects of shape and flight behavior that convinced him the bird was simply a dark young Pomarine Jaeger. But a few minutes later, talking to me, he repeated his original point: the important thing was that it had not *felt* like a skua. "When there's a skua in the neighborhood," said Rich, "you know there's something happening. It's a big, tough bird, it's a pirate . . . you can feel the excitement pouring out from it. You'll know it, for sure, when we see one."

About an hour later an actual skua did appear. The big dark seabird, big brother of the jaegers, came hauling in on heavy wings, to turn and circle for a minute among the gulls in the boat's wake. The bird was just as Rich had described it: blunt, stocky, powerful, roguish. The observers on board seemed duly awed. Just a little drunk on wine, I could have sworn I saw some kind of mutual salute pass between Rich and the skua.

Sometime that afternoon, when the boat was cruising back toward the harbor, Rich and I were leaning on the rail near the bow, watching Buller's Shearwaters skim gracefully over the water, when I decided to ask him about something that was puzzling me: "Rich, I don't understand. Nobody around here seems to be very competitive. *You're* not into competing. So how come you're working so hard on this year list?"

Rich smiled. "That's worth thinking about," he said. "But look, the list itself doesn't matter. The record doesn't matter. It's

Skua in flight

like when a bunch of friends are playing football in the back yard, you go all out to win, but afterwards it doesn't matter who won. Here's what's different about it, though," he said, turning serious. "The list total isn't important, but the birds themselves *are* important. Every bird you see. So the list is just a frivolous incentive for birding, but the birding itself is worthwhile. It's like a trip where the destination doesn't have any significance except for the fact that it makes you travel. The journey is what counts."

When the boat pulled back in to the dock, I was deep in thought. Clearly there were perspectives on this bird-listing game that I had never considered. As the fall of 1972 went on I would travel some more, look at birds some more, and then go back to Arizona to think about my next move.

Just Like Christmas

It was a thick volume that arrived in the mail every year when I was a boy, and for me it represented all the magic of the Christmas season. Many were the nights that I would lie on the floor, poring over its pages, again and again. It was a wish book, a dream book, filled with delights and possibilities. Was this some Christmas catalogue, a compendium of toys? No — better than that. It was the volume of results of the annual Christmas Bird Count.

Roger Tory Peterson's book *Birds Over America* had been my introduction to the Christmas Count. Peterson described how in 1900 the ornithologist Frank Chapman had conceived the count as a substitute for the "side hunt" popular then — a grisly sport in which the Christmas guests would divide into teams and go out to shoot anything that moved, to see which side could kill the most. Chapman's little bird count was a feeble antidote at first, but it persisted and grew, sponsored by the National Audubon Society, eventually becoming the biggest birdwatching event in the world.

Before I turned twelve, I started going on Christmas Counts myself, tagging along with Ralph Wiley or Dan Kilby, or other members of the Audubon Society chapter in Wichita. The Wichita count, like all the others, was conducted within a fifteen-mile-diameter circle. The birders would divide into teams and fan out over the circle, counting every bird they could find in a day — not just every species, but every individual. That was a part of the excitement: every single bird was important. If our team found a snipe and no one else in the circle did, I could open the Christmas Count issue of *Audubon Field Notes* a few months later and find it again in the tally for the Wichita count: "Common Snipe, 1." And our 53 Harris's Sparrows would make up a major part of the total of 128 reported by Wichita. And then, of course, I would pore over the rest of the volume, reading results of counts from exotic places like Florida and Arizona.

Every year since, I had joined the Wichita count. But as Christmas 1972 approached, I was in Arizona. Anyone with binoculars was welcomed on a Christmas Count — the organizers and compilers of the counts were always hoping to maximize coverage of their circles — and I decided to stay in Arizona and join as many counts as possible, to meet more of the local birders and learn more good birding areas.

The other guys in the Tucson Five were going home for the holidays, but they were still in town when the official two-week count period began. Ted and Mark and Joel and I decided to go down to Nogales to take part in the first count on the sixteenth.

We had planned to leave Tucson a couple of hours before dawn. But the day before the count, Ted went off and slept for much of the afternoon. Getting up refreshed in the evening, he insisted that we should go to Nogales much earlier, to see how many owls we could find before daylight. "This is the West," I said, resigned to another night without sleep; and by a few minutes after midnight we were out on the Ruby Road west of Nogales, looking for owls. By the first cold daylight we had hiked down to a stretch of creek below the Lake Patagonia dam. We walked for miles, up and down the hillsides, back and forth across the stream, feet constantly soaked, moving fast to keep warm. Ted found a Winter Wren, tracking it down by call in a dense thicket, and we turned up a couple of Fox Sparrows. Finishing our area with time to spare we went "poaching" in areas assigned to others: grassland near the airport, neighborhoods on the edge of town. Right at the end of the day Mark spotted a Merlin, and we watched it as the sun went down behind the rooftops of Nogales.

As with every Christmas Count, at the end of the day the participants gathered to compile totals and compare notes. The Nogales compilation took place at the home of local birding guru Bill Harrison, who had built Nogales into the biggest count in Arizona by the early 1970s, regularly running up a species list near 150. Every top birder in the state seemed to be in the Harrisons' living room that evening.

Naturally, Ted Parker already knew most of these birders. "Hey," he said to me, pointing out a couple who had just arrived, "you ought to meet those people. That's Bob and Janet Witzeman."

I already knew the Witzemans by reputation. Bob was a physician, but his considerable spare-time energy went into birding and, more recently, into high-powered work on bird conservation. Janet wrote a column for the Phoenix Audubon newsletter, and she had just coauthored a book on the birds of the Phoenix area. They were laughing and joking with the other birders, and pretty Janet had a smile that lit up the room. I decided that I liked these two immediately.

Of course they had never heard of me, but they were friendly when Ted introduced us. When the Witzemans found out I was going to be in Arizona through the season, they urged me to come up to Phoenix for their Christmas Count on the twenty-third.

"Phoenix doesn't get as many species as Nogales," said Bob, "but we come close. We're contenders. Counters and contenders." This year, Janet would be co-organizer of the count. Hopes were running high. I promised I would come to Phoenix to help.

Hitching rides up from Tucson on the twenty-second, I reached the Witzemans' home in late afternoon. The house was abuzz with activity. Several out-of-town birders besides me were going to be camping on the floor that night, and many local birders had come over for last-minute strategy sessions. Maps were laid out on countertops and chairs, and the phone was ringing constantly with suggestions and questions and reports from birders who had been out doing last-minute scouting of the count circle. Janet and her friend Bix Demaree were conferring over the schedules for different field teams. I had never seen a Christmas Bird Count organized to this level of detail.

"Our prospects look really good," Janet told me. "We might break 150 for the first time. Nogales had 149 this year, so if we can reach 150, we'll have the top Arizona count."

All the best birding spots in the circle had been assigned to proven bird-finders. Since I was an unknown, a gerrymandered area was devised for me: brushy suburban lots, part of a golf course, morning coverage of a wooded cemetery that otherwise would not be checked until afternoon. These places would keep me busy all day and, I surmised, nothing would be lost if I turned out to be incompetent. But I appreciated the chance to partici-pate, and I appreciated the fact that they loaned me a car for the day. It seemed best not to tell them that I didn't have a driver's license.

Determined to make a good day of it, I was in position in southwest Phoenix before first light on the twenty-third.

In the right place, and at the right time. Not just the right time of day: the right time of the decade. That winter of 1972–1973 was a remarkable season in Arizona. All the finches, all the thrushes, all the mountain birds that might wander to the low-lands, all of them arrived at the same time. It was a winter that the local birders would talk about for years. Blissfully unaware of the uniqueness of the season, I had been wandering around the state, finding birds, thinking how easy it was. And it would turn out to be even more so around Phoenix that day. Pure luck, and the coincidence of that productive season, gave me a great day on the Phoenix Christmas Count.

Flocks of White-crowned Sparrows were everywhere in the brushy places. In one of these flocks, a Harris's Sparrow had been staked out by local birders. The Witzemans had asked me to stop by and look for this bird, even though two other parties were trying for it as well. They wanted to take no chances on missing this rarity. As luck would have it, I turned up not only the Harris's Sparrow, but also a White-throated Sparrow, a species found by no one else on the count. Later, scrutinizing every flicker (as I always had back in Kansas), I found a Yellow-shafted Flicker near the golf course — still considered a full species at that time, and a rare bird for Arizona. But my best luck came at the cemetery.

The Greenwood Cemetery was an anomalous rectangle of green, heavily watered, planted with pines and other coniferous trees, a striking contrast to its arid surroundings. Most winters it was not a birdy place (birds of the low desert had little use for pines), so ordinarily the Christmas counters would only stop by for a brief look in the afternoon. But this was not most winters. This was an invasion year. For mountain birds wandering the lowlands, this patch of conifers acted as a magnet.

At the back of the cemetery, a flock of Red Crossbills fed inconspicuously in the pines. An occasional *kip-kip* callnote, and the soft rustling and snapping of seeds being extracted from pine cones, gave them away. There had been Red Crossbills all over the pines in some Tucson cemeteries and parks that season, so I was not surprised to see them here (but no one else on the Phoenix count saw those birds, or even looked for them). In a row of cedars, a Mountain Chickadee was foraging. This bird had been reported here a week or two earlier (but the other counters assigned to the cemetery, during their quick visit in the heat of the afternoon, couldn't find it). Then a Cassin's Finch appeared, and a Slate-colored Junco, and a Brown Creeper. Best of all was a Williamson's Sapsucker — almost unknown in the Phoenix area, far from its usual haunts in the mountains. I assumed that the other counters would see this bird as well, but they did not, and I arrived at the count compilation with several choice "exclusives."

But everyone had had a good day. Janet had found an Oven-bird, only the second one ever for Phoenix. Bob had found a Groove-billed Ani and had documented it with his camera. Bix Demaree's group had turned up Western Bluebirds, Steller's Jays, a Black-headed Grosbeak, and other local rarities. As the tallying of the count proceeded, one group after another came through with hard-to-find species. When we were finished, we counted and recounted and checked our addition, but there could be no doubt about it: we had recorded 165 species, a new record, the biggest Christmas Bird Count ever for Arizona. I blessed my luck for being there, as birders who had been working hard in the field all day went jumping around the room and hugging each other and acting like they had all the energy in the world, as if they were ready to go out and do it again.

Luck was with me the following day, too, because I *did* have to go out and do it again. Trying not to sound skeptical, Bob Witzeman asked if I could show him the rare birds I had reported. I was worried at first: all those birds easily could have disappeared overnight; but as it turned out, we were able to relocate practically all of them, including the rarest ones. So my luck had held, and I had gained a reputation and gained a couple of good friends.

In the afterglow of the Phoenix count I decided to make another try for the North American Big Year record in 1973. Not that I imagined myself some super birder. I knew I'd been lucky in finding the rarities on the Phoenix count. But I also knew that this kind of luck happened only when one was out in the field, trying hard. You had to make the effort to have the luck. And if effort contributed to luck, a record-breaking attempt would contribute to effort. It would be the incentive. I would give myself the challenge of this Big Year, and the attempt would put me out in the field where I might get lucky again.

So my head was filled with plans and schedules and ideas as

I hitchhiked over to the Chiricahua Mountains for the Portal count, scheduled for New Year's Eve. Throughout the day of the count I was preoccupied, having to force myself to concentrate on the birds around me. It was a big invasion year here as well, with flocks of Evening Grosbeaks and Cassin's Finches around, and many Sage Thrashers lurking in the brush. Townsend's Solitaires were calling their soft bell-like notes everywhere in the juniper stands. As much as I was enjoying these birds, I could hardly wait for the day to be over so the new year could start.

At the compilation that evening, everyone patiently listened to me rattling on about my coming Big Year, offered advice and encouragement, and wished me luck. The owners of the Cave Creek Ranch kindly offered to let me stay in an unused cabin across the creek that night. After the compilation party, Bob and Janet Witzeman — who had driven down from Phoenix for the count — invited me to their cabin to toast the coming new year.

We had a few drinks while Bob grilled me about my plans, asking rapid-fire questions: "Where are you going to see a Blue Grouse? How can you watch the spring migration in the East and West both? Have you ever been to the Everglades?" We talked for more than two hours. When I strode out of the Witzemans' cabin I was filled with encouragement and enthusiasm and alcohol, buoyed up by visions of my noble challenge for the year. Ironically, in my euphoria I turned the wrong way outside their door and wandered around in the dark for half an hour before I found my own cabin and collapsed on the sofa in my sleeping bag.

When I woke up it was 1973, and my first bird of the year was flitting nervously in branches outside the window: a Ruby-crowned Kinglet. The big white ring around the eye of this tiny bird gave it a wide-eyed, excited look, as if it were surprised to have achieved fame so quickly.

Dressing hurriedly in the cold cabin, I went out for a quick walk a mile up the Cave Creek road to South Fork, to look for the Mexican Chickadees that had been there the day before. On the way I was reveling in the robins, jays, juncoes, towhees, and all the rest — birds that had been old hat yesterday but were brand new today. Every time I raised my binoculars I had a new bird for the year. This was the fun part of year listing, I told myself; this was the easy part. It would get tougher later on.

The Mexican Chickadees were right where they were supposed to be, calling in husky voices as they clambered about the pine branches, loosely consorting with a mob of Bushtits. I watched them a while before starting back toward Cave Creek Ranch, where the Witzemans had offered me a ride as far as Tucson.

As I was walking back a light snow began to fall, pulling a veil of mist and mystery across the silent pines, the canyon walls, and the road ahead — the road that was to be my home for the next twelve months.

Ruby-crowned Kinglet

There's a Birder on the Road

OUT OF the West, this highway had followed me for fifteen hundred miles. From where I stood now, looking back, the pavement seemed to shift and waver in the glare of the evening sun, as if to avoid description. But I didn't need to see the road now to describe it. I knew it by heart: this mongrel road, this patchwork of old and new, Interstate 10.

I knew it well. I had watched it, felt its growing pains, for three years. Interstate 10 was being built along the general route of old U.S. 90, and eventually the freeway was meant to stretch uninterrupted from Los Angeles to the Atlantic. In the early 1970s, though, I-10 existed as a series of fragments, some long and some short, all across the southern tier of states. You could travel only so far on the smooth, modern, four-laned interstate before being shunted off onto narrow, chuckholed, two-laned U.S. 90 again.

Heading east out of Tucson, I-10's twin ribbons of pavement arrowed to the horizon, giving no hint of what lay ahead: long detours through fading western towns, convulsive miles of road repairs or the need for them, the road losing itself in the badlands of west Texas. I knew about these things. Still, the freeway interchanges of Tucson always inspired me with false confidence. I had been feeling pretty good when my friends, the other four-fifths of the Tucson Five, had dropped me off at the on-ramp on South Stone.

The situation had gone steadily downhill since. It was three nights ago now that I'd been standing on the edge of Tucson, thumb held high. Three entire days and nights, and I had only come 1,500 miles. That was terrible. Generally I hoped to make a thousand miles per day — per twenty-four-hour day, that is, because I rarely stopped overnight until I reached my destination. There was no mileage in going off somewhere to sleep, so I would just stand by the road until I got a ride. As long as I could stay awake, I could make good time. Until this time. This was turning into one of the slowest trips I'd ever had . . . and just when all possible speed was really necessary.

I had to be in Pennsylvania in six days, after a detour to the tip of Florida, and I was running out of time.

Apparently the first thing Ted Parker heard when he came back to Tucson in mid-January, 1973, was that I was out to break his Big Year record. I had only mentioned the idea to a few people, but the word had spread. By the fifteenth of January, bets had already been laid as to whether I would beat Ted's one-year total of 626.

I'd made a considerable start at it. The Christmas Bird Counts in late December had turned up some uncommon species, and I had been able to follow up on several in early January. Best of the lot was a Rufous-backed Robin. This stray from Mexico had been reported from a residential area in Tucson; I went to look for it and found that at least a thousand American Robins were also ranging the neighborhood. My search took on a needle-in-a-haystack quality — except that a haystack would not have been flying back and forth over an area of more than a square mile, panicked and scattered by a Sharp-shinned Hawk.

While I was chasing the robin flocks around, the police showed up to ask what I was doing. I told them about the Rufous-backed Robin. They were openly skeptical, but just then a couple of other birders came by, also looking for the robin. The police drove away, shaking their heads.

I did eventually see the Rufous-backed Robin. Then I hitched up to Phoenix, where Bob and Janet Witzeman helped me find Le Conte's Thrasher and some other specialties. So by the time Ted Parker came back after the Christmas break, my record attempt was well under way.

I'd been wondering uneasily how Ted would react to the news. The previous record-holder, Stuart Keith, had been allowed to retain the crown for fifteen years . . . here Ted's binoculars had hardly cooled off from 1971, and already his record was under siege. But it did not seem to bother him. He gave me advice on finding birds, wrote down the names of other birders that I should contact, and analyzed the pros and cons of my hitchhiking approach. "If you just stick with it, you'll break the record easily," he said. "You can hit 650 if you get to Alaska." Ted had not been to Alaska at all in 1971.

Ted also had exciting news: a Loggerhead Kingbird was in Florida. This Caribbean bird had never been seen in the United States until the previous winter, when one had been found on the Florida Keys. This winter, one was back on the same street corner in Islamorada. Ted had heard about it via the birding grapevine and had gone to see it over his Christmas break; this was a perfect stakeout, he said, impossible to miss. And it would be a definite bonus for a Big Year.

Parker had yet another suggestion. Some birders from his hometown of Lancaster, Pennsylvania, were planning a fast-paced trip through New England for the weekend of January 27. If I could get up there in time to join them, it would be a relatively painless way to see the northeastern winter specialties — certainly more comfortable than hitchhiking around freezing cold New England in midwinter.

It sounded great. But I would have only ten days to get from

Tucson to south Florida, find the kingbird, and then hitch to Pennsylvania. It would take concentration and luck. My year on the road was now starting in earnest.

Mark Robbins gave me a lift down to the best freeway on-ramp for catching rides east. The other guys came along to see me off. They wished me all kinds of luck, and I said, "All right, you guys, I'll bird like a madman for the honor of the Tucson Five." Finally Joel Greenberg said, "Hey, c'mon, let's get *out* of here before we start getting *emotional* about these fond farewells!" So they piled back into the station wagon — around the corner and back through the parking lot, honking the horn and yelling and grinning — and then they were gone, and I walked out alone to face the highway.

To slide downhill again into that lowered consciousness, to lose myself in the rhythm of the road.

Looking back from the 1990s, it is difficult to picture just how commonplace hitchhiking was two decades ago. On a favored on-ramp in summer, a dozen or more thumbers at a time would be waiting for rides and getting them. America may have been a gentler place then. In the years since, hitchhikers have become far scarcer, with the perception that this mode of travel has become far more dangerous. But in January 1973, I was just one among thousands of kids traveling the continent by thumb.

This was the first long-distance hitching I'd done in more than a month, but despite the slow going, I slipped back into the rhythm easily. Hitchhiking does not require much mental energy; there are a few strategies for getting rides but the main ingredients are persistence and luck. You don't gain much by thinking about what you're doing. Everything is reduced to basics . . .

The interstate highway is your thread of familiarity. It has a sameness, a pattern. All across the continent there are on-ramps and off-ramps and interchanges that look exactly alike, with the same points where you can hitch rides safely and/or legally. Underpasses and overpasses are similar everywhere, and if you have slept under bridges in Oklahoma you can sleep under bridges in

Oregon. Certain chains of truck stops and coffee shops are found nationwide. You learn which ones serve cheap coffee with free refills, which ones tend to be tolerant of hitchhikers, which ones tend to have sympathetic waitresses. The survival skills are the same all over the interstates.

Away from these highways, though, everything changes. You know where the interstate goes, and there are signs everywhere to remind you; but you don't know where the back roads go — they might lead to nowhere, and you might go there with them. You know what's happening on the interstate: it's your home turf; but when you get off of it you're on someone else's turf, and you're at the disadvantage. So you stick with the familiar. You stay with the interstate until you reach your destination.

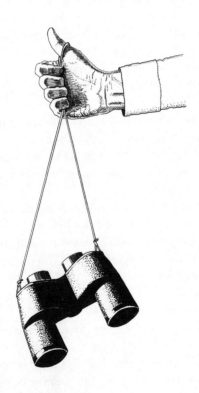

And you stay awake. If you go off somewhere to sleep at night, crossing the continent could take you more than twice as long. After midnight there may be fewer vehicles on the road, but they're usually going longer distances — and the drivers may want someone to talk with, to help them stay awake. Some of your longest rides have started at three in the morning, after you had waited by the freeway for six hours. You know it can happen, so you stay awake and wait.

It helps if you've been dropped off at an interchange that has a truck stop or cafe. There you can get a cup of coffee for very little money, several refills for nothing. The cream and sugar are free, and they may add some nutritional value. You need it. Hunger is just one more kind of discomfort. If you're tired enough, you want sleep more than you want food; if you're standing in the rain, you want a ride more than you want a meal. You alternate your discomforts, play them off against each other.

You build up a resistance to cold and boredom and hunger and lack of sleep, but then other things start to catch you off guard. Standing past midnight beside a deserted highway, a little high on caffeine, you suddenly notice the sky overhead — a billion stars, spread out across the heavens like diamonds and like dust — and it can leave you shaken. And you'll be shaken again when you're riding as night turns to day and you get to watch the sun come up all the way across Ohio, leafless trees and winter fields rolling past against the dawn.

You see a lot of sunrises when you're on the road. It's a compensation for being out there. Sunrise brings traditional messages of hope and resurrection — and more basic meanings, like the possibility that it might get warmer, and you might be able to spot police cars farther away.

The police can spot you now, too, and you're generally illegal. On the interstates, the law forbids pedestrians (including hitch-hikers) to stand anywhere except down by the entrance ramps. But the law of averages tells you that your chances are much better if you stand up by the freeway itself, where many more cars will pass within range. You take the chance. But when the cops do come across the horizon, you stay calm. You keep your non-chalant thumb raised as the police car approaches, slows, pulls to a stop — then you walk back as the cop gets out of the car and, being very careful not to sound insolent, you say, "Hi! Going toward Jacksonville?"

Always, the officer checks your I.D., calls in to headquarters to see if you're wanted for anything. Often, he searches your gear. Sometimes, he gives you a little verbal abuse. But then (almost always) he lets you off with a warning. Even if you're being insulted and you feel like talking back, you've learned to stay blandly respectful and courteous.

Antagonistic police are not a major threat. It's the friendly people that you have to watch out for — especially the friendly drunk, a buddy to all humanity, who wants someone to talk to, and who'll insist there's nothing wrong with the way he's driving. You've ridden almost to death's tollgate a dozen times on the wheels of dangerous drunks. Another kind of overly friendly driver may drop you off in the middle of nowhere when you tell him you're not interested. Then there are those people who pick you up not because they like the way you look, but because they *don't:* in the 1970s, beating up long-haired hippies is still considered a sport in some quarters. With all of these possibilities, you have learned to look at the driver before you jump in any car, and sometimes you will turn a ride down.

Some genuinely friendly drivers are all too eager to share. Often, they'll hand you something to smoke and look suspicious if you turn it down. But everyone hands you something. Texans may hand you a beer. Vegetarians or born-again Christians or Communists or right-wingers may hand you their philosophy; traveling salesmen may hand you advice on going back to school. You can always get the things you don't need. The truck drivers, now, they'll hand you a thermos of coffee. You get along with truck drivers. They're serious travelers, like you are.

Yes, you're a serious traveler. You're serious enough to stand there while a thousand or two thousand or five thousand cars go by, waiting for the one that will give you a ride. You stand there and smile blindly into the glassy stares of the approaching drivers. Those drivers may or may not look at you in passing — probably not; hitchhikers are at the low end of the social scale on the road. If you're smart, you won't look too closely at the drivers who pass. Especially not the women. A woman traveling alone will almost never pick you up . . . not in reality, anyway. Only in your idle dreams.

Dreams and coffee and sunrises make up the rhythm of the road.

Music is a part of it, too: the popular music on the jukeboxes and radio stations. You hear it constantly, in diners and on car radios. The music has a rhythm that fits the steady drumming of tires over pavement. It seeps into your bloodstream. After a while it ceases to make any difference whether or not you *like* the stuff. When you're traveling alone, a nameless rider with a succession of strangers, it can give you a comforting sense of the familiar to hear the same music over and over.

At any given time, a few current hits will be overplayed to exhaustion by the rock & roll stations. In hitching across the continent, you might hear the same song fifty or sixty times. Certain songs become connected in your mind with certain trips.

When I hear the Stones doing "Tumbling Dice" now, I remember driving across west Texas at night, stopping at a cafe where there were Mexican paintings on the walls and where the young oilfield workers, marooned in this wasteland, asked for news of the outside world. Hearing Alice Cooper's "Eighteen" brings back an image of crossing Tennessee in early spring, when white dogwood blossoms were just beginning to appear in the dark woods. I was traveling when the Doors released "Riders on the Storm" — every time I got picked up that song would be on the radio, and at the verse "there's a killer on the road," the driver would look at me with sudden suspicion. Then a few months later, Creedence came out with "Sweet Hitchhiker" and sealed up the wound with bubblegum.

. . . And now I was three days into this run from Tucson to Islamorada, and a song had emerged to characterize this trip, a new one from the jazz-rock combo Steely Dan. The lyrics said nothing about Loggerhead Kingbirds, but I heard something personal in the cynical tone of the song: "You'll go back, Jack, and do it again." Maybe it was true. Here I was starting off to try for a Big Year record, for the second year in a row; and if I could not make better time than this, I was going to fail, for the second year in a row. Would I make it to Islamorada and then to Pennsylvania in time? Why wasn't I getting decent rides?

Slow travel was just one of the things that threatened to derail my year-list attempt. People often would pick me up because they were tired and wanted someone to help drive; but I didn't have a driver's license. I always went ahead and drove for them, but carefully. Had I been stopped for even a minor offense, I might have been locked up for weeks. So when I was at the wheel, I was the most law-abiding joker on the road, except that technically I shouldn't have been driving at all.

Late the night before, going into Louisiana, a guy had asked me to drive his brand-new shiny Torino GT while he had a nap. Fine, I said. It had rained, and the pavement was slick, but I had no problems with it — not until a rabbit darted across the highway. My kindness-to-animals instinct hit the brake before I could think. We went off into the median strip, flinging up mud and jolting the Torino's owner into wide-awake panic as we bounced up into the opposite lane. Fortunately, very few cars were on the road. I drove half a mile down the wrong side of the freeway, with this guy screaming at me the whole way, before finding a place to get back across. So much for *that* ride.

There had been other minor disasters. At San Antonio, Texas, I'd intended to go around the bypass rather than going through town. But this guy who gave me a ride on the bypass assured me there was a good shortcut across one edge of the loop. I should have known better than to take his advice: locals never know anything about hitching through their own cities. When I tried the shortcut, I wound up having to walk the last five miles out to the other edge of town.

Finally through San Antonio, hitching east, I got a ride that was almost funny. It was in an ancient clunker with California plates, driven by a longhair who looked as dilapidated as the car. Whatever he had been smoking, it clearly held the upper hand now. "I dunno, man," he muttered, in a singsong voice. "I was thinking of maybe going to Florida, but I dunno . . . don't have any bread for gas. Maybe I oughta book it back to Cal . . . I dunno, man. I don't think this old car is gonna make it very far." He was correct on the last point, anyway. We had hardly gone twenty miles before the car caught fire — and we both wound up hitchhiking, out there miles from anything.

I was having far more bad luck than anyone could reasonably expect, and I was starting to doubt that I could keep my rough schedule for this trip. One option was to skip the Loggerhead Kingbird at Islamorada and head straight for Pennsylvania. But kingbirds had always ranked among my favorite birds, and there might never be another Loggerhead Kingbird in the United States. On the other hand, if I didn't make Pennsylvania in time to join the Lancaster bunch on their New England trek, I'd have to get the northeastern winter specialties on my own. That would mean hitchhiking around all those frigid little states (about which I knew very little, except that they were cold in winter) without the security of a warm car to return to. I was too tired to think about it.

Out of the west, now, high clouds paraded across the sky, in a ceremonial sunset. From where I stood, facing the eastbound traffic, the highway seemed to come straight out of the sun. The pavement glared, and sunlight flashed from the chrome and glass of the passing cars, setting off little fireworks behind my tired eyes. But it was all right. I was free and aimed in the direction that I had chosen. Like a leaf floating in a creek, I might be stalled briefly in a backwater eddy, but eventually the flow would pick me up and sweep me on downstream — toward my destination.

Time of a Rival

BAD LUCK on the road can last only so long; then you die, or your luck improves. After a very slow start east from Tucson, I eventually made faster progress. But I reached my destination in the Florida Keys at the most frustrating time of day possible. After four days on the road, I walked up to the stakeout for the Loggerhead Kingbird at dusk — just after every bird in town had gone to roost for the night.

The cross-country grind had worn me down. When it was dark enough, I slipped into a vacant lot between houses to roll out my sleeping bag on the hard ground. I listened a while for dogs — the noble dog is a major drawback to camping in strangers' yards — but none came around. I dismissed the possibility that I might be discovered by humans; no one checks, no one expects to find hitchhikers dozing in the shrubbery.

My sleep was not interrupted. But in the morning, it seemed my luck was still bad. Ted Parker had told me that numbers of Scissor-tailed Flycatchers and Western Kingbirds were wintering in Islamorada and that the Loggerhead associated with two of the Westerns, near the corner of Atlantic and Jerome. To my consternation, I could not even find any Scissor-tails or Westerns at first. Had all the birds moved out? Finally, around eight o'clock, Scissor-tails began to appear. Hiking around town, I counted at least twenty-five Scissor-tailed Flycatchers and five Western Kingbirds. Not bad for birds that were once considered rare east of the Mississippi. But the genuine rarity, the Loggerhead Kingbird, did not show up.

By noon I'd walked the whole town repeatedly and found myself back for the tenth time at the corner of Atlantic and Jerome. Two Western Kingbirds had taken up stations there, but the Loggerhead was not with them. I looked at the Westerns for a minute and walked on.

A big spreading fig tree stood on the opposite corner, and in its shady branches some small birds were moving. The first one I put my binoculars on was a Yellow-throated Warbler, shining like a drop of gold among the dark leaves. The second one . . .

It was a good fifteen seconds before I realized I did not know this bird. I was too busy admiring its pattern: clean-cut white lines on a black face, burnt-orange collar, broad white edgings on the wings. Finally it clicked — it had to be a Stripe-headed Tanager! Another stray from the West Indies, one that would not reach the United States at all in an average year.

After I'd watched the tanager for ten minutes, it flew away, and I walked to a pay phone. Bird-listers usually feel obliged to spread the word about rarities. When I phoned Sandy Sprunt in Tavernier, he told me that the tanager had been reported already — some birders had seen it on the same corner, maybe in the same tree. Sprunt had no new advice on the Loggerhead Kingbird, but he had news from down the Keys: a Lesser Black-backed Gull was at Key West. At that time, this invader from Europe was still considered quite rare in North America. Temporarily abandoning my kingbird quest, I thumbed on down the Keys.

The next morning in Key West, with the help of local birder

Frances Hames, I was able to see the Lesser Black-back at the city dump. Among the hordes of Ring-billed Gulls and handfuls of Herring Gulls, the European outlander was not easy to pick out at first. Frances thought there might be more of these strays around than anyone realized; indeed, by a few years later, Lesser Black-backed Gulls were being seen routinely, in numbers, all over the eastern half of the continent.

Frances also gave me a clue on the missing Loggerhead Kingbird. It had been seen recently, she said, but not at the earlier stakeout. The bird had been spotted farther up U.S. 1, toward the northeast edge of Islamorada.

It was almost anticlimactic when I found the kingbird that afternoon, perched on a wire next to the Townsite Shopper Supermart in Islamorada. The Loggerhead, with the cocky self-assurance of all kingbirds, looked nonchalant about being there. You never would have guessed how out of place it was — not until you tried to look it up in a North American bird guide.

Luck is always a factor in birding. If the Loggerhead Kingbird had been easy to find, I might have turned around and left without having seen the Stripe-headed Tanager or Lesser Black-backed Gull. Those two, like the kingbird, were species I would not see again during the year.

Now I turned my thumb northward. The birders from Lancaster, Pennsylvania, were going to leave for New England Friday afternoon, the 26th of January, and it was late Tuesday when I found the kingbird; I'd have to hurry to join them. But I made it in forty-eight hours. By Thursday evening I was in Pennsylvania.

On the way north I had no real sleep. I had other things instead, like a run-in with the Florida state police, and a five-hour walk at night in a North Carolina drizzle. By the time I landed, like a burned-out rocket, at the edge of Millersville, I was unwashed, unshaven, incoherent, in no condition to be meeting anyone for the first time. Ted Parker had told me I'd get along fine with Harold Morrin. Still, I had doubts, even as I found a pay phone and dialed the number.

"Stay right there," Harold told me. "We'll come get you." A couple of minutes later a van pulled into the lot, with two smiling faces behind the windshield.

I could tell that Harold Morrin was a little surprised by the way I looked, but he didn't make a big deal of it. As he told me later, he dismissed it as "the trademark of youth." Harold looked to be about forty; starting to get bald on top, but with a young-looking face. His aged mother, a retired schoolteacher, lived with him in a tidy house in Millersville, and Harold commuted every day into Lancaster, where he was a company executive. Evidently he had just come from work, and he was still wearing a white shirt and tie. But appearances didn't matter for either of us. With a shared interest in birds, the businessman and the hitchhiker were friends right away.

Harold introduced me to his pal Charlie Mellinger, who had whitening hair and a weathered face, but with a roguish twinkle in his eye that suggested he might be a teenager in disguise. Charlie had not held a regular job in thirty years. He kept busy as a freelance carpenter/painter/gardener/plumber/mechanic/handyman around Millersville. He made his own schedule, took time off when he wished, and spent a lot of his spare time birdwatching.

Friday morning Harold had to go in to work for half the day, so I walked over to Charlie's house. One step into the living room, I found myself staring at what had to be one of the world's greatest Christmas trees. The abundant ornaments hung in a harmonious balance of color; the tinsel accented the sweep of the branches; the effect was of great festive decoration, yet somehow maintaining its natural dignity as a tree. Getting a little dry now, a month after Christmas, but still a marvel to behold. "Yeah," said Charlie, "when I get my tree decorated right, I keep it around for a while and enjoy it."

That was Charlie. If he hadn't wanted a Christmas tree, he wouldn't have bothered; since he had one, he'd keep it as long as he liked — and so what if everyone else had taken theirs down?

We went out birding around the county, eventually winding up on the banks of the wide Susquehanna River. Looking up and down the river, we could count well over a hundred Tundra Swans. In the morning sun the swans shone white against the gray river, against the dark trees on the far shore. I remembered how Ted Parker had talked about coming out here, seeing flights of swans migrating down the Susquehanna. Thinking of Ted reminded me of something else: "Hey, Charlie!" I said. "That's my two hundredth bird for the year."

In the afternoon, Charlie made one last check of the engine in the camper. About 2:30 we drove into Lancaster to pick up Harold. "We're on our way," he smiled, pulling off his necktie and unbuttoning his collar.

North of Lancaster in the town of Lititz we picked up Russ Markert and Andy Mack. Russ was a thin, courteous gentleman, soon to be retiring from his career as a clocksmith; Andy was a wisecracking high-school kid, who turned to me immediately and said, "Well, you're an IDIOT now."

I considered that. "Uh, thanks. What do you mean?"

"Incredible Distances In Ornithological Travel," Harold explained. The acronym seemed appropriate for this weekend, since we were planning to cover 1,500 miles in three days. But to hear the guys talk about it, this was nothing unusual for them.

As we drove north, Harold Morrin told me the history of these IDIOT birding runs. It was hardly a monologue, because Harold always understated his own contribution, so Charlie and Andy and Russ were constantly interrupting to clarify Harold's comments. But the composite story was something like this.

The Lancaster County Bird Club had a tradition of welcoming anyone who might be interested in birds, and no one was a better ambassador than Harold Morrin. ("Oh, I really haven't done much," Harold protested.) Everyone was invited to go birding with him, and Harold would put in huge amounts of time helping people find the birds they wanted to see. ("Now, really," said Harold, "anyone would have done the same thing.") He was especially willing to help beginners who didn't know where to go and kids who were too young to drive. ("Even rotten kids like Andy," Charlie said, giving him a friendly shove.) With Harold's recruiting, LCBC trips were always well attended, whether they were someplace right around the city or to the distant corners of Lancaster County. Sometimes, on big weekends, they would even go as far away as New Jersey or northern Delaware.

But in the late 1960s, one of those kids too young to drive had been Ted Parker. Ted had a level of intensity Harold had not seen before. Almost from the start, Ted had suggestions: *Let's go over there, I hear some callnotes, there'll be a warbler flock.* Or, *The habitat looks better up the road, let's go there.* Then bigger suggestions: *With this weather, our best chance would be up at Middle Creek; let's see what we can find there.* Or, *At this season, we should be down in the southern part of the county; let's go there.*

Harold was surprised at first. But he went along with these ideas, and Ted would produce: speeding through the habitat, looking at everything, and listening, always listening. He would sift through every familiar sight and sound to zero in on the unusual birds. Harold Morrin was wise enough to recognize genius when he encountered it. Their roles shifted; Harold became the follower, and this confident teenager became the leader.

And Ted's suggestions grew more ambitious. *We shouldn't stay in Lancaster County today; we should go over to Tinicum and look for Ruffs. After this weather front, we should drive down to Cape May and see what's moving; we can be there in four hours. We should drive out to Montauk Point to look for eiders; we can be there in six hours. There are great birds in North Carolina, and we could be there in eight hours. Get a couple of people to share the driving, and it'd be easy to do it over the weekend.* Harold kept on accepting these escalating plans, because he was seeing lots of birds, great birds, and having a great time.

Other birders started joining these forays: birders from around eastern Pennsylvania, Delaware, New Jersey, anyone who had the stamina for the kinds of trips that Parker dreamed up. Ted was sixteen now and had his license, and once his hands locked onto the wheel he would drive to the end of the world or to the next birding spot, whichever came first. *There are Greater Prairie-Chickens as close as Illinois, and we could be there in only fifteen hours' drive. We've got a three-day weekend, and if you took one extra day off, we could fit in a quick trip to Florida.* Half the continent, it seemed, was within reach.

Behind them lay the picture-postcard countryside of Lancaster County, where the horse-drawn carriages of the Amish farmers moved peacefully down quiet lanes; ahead of them lay the open highway. Ted Parker and Harold Morrin and their friends would go roaring down that highway almost every weekend, looking for the birds of America.

And in 1971, the year that Parker turned eighteen, they found so many of those birds that they attracted national attention. Ted had just been trying to see every bird he possibly could, as he always did; so Ted and Harold and friends had birded all over the Atlantic seaboard on weekends. They had taken winter trips to New England, a quick spring trip to Florida and a longer one to Texas, and a big summer trip to the northern Rockies and the Pacific Northwest. Then Ted had gone off to school in Arizona in the fall, and instead of going to classes he had tracked down every possible bird in the Southwest and California. By the time the year was over he had set his record of 626 species.

Harold Morrin had watched with pride as his young friend had achieved this milestone. He had watched with pride as the birding community had awakened to the fact that this kid was remarkable — a fact that Harold had recognized first. "Everyone was amazed," he was saying now. "The previous record had held for fifteen years, and then Ted broke it by such a wide margin. He really showed what was possible." Harold shook his head with a smile, then stopped and looked at me. "But I guess Ted's record won't stand for long, now."

Parker himself, I knew, couldn't care less if anyone broke his record. But there was a touch of melancholy in Harold's voice. "I suppose it's inevitable. Everything is moving faster these days. But you know, it was only thirteen months ago that we were looking at an Ipswich Sparrow at Cape Henlopen. That was Ted's last new bird for 1971. Just thirteen months ago."

I had to make Harold feel better. "Whatever I come up with this year," I said, "it won't be as impressive as what Parker did. You guys had to pick up those birds in quick trips. You were working all year, Harold, and Ted was sort of going to school. Me, I can go back for these birds over and over. I didn't see a Short-tailed Hawk in Florida this week, but that's okay. I'll be back. Time is the big advantage I've got."

Charlie pointed out that I'd waste a lot of that time on road-sides, watching cars instead of birds. It was a comment I would hear repeatedly: people overestimated the difficulty of getting rides. "This is the West," I said, although it wasn't. "Seriously, it's not that slow. For a trip across the continent, it's almost as fast as driving. I've got all the time in the world. If I don't die before the year is up, or wind up in jail, I should dig out 635 species, maybe 640."

"Six hundred twenty-seven is all it would take," said Harold.

"Anyway," I concluded, "whatever list I come up with this year, it'll be easy enough for someone to top. The only advantage I have is that nobody else has thought to try a Big Year this year."

Charlie and Harold took turns driving, and the rest of us tried to doze as the miles of interstate rolled away. From midnight on, we camped in the front yard of a birder in northeast Massachusetts. Saturday morning we were up early, and it was cold. The weather was clear, the sun on the horizon very bright, bleak white winter sunshine reflecting on the snow, the ice, the frozen marshlands.

We took the coast road north. Above the morning marshes, parties of American Black Ducks were up and flying. But this morning I was paying as much attention to the countryside as to the birds. This was new territory for me, and it looked the way I expected "typical New England" to look: everything orderly, a conscious arrangement to the farms and fields and leafless woods. In the towns, new buildings in imitation colonial styles stood next to genuine old buildings, restored and maintained. They seemed to take their history seriously here. It was proudly displayed, hung out in the shop windows. Not like the American Southwest, where the history was too recent to be honored, where the real historians lived out on the mesas and came in to the bars on Saturday nights.

Within a few miles we had crossed into New Hampshire, traversed the short coastline, and arrived in the port city of Portsmouth. Harold, who knew this area, took us more or less unerringly around to the east-central part of town. We turned onto a street where reflections of sunlit water rippled on warehouse walls. A block or two down the riverfront, we pulled into a parking lot by the dock where our boat was waiting.

The *Viking Star* had been chartered to take a group of birders out for the day to the submerged banks known as Jeffrey's Ledge, some twenty-five miles offshore. Special birds lived out on those cold gray waters, mostly hardy seabirds, especially alcids — birds that nested on Arctic islands and came south well offshore. Earlier generations of birders had waited for storms to bring alcids within sight of land. Birders of the 1970s were starting to pursue those birds into their own element: boats could be scheduled for weekend trips, but storms could not.

On the dock, birders were milling about, organizing their gear, greeting friends. Harold Morrin seemed to know everyone. At this moment a burly fellow was greeting him effusively, clapping him on the back.

"That's Benton Basham," said Andy. "Jeez, he gets around. We run into him every time we go birding on the coast."

"Basham?" I said. "Isn't he some big deal in the ABA?"

"Yeah, membership chairman or something. He's supposed to live in Tennessee, but I think he spends all his time birding."

The man in question was being steered in our direction by

Harold. "Benton, you remember Andy Mack. And this is Kenn Kaufman, a birder from Kansas. He's a friend of Ted's."

"Hey, yes indeed, Andy, how're you doing? Hey, Kenny, how d'you do. Good to meet you!" He was beaming, as if he could not imagine anything better than meeting another birdwatcher. "What brings you out this way?"

"Harold brought me," I said. But I was smiling; it was impossible not to like the guy immediately.

"Oh, he brought himself, really," Harold put in. "You're going to be hearing more from this young man, Benton. Kenn is out to break Ted's record. He's doing a Big Year."

"Boy, that's really *serious* fun," said Benton. "My buddy Floyd Murdoch is doing the same thing."

"What?"

"My good buddy — Hey, Floyd! Hey! C'mere a minute." A pleasant-faced man, who looked to be in his early thirties, detached himself from a nearby conversation and ambled over. "Kenny, I'd like you to meet my good friend Floyd Murdoch. Floyd is doing a Big Year this year, too."

And he *was,* too.

Floyd Murdoch looked conservative: clean-shaven and short-haired, with steel-rimmed glasses. He was from a British background, but was now teaching at a small college in Michigan and doing final research for his doctoral dissertation. His topic was the history of bird protection in the United States. To get information, he was going to visit National Wildlife Refuges all over the country. The enthusiastic Benton Basham had pointed out to Floyd that, since the refuges were all good birding spots, his research would net him a decent year's list — and if he put in some extra effort, he might post a record. Floyd had made calculations and decided he would have enough time and money left over to make an attempt.

Our conversation was cut short by the imminent departure of the boat. Fifty-eight winter-clad birders shuffled on board, filling the decks to capacity. Lines were cast off; the *Viking Star* edged sluggishly away from the dock, and we headed downstream, toward the harbor mouth.

Before we were out of sight of the dock, I had seen a life bird for me: Great Cormorant. Three were perched, like gaunt statues of themselves, on a stone structure in the river. This big black "shag" was common, I knew, along the northeastern coastlines; the fact that I had never seen it before reflected my lack of experience in that quadrant of the continent.

As a newcomer, I was eager to look at the common birds here. The Great Black-backed Gulls might be old hat to the locals, but they were impressive to someone from the Midwest. The biggest gulls on this continent, they flapped along with heavy wingbeats, circled back in glides like eagles. Herring Gulls and Great Black-backs were converging on our position now from all points in the harbor. Gulls, being great opportunists, make a habit of following boats near shore and picking up any scraps thrown overboard. Birders, who are also great opportunists, take advantage of this by "chumming": tossing out food to keep the gulls interested. Once we are far enough out to sea, the escort of gulls might lure in some of the more oceanic species. Back at the stern, now, Charlie Mellinger was throwing out handfuls of bread crumbs to the flock.

We passed the jetties guarding the river mouth, where Horned Grebes and Red-breasted Mergansers were riding low swells. Rafts of Common Eiders floated offshore. These big chunky sea ducks were another novelty for me, and I was to spend a lot of time that day admiring the eiders, especially the spectacular black-and-white adult males.

Before we were very far offshore, the work of the "chummers" paid off: a Black-legged Kittiwake came in from the horizon, heading straight for the gull flock behind the *Viking Star.* This small ocean-going gull was a hint that we were far enough out to expect some real seabirds. I went up to the bow, where birders were eagerly scanning the waves for alcids. For many on board, alcids were the main reason for taking the trip.

Only three years before, I'd never even seen an alcid. Mainly birds of northern coastlines, alcids were so remote from most birders that they even lacked a good group name. "Alcid" was ornitho-slang from the technical name of the family Alcidae, and the species were called murres, murrelets, auklets, guillemots, puffins, razorbills, dovekies. As a kid, puzzling over my Peterson guides, I'd concluded that one would have to see the alcids to learn their names.

As it would turn out, this was not to be a day for really learning the alcids. Few were present. We saw no murres of either sort, and no puffins. A few Black Guillemots were around; in winter plumage, mocking their name, they looked mostly white. We saw a few Razorbills, chunky big-headed alcids, flying low over the water with fast wingbeats. For a long, frustrating moment, I watched a couple of dots buzzing along the horizon. Someone said these were Dovekies, and I believed them, but I could not count a bird seen so poorly. Luckily, late in the day, a single Dovekie flew from a wave crest off our bow, giving everyone a good view.

Even with few alcids, it was a great day. It was something bold, something removed from the ordinary, to be batting about the winter ocean in search of strange seabirds. When we tired of

Eiders along rocky shoreline

scanning the horizon, we could always go to the stern and watch the attendant gulls. Among them, a couple of frost-colored Iceland Gulls showed up. Black-legged Kittiwakes came and went, weaving gracefully among the larger birds. At times a Northern Gannet would come in, large and long-winged, circling high above the gull flock before continuing on its way.

Many of the birds were new for my year list, of course. And they were new for my newfound competitor. I spent quite a while talking with Floyd Murdoch while we watched these birds.

If I felt nonplussed to meet a rival, so did Floyd. In planning his Big Year he had calculated costs and had figured he could just barely afford it. He saw it as a campaign on a shoestring budget. But my shoestrings were so much shorter than his that he looked wealthy by comparison, and that made him uncomfortable. Fortunately, Benton Basham rescued our conversation.

"Yessir, this ought to be fun," Benton opined. "You two are about evenly matched. Now, look here. Kenny, you don't have so much money, but you have time. You can spend a lot of time on every bird. You can go back for some if you miss them. Now, Floyd, you have a little more money, but you don't have so much time. You have to work these trips into your schedule, and you may not get second chances for a lot of these birds. Boyoboy. This'll be fun for people to watch. You two are evenly matched."

I thought of saying something about the even matchup of motel beds versus roadside ditches, five-minute detours versus five-mile walks . . . but then kicked myself, mentally: *This is the West, right?* I was doing what I had chosen to do, and if I were doing it in less comfort, it was no one's fault but my own.

Still, this competition changed my quest. No longer would 627 species be enough. No longer could I plan to pass up birds that would be too inconvenient for a hitchhiker to reach. To have a chance of holding the new record I would have to go after every bird imaginable, trying for the most remote possibilities. Now the year ahead began to look like a real challenge.

The day after the boat trip, the Lancaster birders and I drove up to central Maine to look for a Northern Hawk Owl staked out near Bangor. On the drive I was silent, contemplating my next move. For a while, I thought about giving up on my quest and going back to Kansas. A girl I had known there might still be single, might take me back if I dropped these wandering dreams. Not understanding the nuances of bird listing, she would never know that I had given up, failed. But I would know . . .

Then I thought about what Ted Parker or Rich Stallcup, previous Big Year champs, would do in this situation. Ted would glide to victory, propelled by birding genius. Rich might do the same, but he would also point out that the competition was not the main thing. What mattered was the birds to be seen, the things to be learned. And that was true. But could I pursue this quest for eleven more months, facing discomfort and danger, at the risk of coming off second best?

By the time we reached Bangor my mind was made up and, free of ambivalence, I could enjoy the Northern Hawk Owl. This owl was a rare visitor anywhere south of the Canadian border, so the news of its presence was drawing birders from throughout the Northeast; we were not surprised when Floyd Murdoch and Benton Basham showed up about the same time we did.

We had directions: precise directions, even pinpointing the large spruce on which the owl usually sat. The owl, unimpressed by such precision, was actually perched on a nearby powerline pole when we first saw it. Apparently our arrival did not impress it either. It merely glanced down at us occasionally with benign indifference, while we gazed back through a battery of binoculars and telescopes and cameras.

The bird was what its name implied: an owl with hawkish character. It lacked the ear-tufts of "horned" owls, and it perched almost horizontally, holding its long tail level behind it. The owl was nearly motionless except that its head moved constantly, its yellow eyes glaring in all directions. Sharp gray and white barring below, and bold black rims to the face, made it the most distinctly patterned owl I'd ever seen. We had been watching it about fifteen minutes when it dropped from its perch and flew with quick wingbeats, low over the snow, toward the large spruce, rising to alight at the top of the tree.

For us, standing in the snow in temperatures well below freezing, it was hard to recall that this was really unusually far south for the Hawk Owl. Before the winter was over, no doubt, the owl would go north again. I would go in every direction from here: south, and west, and back east again, back and forth, and of course north again, because my plan for the year was decided. When I saw a Northern Hawk Owl again, it would be in the Yukon Territory — five months later, and tens of thousands of miles farther along the road.

Strategy and Hard Weather

W HEN *Scott Juelfs and I arrived on the Outer Banks, the long strip of barrier islands off the North Carolina coast, we found Myrtle Warblers wall-to-wall in the bayberry thickets. It was the evening of February 9, 1973. One of the heaviest winter storms on record was advancing on the southeastern states, but we were hardly aware of it. As darkness fell, we sat in Scott's car beneath the flashing beacon of the Bodie Island lighthouse, playing chess.*

It was snowing out. Every time the eye of the lighthouse glowed, the beam caught hundreds of flakes. The snow was not heavy yet, but it was falling at a hard slant on the wind. Must be more sleet than snow, I told myself. The Carolinas are southern states . . .

I simply was not paying enough attention. There is a tendency to assume that the world has been discovered already . . . so when something significant happens, we may not be prepared even to notice. That night on the Outer Banks we were witnessing the start of a major disaster for thousands of birds in the area. But we

did not know it — so our attention was focused on the micro-
cosm of the chessboard.

Scott and I had been holding an intermittent chess tournament
for several years; the score now stood at about twenty-two games
apiece. Scott played an intensive, direct game: guarding his own
king, firing away at mine. My only working strategy was to whit-
tle away his important pieces first, and then corner the king. Our
different methods made for an even match. Chance, as much as
anything else, determined which strategy would prevail in any
one game.

Chance, as much as anything else, had put me on the same January boat trip as Floyd Murdoch. In a way, I was lucky to meet my
competition so early. I would have heard about him eventually;
but it was good to know, early in the year, what I was up against.

After our concurrent New England trips, Floyd returned to
Michigan. He had to teach the spring semester, but he would
make quick trips by car or plane, on weekends, after birds he
needed. I would continue with my own very different strategy —
spending time instead of money. I had plenty of time, I thought,
all the time in the world.

After another day birding around Lancaster with Charlie
Mellinger, after getting more bird-finding directions from Harold
Morrin, I started south. Right away, my luck turned strange.

For one thing, it rained. No one picks up hitchhikers when it's
raining. It took me more than half a day just to get to Baltimore,
which should have been a ride of less than two hours. Getting
around Baltimore took even longer, with long waits for short
rides on the bypass loop.

It was dark before I reached Washington, D.C. Trying to take
the beltway around Washington, I got lost and wound up walking through the heart of the city at midnight. It gave me the
feeling of some patriotic pilgrim. Standing at the iron gates and
peering in at the White House, I saw it for the first time as a real
building, where a real human wrestled with the problems of

statesmanship. Reading the inscriptions on the Lincoln Memorial, walking over to the Washington Monument, I realized with surprise that I was not being harassed by anyone. No guards or police barred my way. It seemed even the vagabonds could come into the capital and admire the monuments.

That feeling of freedom and national pride did not last long. The next day, as I continued south, it was raining buckets again. Halfway across Virginia, south from Richmond, ran a tough toll road. Signs on the shoulder warned against picking up passengers. I managed to get rides anyway, but when the toll road ran into a tangle of interchanges in the middle of Petersburg, Virginia, the old man who was driving got flustered and decided I should get out right there, right now. Right out in the middle of the turnpike, where I was promptly arrested.

The cop was a rookie. Having just been issued his badge, he apparently was ready to go out and arrest the world. An earnest clumsiness marked everything he did, as he pulled the sleek cruiser over and parked not quite out of the way of traffic; hunted around on the dashboard before turning on the flashers; turned on the siren for a second, thought better of it, and turned it off. Put on his Smokey-the-Bear hat, checked it in the rear-view mirror. Started to pull on his raincoat — here he encountered a problem, and made an awkward job of getting out of the car and putting the raincoat on at the same time. Finally he walked around to where I was patiently waiting, and said, "It's mah duty to arrest you fer hitchhikin on the innerstate hahway in the Comwealth of Virginia."

Well, This is the West, I said to myself. We turned around and drove to the Petersburg police station, where the rookie sat befuddled, rainwater dripping off his hat brim, trying to fill out the paperwork. I thought it was all pretty amusing, until the moment when the cell door clanged shut behind me, and it occurred to me that this was for real.

Never having gone to a genuine adult jail before, I didn't know that I should demand my one phone call right away. Once I was in the cell, arranging for access to a phone proved to be difficult.

Since I did not have enough money to pay the fine, I was told, I would be locked up until the following week — then a judge would tell me how much jail time I'd have to serve. This was bad news. Time was the one advantage I had on my year list, and I could not afford to spend any of that time sitting in prison. After two days in the Petersburg jail, I finally convinced a guard that I hadn't had a chance to make a phone call yet; swallowing my pride, I called my parents and asked them to wire me the bail money. I knew they couldn't very well afford it at that point, but they sent it anyway.

When the money came over the wires and someone told me that, technically, I was free, it was one o'clock in the morning. Although I could have stayed in the cell until daylight, I didn't even consider the idea. I just wanted out. The rain had ended; it felt wonderful to be out in the open air again.

Three blocks from the jail I encountered a wild-eyed young man, carrying a knife, who tried to hold me up. I suppose I should have been scared . . . but having just gotten out of jail myself, I was in no mood to take any crap from a bona fide criminal. We had a lengthy argument, which deteriorated into a scuffle for possession of the knife. The mugger was distracted by a car coming down a side street; I had enough time to drop my backpack and whip off my belt — my leather belt with the heavy, square-cornered buckle — and get it swinging around my head. The belt outreached the knife, and my erstwhile attacker backed off, shouted profanities at me for a while, and then disappeared down an alley.

When I was sure he was gone, I retrieved my backpack and walked on. In the next block I was stopped, questioned, and searched by the police.

From Petersburg I continued south. Harold Morrin had told me that a Eurasian Green-winged Teal was being reported on the Outer Banks of North Carolina. At that time, this bird was regarded as a separate species from the American Green-wing, so it would count on my year list. I'd been wanting to visit the Outer Banks anyway, and the teal gave me a good excuse.

Reaching the Raleigh-Durham area of North Carolina, I tried to call a couple of young birders who had been transplanted here from Kansas. After several tries I connected with Sebastian Patti, a student at Duke. Sebastian had been spending some of his weekends birding the Outer Banks, and he gave me detailed directions on where to find the birds there.

Thumbing rides over to Chapel Hill, I managed to locate my old comrade Scott Juelfs. Scott was a better general naturalist than I; here at the University of North Carolina, he was taking a double major in zoology and botany. He was only mildly impressed with my Big Year project, but his interest picked up considerably when I started talking about the Outer Banks. Although he had explored the Appalachians and the South Carolina coast, the North Carolina Banks would be new territory for him. We agreed to make an expedition there the following weekend.

After a week of temperatures in the 40-to-60 range, it was a surprise to step outside Friday morning and feel a biting chill in the air. The wind was still cold at 11 A.M., when Scott came back from classes and we headed for the coast.

Along the road we saw few birds, aside from a handful of Eastern Bluebirds. Beyond Williamston on U.S. 64, towns were few, traffic sparse. The leafless woods were low and swampy. A few miles beyond the wide Alligator River, where the Intracoastal Waterway went through, we took the long bridge that left the mainland and went out to Roanoke Island.

Roanoke was historically famous as the site of the ill-fated Lost Colony. The tourist town of Manteo looked rather lost today, this being a cold day in the off-season. Roanoke Island was well wooded, as the mainland had been. But as we came to the bridge leading on across to Bodie Island, the sky opened up ahead of us. Beyond Bodie was nothing but a great wall of gray sky coming down to the sea.

On Bodie Island, U.S. 64 ended at a T-junction, with small

highways running north and south. Barrier beaches between the ocean and the coastal sounds, the Outer Banks paralleled the coast, thirty miles offshore in places. North from this T-junction were more small towns and the historic dunes of Kitty Hawk. We turned south toward the Pea Island refuge, which Sebastian Patti had recommended.

A strong, cold wind carried a hint of misty rain. Despite the cold, however, the next thing we saw was a flock of Tree Swallows, at least seven hundred of them. This seemed like an omen of good climate, because swallows ordinarily eat flying insects. Actually, Tree Swallows cheat — they eat berries during cold spells, so they can winter farther north than their relatives. Still, we figured these birds would not be around unless the Outer Banks were generally warmer than they seemed this evening.

Southward on Bodie Island, the highway was walled by dense thickets of yaupon and bayberry up to twelve feet tall. Everywhere along the edges was a movement of small birds. They flitted among the branches, darted across the road, in a feathered approach to perpetual motion. Slowing down to look at them, we concluded, after glancing at several hundred, that they were all Myrtle Warblers. The Myrtles (to be known in later years, less poetically, as the eastern subspecies of Yellow-rumped Warbler) were in winter plumage, brownish gray, markings blurred. When they flew, they signaled their identity with a triangle of light spots: a yellow patch on the rump, and white spots in the corners of the tail. This code was flashed at us from all directions. The calls of the Myrtles, hard *check* notes, filled the thickets.

We wanted to get to the National Wildlife Refuge headquarters before it closed for the weekend, so we continued south across the high bridge over Oregon Inlet. South of the inlet, the thickets were more scattered; there were more marshes, diked-in ponds, open fields, with flocks of Snow Geese on the flats. The guys at refuge headquarters had little to add to what Sebastian had told us about the birds there. We thanked them, picked up refuge maps and bird checklists, and drove north again.

With the overcast and the late hour, light was beginning to fade when we turned off toward the Bodie Island lighthouse. This side road was lined with neatly planted pines, the only trees we'd seen since reaching the Outer Banks. At the end of the corridor of pines was a large parking lot, deserted now. We walked around the lighthouse to a raised wooden platform overlooking a large marshy pond, one of the spots we'd been told to check for the Eurasian Green-winged Teal.

It was getting too late to check, though. Daylight was failing, and the wind, still strong, now carried a veil of sleety rain. We could see duck silhouettes along the pond margins, and it would be worth spending time here tomorrow, but — "I think today's birding is over," Scott said.

We descended from the observation platform. Even now, with sleet and darkness both falling fast, the thickets around the lighthouse were alive with Myrtle Warblers. Their calls, sharp *check* notes, came from far and near in the bushes as we walked back to the car.

Leaving Bodie Island to the warblers, we drove back into Man-

Myrtle Warblers

teo. Few places were open, but we found an unfriendly little diner — deserted except for a few glum locals — where we drank coffee and wrote up our notes from the afternoon.

Our original plan, or lack of one, had been to camp out on the beach. But the wind was still increasing, now heavy with sleet. We couldn't afford a motel. "Let's go back to the lighthouse," I suggested. "Those pines should block the wind, and there ought to be enough light to play chess by." Scott had brought his portable chess set for such a situation.

The Bodie Island lighthouse was easy to find in the dark. The giant light behind the huge lenses flashed on every few seconds, and we sat in the car below, puzzling over our chess moves by the intermittent light. In the back of my mind, though, I was puzzling over all the Myrtle Warblers we had seen that evening. It was ironic to come to this refuge, a wintering ground for great thundering flocks of waterfowl, and to be most impressed by a bird five inches long. Hardly an unusual bird, either. Back in Kansas, it had been one of the first warblers to come through in spring, and one of the most common. So what had caught my attention here? Sheer numbers. The uneasy feeling that there were, somehow, *too many* Myrtle Warblers here, more than the thickets could hold.

The Myrtle is typical of the warbler family in some respects. It is classified in *Dendroica,* the genus that includes nearly half the fifty-odd kinds of warblers in North America. Like many other Dendroicas, the Myrtle spends the summer in evergreen forests of the far north and moves south in autumn. The difference is in distance traveled. Black-throated Blue and Cape May warblers fly to the West Indies for the winter; Magnolia and Bay-breasted and Black-throated Green warblers fly to Central America; Blackburnian and Blackpoll warblers go to South America. But the Myrtle Warbler's main wintering area is along the Atlantic and Gulf coasts of the United States.

Score a point for the vegetarians. The Myrtle Warbler — one of the most successful members in a family of insect-eaters — is one of the few that eats berries regularly. This diet shift gets it through cold weather, when insects are hard to find, when most warblers would starve. Such a strategy might be a big advantage: migration is dangerous; most kinds of warblers probably lose much of their population every year to the casualties of long migrations and overwater flights. With its much shorter migration, the Myrtle Warbler manages to reduce the dangers of travel. In the winter bayberry thickets, surrounded by edible berries, the bird seems to signal that all is well by giving its distinctive call-note: *Check!*

"Checkmate," said Scott.

It was what I deserved, for not focusing on the chessboard. We set up the pieces again and started a new game.

Trying to concentrate this time . . . outside, the sleet continued, increased, swept past the lighthouse lenses in driving clouds. Only it was not sleet any more: big flakes were sticking to the car windows, and the parking lot was turning white. "Snow," I said. "Ridiculous. I thought the Carolinas were southern states. Where's this Yankee weather coming from?"

By now we had the engine running, so we could turn on the heater. Switching on the radio, we picked up a weather report that it was snowing all over the Carolinas: temperatures dropping, drifts piling up, road conditions deteriorating. The soft-drawling radio commentators clearly regarded all this as highly unusual. Turning off the radio, I said, "You know, I wonder if this storm could be the reason we were seeing so many Myrtle Warblers this evening."

Scott looked up. "You think it's an influx from farther north? But the heaviest snow is supposed to be south of us, and inland."

"Well, look," I said, "it's bound to be warmer here on the coast — the elevation, you know, and the effect of the ocean. I was reading about the situation in Europe — when the weather gets exceptionally cold on the Continent, there's a big flight of birds out to the British Isles. It's not any kind of regular migration, just a mass movement to the northwest, to escape the cold. Lapwings, and some kinds of thrushes . . . I think it's called a hard weather movement."

"So you think the Myrtle Warblers might be pulling the same kind of flight, moving out here from the mainland."

"Seems plausible."

Scott considered that for a minute. "Great Britain is big," he said. "The Outer Banks are not. I can't picture all the Myrtle Warblers from hundreds of miles inland being programmed to fly out to these little sandbars when the weather gets rough."

I conceded that he had a point. "But it could be happening on a minor level. A general movement out to the coastal plain . . . if the birds keep moving seaward to the last land, the flock stops here."

"Well, consider this," said Scott. "Checkmate. You lose again. That's twenty-five to twenty-two now, Kaufman; I'm leaving you in the dust. Anyway, we don't know if we're seeing unusual numbers. I admit that they're incredible, but maybe they're always like this here in winter."

This point was hard to debate, since we had no data for comparison. The discussion stalled. Outside, the wind increased. We could feel it buffeting the car, eddying around the corners, edging in at the cracks. Wind was an incessant background noise, a nervous, gnawing sound, eating holes in our concentration. We fought one more chess game to a stalemate before calling it quits.

The night dragged out to be a long one. I was lying cramped in the front seat under my sleeping bag, trying not to become entangled in the steering wheel. Sleep was elusive. Every time the wind shifted I was shaken awake, feeling uneasy, and sat up to stare out at the accumulating drifts of snow.

Morning arrived with an unpleasant insistence. The interior of the car was as cold as an Eskimo's tomb. Outside, the snow had changed back into freezing rain. Slushy ice was settling now into the marshes, the thickets, the roads. Especially the roads. "Looks like a fun morning," said Scott.

It was one of those mornings when you realize, with chilling clarity, that birding is a ridiculous activity. But ridiculous or not, it was what we had come for. Climbing out of the car into the wind, hunching up our coat collars, we hurried to the observation platform to see what was on the lighthouse pond.

Up on the platform we were lashed by stinging rain. Visibility was poor. Ducks on the pond, Blacks and Pintail and Green-winged Teal, were staying close to the marsh grass. The teal had to be scrutinized one by one. Holding binoculars steady in clammy hands, we would squint at one teal drake at a time to be sure it was just the American form.

All the time we were on the tower, the surrounding thickets were filled with the activity of Myrtle Warblers. I wondered if I detected a note of anxiety in their calls. There was ice on the branches in the thickets, and more icy rain in the air; no matter how good the bayberry supply was, it would do the warblers no good if the berries were all encased in ice. The flocks seemed to have a direction to their movements today, a deliberate exodus from one thicket to the next, searching for food.

Scott and I were numb by the time we finished checking the ducks on the lighthouse pond. Hurrying back to the car, we cranked the heater up and headed for the ponds on the refuge.

At one of the flats along the road at least a hundred Snow Geese grazed, hunched down against the wind. A car with Florida plates was parked on the road shoulder. The two women in the car, armed with binoculars and Audubon patches, told us they had made a special trip here to look for Ross's Goose. This western goose was still considered a great rarity in the East in the 1970s, but one had been reported among the Snow Geese here this season. We spent a few minutes scanning the flock. While we were there more Snows came in and with them another goose, a dark one: Greater White-fronted Goose. Scott was excited, because the White-front is fairly rare in the Carolinas. The Florida women were unimpressed. They'd come here to get a life bird, and they didn't want to see anything but a Ross's Goose.

We returned to our search for the Eurasian Green-winged Teal, agreeing to check with the Florida women later in case we saw their bird. But it was becoming obvious that our own search would be more than enough to keep us busy. Hundreds of teal were present, dark little ducks sitting on distant water or flying up against the wind. In some places we could study the teal from inside the car. More often, we had to make sorties out along the pond edges. Each time, we came back chilled clear through, soaked with icy rain. We would put the heater on full blast, listen to the radio reports about the disastrous effects of this record-breaking storm, wait until our teeth stopped chattering, and then look for another concentration of ducks.

We went down past the refuge headquarters, checking all the teal, and then returned north through the same areas. On the way back we ran into the Florida women again, still searching for the Ross's Goose, still grimly unsuccessful.

It was about that time that I began to feel that we birders were missing the whole point.

A storm of impressive dimensions was going on around us — and we were ignoring it. We were running around like idiots, looking for the odd bird that did not belong here. "Listen," I said, impulsively, "let's go up to Oregon Inlet and watch what's happening there."

Scott raised one eyebrow. "There aren't likely to be any teal there."

"I don't care."

At the inlet, violence and confusion prevailed. Spray mingled in the air with sleety rain. Waves running ten to twelve feet high were coming in from the northeast, to smash on the seaward side. We tried scanning the ocean, thinking that seabirds might be pushed in close by the weather, but we could see little in that direction. Surf Scoters and Red-breasted Mergansers occasionally would be tossed into view between wave crests. The inlet itself boiled with currents and countercurrents; four Red-throated Loons and several Horned Grebes had moved into the protected waters of the small-boat harbor on the north side of the inlet.

Where the wind struck the high arch of the Oregon Inlet bridge, big gulls were riding on the updrafts above and alongside the bridge: dozens of Herring Gulls, a few Great Black-backs. Smaller gulls seemed unable to handle the air currents there. We saw a flock of the small Bonaparte's Gulls come over the inlet, fluttering hard, scudding sideways on the gusts.

Back to the north on Bodie Island, Myrtle Warblers were swarming along the road. Scores of them were down on the road shoulder, in the grass, searching for food. We tried making sample counts, but it was impossible. Our best wild guess was that we were seeing three thousand warblers per mile of road — and even over the sound of the wind we could hear more, thousands more, calling in the thickets. With so many present, and food so hard to find, and the weather so rough, it seemed certain that many would not live to see the following day. We were not surprised to find several sitting on the road, inactive, eyes dull. Even the ones still up and flying were having problems; twice in ten minutes we heard a soft *thud* as the wind tossed flying warblers against the side of the car.

We encountered a line of cars parked along the road: Sebastian Patti's group from Duke. Sebastian, wrapped up against the cold and rain, came over to talk — mostly about the day's weather. I mentioned my amazement at the numbers of Myrtle Warblers: "This has *got* to be unusual. An influx from somewhere." Sebastian looked thoughtful. It was possible, he said, but there were *always* incredible numbers of Myrtles here in winter. He had one concrete suggestion: his gang from school had taken over most of a motel in Manteo; if Scott and I didn't mind sleeping on someone's floor, he said, there'd be room. We thanked him, said we'd probably take him up on it.

Driving north toward Nags Head, we found some of the Tree Swallows we had seen the day before. They were not doing well. Their buoyant flight, which made them so maneuverable in calm air, only seemed to make them vulnerable in these winds. They were staying low, even sitting on the ground, around the edges of bayberry thickets. We saw a few swallows circle up higher, and a sudden gust carried them away like so many leaves.

Going back south on Pea Island again, we were noticing the high water in the roadside marshes. All that rain and sleet, and runoff from snow, coupled with what had to be high storm tides, had raised the water level significantly. That could be a bad thing for the creatures of the marsh. Their habitat was created by a fine balance of water and land and plant life; when water went on a rampage, the other elements could hardly compete . . . "Wait a minute," I said. "Stop. Back up. What was that?"

A dark shape was stalking along the road shoulder. Scott jammed the car into reverse, and the shape resolved itself into a chunky, angular, beaky marsh bird, a Clapper Rail. Evidently the rail had been flooded out of the marsh and had come up on the road as the only available high ground.

The rail looked miserable. I thought of Clappers I had pursued in the tidal meadows of summer. The Clapper in summer was often hard to see, but easy to hear, as it darted devilishly from one reed-bed to another or raised a clattering cackling chorus to the sunrise. How different to see it now, forced out in the open, hesitating between flooded marsh and fearsome road. Looking cold and ratty and bitter, the rail splashed back into the water-logged marsh. Before the day was over, we would see several more refugee rails wandering the roads.

Late in the afternoon, Scott and I were standing at the south end of Bodie Island, looking across Oregon Inlet. Snow was driving almost horizontally on the wind, and we could barely make out land on the far side of the gap. Out above the roiled waters of the inlet, up in the raging wind, the gull flock was still there: we occasionally could see them wheeling and gliding, dim shapes through the screen of snow. The gulls apparently were the only birds that were faring well in this mad weather.

From behind us, loose groups of Myrtle Warblers would approach, coming from the thickets of Bodie Island. It appeared they had given up on foraging there and were moving on in a desperate search for food. The Myrtles would come past us and strike out across the inlet, struggling in the crosswind. Some were flying too low, and wave crests picked them out of the air. A few, overpowered by the wind or just disoriented, crashed into the bridge supports and fell, to be scooped up by the predatory Herring Gulls. Some of the warblers continued flying until they faded in the veil of snow.

Just the night before, I had been admiring the strategy of this species. I'd been thinking that the Myrtle Warbler had it made: adapted to winter on the Carolina coastal plain, it avoided the dangers of the long trans-oceanic migration.

Today we were seeing the other side of the coin. Those warblers that had taken the risky flight, that had made the long crossing to the West Indies or South America, were far beyond the reach of this death-dealing storm. But the Myrtle Warblers were caught out. It seemed there could be no perfect strategy. The variables would take their toll, culling the marginal birds from either side, leaving only the strongest to carry on.

Night was falling as we turned away from the inlet and headed in toward town. On the way, we were talking about the insulation of human experience. We live enclosed in artificial structures with controlled climates, synthetic food, and purified water. No wonder our glimpses of the real world come as a shock. Today we'd been out at the edge of things, looking across into another existence, where a major storm could mean life or death. But now we were going back into Manteo to take it easy — to join all those people who were sitting in their houses, listening to weather reports without feeling the weather . . .

As we drove into Manteo, we noticed that the town looked strangely dark. When we located the group from Duke we found out the reason. The storm had knocked out the transformer up at Kitty Hawk, and the whole region was without electricity.

We never did decide whether the abundance of Myrtle Warblers that day had been unusual. We had not been able to make precise counts, and neither had any previous observers. There was little point in comparing wild estimates.

But a change was noticed later. The following winter, Christ-

mas Bird Count totals of *Myrtle Warblers were lower throughout the middle Atlantic states. Writing about the counts in* American Birds, *Danny Bystrak noted this decline. "Some observers," he wrote, "feel that a large part of the population may have been destroyed in the heavy snow that the Southeast got in the early spring of 1973."*

To the Promised Landfill

THAT MORNING I got the Ringed Kingfisher, the big Mexican kingfisher, down on the Rio Grande below Falcon Dam. Everyone knew the place; every birder who came to Texas in the 1970s would see them — the only Ringed Kingfishers in the United States — along this stretch of river, where Edgar Kincaid had discovered them in the late 1960s.

The night before, I had walked the last three or four miles from Highway 83 along the road that led to the dam spillway. That morning the birds came over: two of them, one following the other by a hundred yards, calling out a measured *tchak . . . tchak . . .* as they flew. They were big birds, with powerful wingbeats, looking twice the size of our familiar Belted Kingfisher. When one of them swooped down to land in a snag at the top of a riverside tree, it gave a wild clattering rattle that would have put any Belted Kingfisher to shame.

In those days we wondered if the Ringed Kingfishers might have been there all along, overlooked because few birders had visited that section of river before. It turned out later that the birds were actively spreading northward. Within a few years they would be found all up and down the Rio Grande Valley, and some would show up well north into central Texas. But in 1973 the big kingfisher was still an exciting specialty of Falcon Dam, flying boldly, making loud noises, and giving the place a tropical feeling.

. . . That was all there was, though: a tropical feeling, and two Mexican-American birds flying high above the boundary river. A feeling of elation — and at the back of my mind, an opposite reaction, a vague letdown because the search was over. A release of tension, and then the tightening of the spring for the next search: chasing a record, the most important bird was always the next one, not this one, and there was always another new bird somewhere ahead.

For the moment, what lay ahead of me was the long hike back out to Highway 83. I shouldered my pack and started walking.

I had come this way before, when I had made my first stab at a Big Year in early 1972, more than a year earlier. A year is a long time, but nothing here seemed to have changed: the same dust still lingered in the air, the mesquite brush still wore the same dead look. The town of Falcon Heights still baked under the sun, dominated by the surrounding desert hills. The Palace Grill there, where I'd stopped for coffee the year before, was closed now, the windows boarded up. The little motel had been repainted, but still looked as abandoned as it had before. It was evident that Falcon Heights had not changed.

But I had.

A year is a long time. I'd spent that time traveling around, sleeping on roadsides and in vacant lots, eating whatever and whenever I could, working only when I had to, birding and learning all the time. It had been exciting, but I was beginning to feel the mileage.

For one thing, I was thinner now. It was only the beginning of March, 1973, but I'd already come to the point of not knowing where my next dollar was coming from. Under these circumstances, I economized to extremes. It was a rare educational opportunity (coming, as I did, from a middle-class family in an affluent generation) to get to learn firsthand what genuine, serious hunger felt like.

I wanted to claim that the hardship of my starvation diet lent some kind of dignity to my listing effort; but just as often, it made it seem like a joke. During the last few days, stalking the trails at Santa Ana refuge and Bentsen park, I'd had to force myself to concentrate on birds; whenever my concentration slipped at all, I found myself daydreaming about food. It seemed ignoble and absurd to have no higher visions, but I was down about thirty-five pounds from what I had weighed as a healthy sixteen-year-old, and I was hungry.

That was something I could still laugh about. But there were other kinds of hunger, and other ways in which I'd changed.

Life on the road was beginning to make me cynical. It had not been that way at first. In my earliest hitching travels, all I had noticed was that there were so many nice people around, always a friendly stranger to come along and offer me a ride. But at some point my focus had shifted and I had begun to notice the other drivers, the ones who did not stop. I had looked into their faces. On a busy road there might be thousands of drivers that passed before I got a ride; most would ignore me altogether, and those who looked at all would look with hostility or contempt. Watching the expressions, I could see that thumbers, beyond any doubt, were the lowest form of life on the road.

I shouldn't have cared, and maybe I didn't, so long as I got the rides eventually. But every day that I stood out by the road, facing the approaching traffic, my subconscious must have been counting up the score of rejections. It may have translated to a subliminal desire to be accepted, to be a respected part of the community.

There are many kinds of hunger. Any of them can be easier to take if you can truly believe in what you're doing. On most days my birding travels seemed worthwhile to me, a valuable use of my time. Today, my enthusiasm was limited. My destination for the afternoon was the city dump at Brownsville; my quarry was a flock of Mexican Crows currently staked out at the dump.

The case of the Mexican Crow was one of those border-patrol birding situations that bordered on the ridiculous. The species had always been there — fifty miles *south* of the Rio Grande; it had always been the first brand-new bird that an ornithologist would pick up after crossing into Mexico. Sometime in the 1960s, apparently, the crows wandered north and discovered that there was food in the huge dump at Matamoros, just south of the Rio. From there it was only a short hop across to the Brownsville dump on Boca Chica Drive, where the pickings were richer, because the Americans threw away more food than the Mexicans did. The Brownsville dump became a regular winter hangout for a flock of Mexican Crows.

As an extension of range, this was pretty minor. But because the crow had crossed a political boundary, it was in the A.O.U. Check-list Area and was suddenly fair game for all the listers. Everyone came down to see it — after all, it counted as one more species — but no one seemed too thrilled about it. Harold Morrin, I recalled, had been mortified that the Mexican Crow at the Brownsville dump had been the landmark 600th bird on his life list.

So this was my project for the day: to hitchhike to a dump on an inconvenient road outside of town, looking for an undistinguished little crow that was a U.S. bird by virtue of only a few miles. If I saw it, my year list would reach 326 — putting me past the halfway mark in the assault on 650. If I *didn't* see it, I'd be wasting a tough hitchhike (and this would be one more species that my competitor, Floyd Murdoch, might have up on me). Either way, this was just listing-for-the-sake-of-listing, with no trace of ornithology involved, and it made me temporarily cynical about the entire effort. A year is a long time, I reflected, and it looked as if 1973 would be longer than most.

By late morning I had left the arid heights of Falcon behind, headed down the Valley toward Brownsville. For the first sixty miles, Highway 83 was a two-lane road running through dry country where towns were sparse. Approaching Mission and Mc-Allen, 83 broadened out to a four-lane and then to a full-scale freeway. From here east a whole volley of towns, large and small, came in a continuous stream along the road. Traffic multiplied. Having come from the silences of Falcon directly to this freeway mob scene, I was feeling shell-shocked as I faced the eastbound cars.

Standing at attention, I faced this onslaught of traffic. The cars streamed past, racing on without me. Although I knew I shouldn't, once again I was watching the faces of the drivers that passed — most of them, of course, ignoring me; some looking at me with open hostility; a few looking with curiosity. And then I saw my ride.

Her eyes were what I noticed first. Even at a distance, I could tell she was looking at me. There were other cars closer; but she caught my attention while she was still some ways off, all alone in a cream-yellow Mustang, driving fast in the far left-hand lane.

Realistically I did not believe in judging people by their cars. But I had a special feeling about Mustangs. In my midteens I had had two girlfriends at different times who had driven Mustangs; as different as these two young women were from each other, they had been alike in being independent and somewhat wild. Each of them was a bit older than I, but still quite young, and together we were learning things about life for the first time. Days and nights of running around, of drinking underage, skating on thin ice, barely staying out of trouble . . . we were underage for everything but at some level we cared about each other, and that was our morality, while it lasted. So an attractive young woman driving a Mustang was bound to catch my attention. I locked my eyes onto hers, knowing she'd be gone in a few seconds.

And as she pulled even, there was a sudden scream of brakes. The Mustang came swerving across the lanes — my God, I thought, is she going to crash? — and pulled to a stop on the shoulder, twenty yards up from where I stood. I grabbed my backpack and ran up to the car.

The driver was young and blond with unsettling dark eyes. I

nodded at her casually, jockeyed my backpack into the back seat, and jumped in the front seat beside her. She whipped the car back out into the flow of traffic, looking independent and confident. I liked her immediately.

Her name was Diana, and she worked up the Valley in Edinburg, but she'd taken today off. I told her I was going down to Brownsville, without saying why.

"Well, I'm not going that far," she said. "I can take you as far as Harlingen, but first I gotta stop down here at Weslaco and pick up a friend. If you don't mind waiting, it should only take a minute." She laughed and added, "I guess it won't slow you down much."

"No, that'd be fine," I said. "Sure beats walking." I didn't mind stretching this ride by a few minutes.

Conversation lapsed for a while, and we listened to the car radio. At length Diana looked over at me and said, "Are you from Brownsville, then?"

"No . . . I'm sort of from All Over. I've been hanging out in Arizona recently. Around Tucson and Phoenix."

"Yeah?" she persisted. "What's happening in Brownsville, then? Do you have friends there?"

Oh, Hell, I said to myself. I had a sudden memory from the previous fall, recalling how Joel Greenberg and I had tortured Ted Parker at the campus bookstore by telling the girls that Ted was a genuine expert birdwatcher. "Actually," I told Diana, "I'm going to the city dump at Brownsville to look at some crows."

She gave me one look — a great look, incredulity coupled with irritation. "Okay," she said, "if you don't want to tell me why you're going, you don't have to."

"Hey, I'm serious," I protested. "Really. There's a flock of crows at the Brownsville dump, and they're Mexican Crows, and they're the only ones in the United States. And I want to go see them."

Her expression right then was priceless. The questions were all over her face; apparently, she couldn't decide which to ask first. Finally she laughed a little and said, "Wow. Far out. Everything in the Valley is Mexican any more. What's a Mexican Crow?"

"Nothing special," I told her. "It's just another black bird. Sort of like the USA crows, but smaller, and it has a deeper voice."

"A deeper voice, huh? Wow, a macho crow. What are they doing at the dump? And how do you know they're there, anyway?"

"I don't *know* they're still around. But they've been there all this winter, and the last couple of winters. And they hang around the dump because they eat garbage."

"Sounds like you're trying to feed me some garbage, too," said Diana; but I could see that she was turning the idea over in her mind, deciding that I must be serious. After a minute she said, "Insane. Are you some kind of birdwatcher, then?"

"Yeah."

"You can't be. Aren't birdwatchers all little old ladies with blue hair? Or old guys with skinny legs and funny-looking shorts and safari hats? If you were a real birdwatcher, wouldn't you be wearing a little birdwatcher's uniform?"

"Come on," I said, feeling tired and angry. "You don't really think that. Nobody thinks that any more, do they? How can the public image be so far off from the reality? Does everybody pay more attention to damn television than to real life? God, I'm sick of that kind of image."

"Well, look, you don't have to get mad," she said.

"I'm not mad. It's just — how do you think I feel, when this really pretty woman is telling me, more or less, that what I spend all my time on is ridiculous?"

Diana gave me a searching look and was silent for a long minute. When she spoke, it was in a softer tone. "I didn't mean to insult you. You're really serious about this, aren't you? But, look, you didn't hitchhike all the way from Arizona just to look at these crows, did you?"

"Not exactly. I left Arizona about the middle of January, and I went over to Florida and up to Maine, and back down to North Carolina, and then over to Kansas, and I've been down here in Texas for about a week now."

"I'm almost scared to ask," she said, "but did you do all that hitching around just so you could look at *birds?*"

"What other reason is there to travel?"

"Wow," she said. "You're out of your mind." The way she said it, it didn't sound like an insult. "But that's almost weird enough to be cool. I mean, it's really different. None of my friends are that interested in *anything*." She paused for a minute. "I wonder if you might have a hard time hitching out to the Brownsville dump. Don't they usually put garbage dumps out in the country someplace? And how many people are going to go there — like, it wouldn't be the most *popular* place in the world."

"This is the West," I said. "If I can't hitch right to the spot, I'll walk the last few miles. I've got the time. I've just got to see that bird."

"It's too bad I'm not going down closer to Brownsville," she said, "but I got to shop for some material and patterns and stuff in Harlingen . . . and I promised Nancy I'd take her a couple of places. Anyway," Diana concluded, "I'll give you my phone number. You might call me tonight and let me know if you got to see the crows."

At Weslaco we got off the freeway and drove through town to her friend's house. Diana went up to the door; but a minute later she was back, looking angry, her blond curls bouncing as she tossed her head. "Nancy isn't home," she said. "I told her I was coming, but she isn't home. Well, screw her. I've still got my own shopping to do." Driving back through town she played with the radio irritably, switched it back and forth between stations, couldn't find anything she liked, turned it off. We rode on for a while in silence.

After a few minutes, she smiled faintly. "Well, it's Nancy's tough luck. She just won't get to hear the inside dope on the Mexican Crows." We laughed, and we talked for a while about her job, about different small towns in the Valley, small talk like that. Finally she looked at me inquiringly: "You must be on the road just about all the time."

"Yeah."

"If you have a wife somewhere, or a girlfriend, you must not get to see her very often."

"I don't have a girlfriend. Not likely to, either. Young women and birding just don't mix." I told her about the apparent lack of young female birders: unsolved mystery, curse of the Tucson Five, bane of all the young male birders.

Diana agreed that it seemed odd. "And I guess you wouldn't be interested in a girl who won't go birdwatching with you." I shrugged, said nothing.

We were almost to Harlingen. Within minutes we came to the main route into town, but we drove past it. When we passed the last Harlingen exit, and continued toward Brownsville, I looked at Diana — and saw that she had been waiting for my reaction. She laughed. "I can do my shopping some other time," she said. "But picking up some guy who says he's hitching all over to look at some crow . . . I've got to find out if you're kidding, or I'll always wonder. You don't mind if I come along, do you?"

I had brief directions jotted down, and recollections from the year before, but even so we managed to get thoroughly lost trying to find the Brownsville dump. Confused, we cast around in what seemed like the right general area, spinning down side roads across the flat and dusty country. Eventually we decided to re-trace our route partway and ask directions.

We pulled up in front of a farmhouse; Diana sat in the dusty Mustang while I went up to the front door. A half-dozen little dark-haired children playing in the yard halted in their games and stared at us. The woman of the house seemed almost as surprised, but once she understood what I wanted she launched into a long and complicated set of directions, talking fast, trying to be help-ful. I caught the general drift of what she was saying and thanked her, and we drove on.

A few miles later, the landscape began to look familiar. When I saw numbers of Chihuahuan Ravens flying, and a few gulls, I knew we had it. By the time we were within a quarter mile of the dump, we could smell it, too; Diana wrinkled her nose a little, but said nothing. We turned in at the entrance, down a bumpy dirt track rutted by truck tires. "This is okay," I said; "you can park it here," and got out of the car.

The uninitiated are surprised to learn that dumps are very birdy places. It makes sense, though. The combined table scraps of an entire city add up to a feast for the omnivores, and in warm weather the dumps attract clouds of insects, which many birds eat.

The Brownsville dump today was a teeming aviary in black and white: black Chihuahuan Ravens and white Ring-billed Gulls, black Great-tailed Grackles and white Cattle Egrets, fluttering around and fighting over the spoils of civilization. A few Turkey Vultures, looking awkward and uncertain on the ground, were over toward the edge of the dump. Numbers of American Pipits were walking daintily among the heaps of trash, seeking insects. This avian free lunch was going on in the midst of an almost equal amount of human activity: men driving garbage trucks and pickups, dumping stuff out, and other guys pushing the stuff around with bulldozers and shovels and rakes.

But I had temporarily forgotten my new friend. She was getting her introduction to birding in the midst of this busy scene — sort of like learning to swim by going over Niagara Falls in a trash barrel. Out of the car, now, she was looking around with a slightly wild expression. "Wow!" she said. "They're all over the place!"

At first I thought she meant birds in general, but then I realized she was staring at the Chihuahuan Ravens. "Oh, those aren't Mexican Crows," I said. "Those are ravens. The crows are smaller . . . No, the smaller ones with long tails are grackles. I think I see some of the crows over toward the back. Let's walk around there a ways."

We had to walk some distance, picking our way among piles of trash. Pipits flew up ahead of us every few paces, and Cattle Egrets stepped haughtily off to the side as we passed. I was about to warn Diana to watch out for rats, until it occurred to me that the idea might send her running back to the car; I kept my mouth shut and watched out for both of us.

"Okay," I said, as a couple of black birds came flying over us, "here are a couple of Mexican Crows. See how small they are? And listen to that voice." The crows were calling, in their low-pitched croaking monotone.

"Wow," said Diana, "they *do* sound kind of funny. And they're little — or littler than those things you were calling ravens. Why should a little crow have a deep voice?"

"Beats me," I said. We walked a little farther. Toward the back of the dump there were more crows, thirty at least. I loaned Diana my binoculars. She fumbled with them for a while — it takes practice to use binocs effectively; I'm not sure she ever got a Mexican Crow in focus, but she appreciated the gesture. The crows paid no attention to us at all.

"Six years ago," I said, "you wouldn't have found these crows here. They only started visiting the U.S. real recently."

"Six hours ago," Diana replied, "you wouldn't have found me here, either. I don't know, though . . . You've got to be willing to try something different. Like, I've never gone birdwatching before, and maybe I never will again, but now I can say I've tried it."

We had turned around and started back when Diana suddenly started laughing. "What's up?" I asked.

"Look at that," she said. "Those guys — they're watching us." Several of the workers in the dump had stopped their work and were now sitting in their trucks or leaning on their shovels, staring at us. "What do you suppose they're thinking?" she asked, and then she grabbed my hand playfully. "Maybe they think you brought me here on a date!"

"Oh, let them think whatever they like," I said, as we headed back to her car. "Some things are better left to the imagination."

Truckers' March

MARCH CAME in like a chameleon, changing its color again and again as it danced on my calendar of 1973. My luck ran hot and cold. In south Texas, I easily found nearly all the birds I sought — but then I struck out on the White-collared Seedeater, a tiny finch that barely crossed the border here. Hitching north, I got fast rides — but then north out of Dallas I got onto the wrong highway, and it took most of a night of walking to get back on track.

When I reached my parents' house in Wichita, a phone call brought news that a Fieldfare, a kind of European thrush, had been found in New York by Paul Lehman, a kid about my age whom I'd met on the New Hampshire boat trip in January. I called Paul, but he said that the bird was gone. Would I be interested in a Boreal Owl, though? There was one staked out near Ailsa Craig, Ontario, right now.

Yes, I would indeed be interested. The Boreal Owl was not genuinely rare, but at that time it had managed to elude most birders. The owl was small, quiet, inconspicuous. It spent the summer in trackless muskeg of the subarctic forest and hardly bothered to come south in winter. In later years we would learn about nesting populations in the Mountain West, and the bird would become merely excruciatingly difficult to find, but in 1973 it was still in the "impossible" category. The American Birding Association had placed Boreal Owl on its "Ten Most Wanted" list.

Naturally I was interested. The problem was that Canadian Customs took a dim view of penniless hitchhiking foreigners (I'd been turned back at the border before). Making more phone calls, I learned that Harold Morrin and the Lancaster IDIOT birders were going after the owl that weekend. They invited me to come along, so I hitched to Pennsylvania.

I knew it would be a grand trip, from the start — from the moment when I walked into Charlie Mellinger's living room and saw the venerable Christmas Tree, still standing in dry dignity in the corner. Piling into Harold's expeditionary camper, we spent all of Friday night driving northwest across Pennsylvania and New York. Shortly past five on Saturday morning we crossed into Ontario, picked up Harold Axtell, and continued on the final four-hour drive to the village of Ailsa Craig.

Past midmorning we reached the quiet little town and located the owl stakeout, a small woodlot behind a house on the outskirts. The women who lived in the house, casual birdwatchers, had found the owl first and had made the mistake of mentioning it to someone. Before long, birders from Detroit, Chicago, Toronto, New York, and elsewhere had appeared on their doorstep, asking permission to tramp around the woods behind the house. The women received us hospitably, but remarked that the *next* time they found a rare bird, they wouldn't tell a soul.

The woodlot was small, but even so, we knew that the bird could be hard to find. Dr. Axtell — who had seen Boreals before — advised us to check each tree with extreme care. The little owl could be deep in the interior branches of a conifer, motionless, all but invisible. It was possible to walk right past a Boreal Owl and never see it.

We never saw it. Through the long afternoon we prowled the woods, studying each hemlock or pine from all possible angles, trying to conjure up an owlish shape somewhere. Each of us must have searched each tree a dozen times, but without result.

And then it was evening . . . and the American Woodcocks, those odd snipes of the boggy woods, were performing their courtship song-flights on all sides of us. We could hear four or five of them at once. Their nasal beeping callnotes from the ground would give way to a twittering, chippering, bubbling song in the air, and occasionally we would see the chunky silhouette of a woodcock in flight against the darkening sky. Although I knew that the woodcocks would start their sky dances before the other birds would consider it to be springtime, this was still an unsettling reminder that winter was drawing to an end, that I was running out of time to find the winter birds.

We searched for the owl the next day in heavy rain, but struck out again. Regretfully, I gave up. The owl might have departed for the north already, and it was time for me to depart for the West.

Late on the 11th of March, I said goodbye to the Lancaster birders and the Axtells. By the seventeenth, I was greeting my friends in Arizona. In the time between, in terms of a distinct identity, I did not exist.

This was my strange double life on the road during 1973. One day I might be sitting in a comfortable living room, talking with respected people like the Axtells or the Witzemans; the next day I could be standing on a dismal freeway on-ramp, watching hostile cops tear my backpack apart. My status changed radically as I moved in and out of different subcultures. The birding world was the one I cared about; but my life was colored by association with the others, with the people of the road.

Leaving Ontario by way of Windsor, negotiating the traffic confusion of Detroit, I headed across southern Michigan and then south into Indiana. It was well past midnight when I reached Indianapolis and got around to the west side of the beltway — but from there, I knew, travel should be steady. That was where I connected with Interstate 70. Anyone driving from New York, Philadelphia, or Washington, headed for St. Louis, Kansas City, Denver, or points beyond, would take I-70. At any hour of day or night, long trips would be happening on that route.

By day, the traffic on I-70 was mostly cars — millions of cars; but come sundown, traffic began to thin out. Motels filled up as the amateurs got off the road, until no one was left but the professionals and the hard-core diggers of distance. Trucks appeared on the highway then, as if they had materialized out of the pavement itself, hundreds of trucks, thousands of trucks. I always had the impression that I-70 had somehow invented the big rigs. It was as if the interstate had put in a solid day's work carrying humdrum car traffic, and then fell at night into uneasy sleep . . . and out of its restless dreams, out of the frustrations of a billion car tires, it created the trucks.

These rigs appeared at night, like prehistoric monsters emerging from their lairs. They charged headlong down the roads, blinking as they passed each other; they gathered in rumbling herds behind the roadside cafes; occasionally one would go berserk and devour a car or two, and as a result the cars lived in constant fear of them. The trucks were the dominant species of the highway ecosystem.

Perched up in the cabs, high above the pavement, the truck drivers rode these monsters. Where the truckers sat, the big windshields spread out before them like giant screens, giving them a whole different movie of the road than anything seen by the little people in the cars. The constant bucking of the cab pounded human guts into jelly; the roar of the diesel masked all sound; the truckers rode, and thought their own solitary thoughts, and the road flowed up like a river to meet them.

A lot of hitchhikers claimed that they never got rides with trucks — but those were the hitchers who got off the road at night. True, most truckers weren't allowed by regulations to pick up riders, so they would rarely stop by day. But late at night, when the hours dragged and drivers began to nod off at the wheel, they'd often pick up someone to help keep them awake. So I'd found that the odds were good for truck rides after midnight.

And I was out there — near three in the morning, I was ten miles west of the Indianapolis beltway on Interstate 70. Traffic was sparse. Each vehicle came up separately out of the dark, like a rising sun; the headlights would leave white tracks across my eyes, and then I'd be left behind in a darker darkness. Each truck threw up a wall of wind, so I'd brace myself as it rushed past; then the wake would catch me, grinding grit into my hair and teeth and eyes. The air was not cold for mid-March, but it was chilly enough to keep me wide awake, and I was ready for a ride as I waited by I-70.

My wait lasted quite a while: I had begun counting trucks, and number sixty-two was approaching, was within twenty yards, when I heard the sound of the air brakes being applied. The truck hurtled on past, but slowing down now, the engine grinding and protesting as the driver fought it down through the series of gears. A hundred yards beyond me the rig pulled to a rumbling stop. Backpack in one hand, I was half-jogging to catch up, smelling the familiar diesel smell — past the rear of the trailer, where the brake lights glowed and the red emergency flashers signaled; past the giant tires in double-pairs; up to the front, to the cab. I reached above my head to open the door, hefted my pack into the cab and swung up myself. The driver nodded at me in curt greeting, jammed the rig up into first gear, and we were on our way.

This trucker was unusual for that era. He had the cowboy boots and western shirt that many of them wore, but he looked hardly older than twenty-five, and his hair was as long as mine. The cab on this rig was not fancy, but it did have a good tape player. The driver kept shoving Rolling Stones tapes into the machine, and we listened to "Street Fighting Man" and "Gimme Shelter" and "Sympathy for the Devil" all the way across Indiana and Illinois. Hard, pounding music to fit the pounding and bucking of the cab. The speakers couldn't quite compete with the noise of the diesel, but I enjoyed the audible parts as the interstate rolled away beneath our wheels.

This driver was not into talking much. That was fine with me; trying to carry on a heavy conversation over the roar of the engine could be a pain in the throat. We did exchange a few words. The guy's name was Rick. He'd been driving trucks for about two years now, and he liked it. He was from St. Louis, and that was where he was going now. He asked where I was headed — Arizona, I said, coming from Ontario. Rick nodded. "Warmer in Arizona," he observed.

Near Effingham, Illinois, we pulled into the parking lot at a big Union 76 truck stop. Rick maneuvered the rig around to a parking place, set the brakes, left the engine running. We sauntered inside.

The familiar truck-stop atmosphere reached out to draw us in. I couldn't be sure whether I'd been in this one before, because

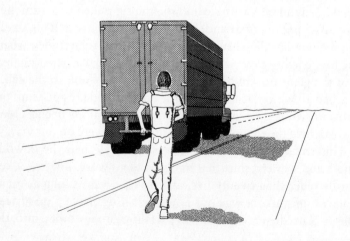

they all had the same feeling: the same T-shirted truckers, arguing about politics or regulations, or staring idly into their coffee cups; the same jukebox, twanging out some Merle Haggard number; the same white formica countertops, and banks of silvery mirrors and ice machines across the back wall.

Rick and I walked back to the section marked "Reserved for Professional Drivers Only," while the older woman at the cash register watched us, looking suspicious. ("Stupid dame," mumbled Rick, "she oughta remember me. I been in here lots of times.") The other truckers glanced up, accepted us. We all shared a common bond: bloodshot eyes, the red badge of mileage.

A pretty redheaded waitress came over to take our order. She looked at our long hair, smiled: "Are you boys really truck drivers?" Rick returned the smile. "Sure, Babe," he said. "We've been driving rigs since we were four years old." The girl laughed, shrugged, wrote down our order.

I watched her walk away. "You know," I said to Rick, "I don't think she believed you."

"Ah, I don't care," said Rick. "People just aren't used to the idea of longhairs driving trucks yet. Things'll change. These guys ain't that different from you, man. Except they got crewcuts and they listen to cowboy music."

Leaving the truck stop later, we continued west. When Rick dropped me off just outside St. Louis, night was fading, and the numbers of trucks on the road were dwindling. Soon it would be daylight, and mere cars would again rule the highway.

My actual destination was the Pacific Northwest, and the straightest route would have been directly west from Chicago. But I was not about to hitch across the northern Rockies in March; by detouring south to cross the divide in New Mexico, I could avoid the worst of the cold and could stop in to see my friends in Arizona before angling north again.

I intended to pause in Tucson only a few hours. But it was a weekend; Ted and Mark were out birding, and I'd really wanted to get Ted's advice on some of the western stuff. Dave Hayward and Joel Greenberg were in town, trying to catch up on studying (although, as Joel pointed out, my arrival shot their chances for any effective study). At my suggestion they put away their books and we went out to Sabino Canyon, looking at desert birds, finding my first Black-chinned Sparrow for the year.

That evening we were out in the parking lot between Graham Hall and the stadium, shooting a few baskets, when Ted and Mark came racing across the parking lot toward us, whooping and yelling. At first I thought it was just normal high spirits. But then Ted shouted, "You should've been with us!" He and Mark had the basketball now, firing it back and forth, jittering around in circles. "You should've been *with* us! What a bird!"

Eventually we pried the news out of them: they had found a pair of Black-capped Gnatcatchers. This Mexican bird had been noted in the U.S. only once before, and under odd circumstances. In June of 1971, a pair of Black-capped Gnatcatchers had turned up along Sonoita Creek near Patagonia, Arizona. Even though that was a famous birding locale, they had managed to build a nest and hatch three nestlings before anyone noticed them. They probably had been seen earlier, but passed off as common birds: the male looked rather like a male Black-tailed Gnatcatcher; the female looked like a female Blue-gray Gnatcatcher.

In fact, the female looked a *lot* like a Blue-gray. Even after the male's identity was confirmed, some maintained that the female was just a common Blue-gray Gnatcatcher. If that were the case, this wouldn't be a record of Black-capped Gnatcatcher nesting in Arizona — just a bachelor Black-capped, lost in the States, pairing up with the first female gnatcatcher it could find. In which case the young in the nest would be hybrids.

Intent on solving the mystery, scientists went out and collected the whole family. The shots touched off instant indignation among birdwatchers — perhaps especially among those listers who hadn't reached Patagonia in time to add the bird to their lists. The criticism got heavier some months later, when it was determined that the female gnatcatcher *was* a Black-capped. It seemed this species had attempted to start a U.S. colony, but had been wiped out immediately. Everyone on both sides of the issue hoped the damage had not been permanent, that more Black-capped Gnatcatchers would turn up.

Now they had turned up. Ted and Mark had been birding below the dam at Lake Patagonia, a few miles from the site where the first Black-caps had nested, and helping some visiting birders to find the local species. It was a quiet day, and it had reached that point in the afternoon when everything had slowed down — everything except Parker, so naturally he found the birds. Mark, a few paces behind him, saw the birds and promptly went bananas. The visiting birders were dragged over to see them as well. But Ted wanted more people to see the gnatcatchers, to make sure there would be no question. As soon as he'd finished telling us the story, he got on the phone.

As plans evolved, it was clear the major group search would not be until Tuesday. That was too long for me to wait — I was already late for the Pacific Northwest. After I'd worked on Joel and Dave for a while ("You can always take Spanish again next year, but the gnatcatchers can't wait"), they agreed to go the next morning.

So Monday morning the three of us were in Dave's car, bouncing down the rough dirt road to the Lake Patagonia dam, while the sky paled behind the hills to the east. Walking in the last mile, we arrived at the dam at first good light.

The surrounding country was high dry grassland grading down into dry mesquite brush. In this setting the hollow eye of Lake Patagonia looked unnatural — which it was — but downstream from the dam, there was typical growth of cottonwoods and willows and hackberries along Sonoita Creek. This strip of green in a dry landscape was a great place for birds.

Joel and Dave and I worked the north side of the stream, where

Ted and company had found the gnatcatchers the day before. Birds were active in the chilly dawn. Some were newly arrived migrants, evidence that the spring movement was under way. Violet-green Swallows were back, hawking insects over the stream, and we heard the rich whistles of Scott's Orioles. A Painted Redstart postured and fluttered in the willows. Broad-billed Hummingbirds glowed blue and emerald in the sun. It was a great morning for birds, but after we'd put in several hours and scoured the area several times, we were starting to get worried. We had not seen a trace of the gnatcatchers.

"Possibly," said Dave, "this bird is related to Rowlett's Owlet."

"Such as," I asked, "a sub-subspecies?"

"No, just a transparent color phase."

"Colorless phase, you mean."

"You've got to admit that this gnatcatcher *sounds* a lot like Rowlett's Owlet," Joel said. "I could've sworn I didn't hear an owlet a minute ago."

"Right," said Dave. "The similarity can't be underestimated. But there's a ventriloquial quality to the owlet's silence. When you *think* it isn't calling from over *here*, it *actually* isn't calling from over *there*."

As frequently happened when the three of us went afield, the day was starting to turn nutty. Today, though, I needed a new year bird more than I needed a good laugh. I made another sortie down the creek; once again, I drew a blank.

When I came back, I found an arrow of rocks, pointing upstream, with a note attached that said "If the children have no bread, let them eat gnatcatchers." The authors of the note were a hundred yards beyond, birding again. Dave told me they would have to leave soon. He'd already missed one class, but if they didn't get back to Tucson they were both going to miss an exam. It looked as if I'd have to camp over and ride back with someone from the major search the next day. "Well, I'll walk up to the car with you and get my stuff out," I said. "I knew I should've packed a lunch. Tell Parker to bring me a sandwich tomorrow, okay?"

With last-ditch optimism, we continued searching as we walked back upstream toward the dam. Dave went over to the south side of the creekbed to work through the heavy brush there one more time. Joel and I walked back up the north side. When we reached the spot where, by my best guess, Ted had found the birds, we stopped to look and listen for a long minute. There was not a movement, not a sound.

But then Dave started shouting.

My first reaction was surprise: surprise that Dave, the quiet one, could yell. His shout was garbled — he sounded almost like Mark — but it was something about gnatcatchers. Joel and I charged like Marines across the stream.

Dave *had* found the Black-capped Gnatcatchers. We were so excited, jumping up and down, pounding Dave on the back and knocking the rest of the wind out of him, that it was lucky we didn't scare the birds away. When we calmed down, we followed the gnatcatchers for fifteen minutes before we lost them. They were flitting actively in the mesquites and hackberries near the stream. Twice they stopped to investigate old birds' nests — we were intrigued by that; if the Black-caps had nesting on their minds, there was a good chance they'd stick around.

Walking back up to the car, Joel said, "If nonbirders had been watching us just now, they never would've understood why we were so excited about those insignificant little birds. I mean, how would you go about explaining it to someone?"

Having left Tucson that afternoon, I did not hear what happened Tuesday until much later. Ted and his search party could not find the gnatcatchers, and in fact the birds were not seen again that year. We had no way of knowing, but we imagined that they might have spent the summer nearby — perhaps upstream from Lake Patagonia, on private land.

Being cheerfully unaware that the news would be of no practical use to anyone, I carried the word of the gnatcatchers with me to California. Having something important to tell raised my spirits considerably. But it didn't help my hitchhiking luck. I got hung up in greater Los Angeles, wasting an entire night just crossing the megalopolis.

In the morning, north out of L.A., it was cold in the low mountains along Interstate 5. There was snow on the ground above four thousand feet — from any distance I could see a horizontal line on the hills, with white snow above and dark soggy ground below, marking the elevation of freezing temperatures at that hour. It continued that way across the hills, with gray skies, freezing rain, slushy snow. But on the north slope, starting downhill for the last time, I could see a change: spreading out to the north was the wide flat expanse of the San Joaquin Valley — and the valley floor was bathed in sunlight. The valley floor was green, suffused with deep blue, hazed here and there with purple or yellow, the colors of wildflowers. Obviously winter was fading fast, spring was rising to replace it. No time to waste — I had to get to the Pacific Northwest.

But it was not a waste of time to stop and telephone the Manolises on my way through Sacramento. And of course they would not let me simply call and travel on — I must come to their house. Mother Anne made a fuss over me, scolding that I hadn't been eating enough or taking care of myself. Georgianne filled me in on birding news. In their California year-list contest of 1972, she said, Rich Stallcup had edged out Richard Webster, 428 species to 427. At that level, obviously, both guys had done very well; but if anyone wanted to quibble about fine points, the record was now in the camp of the northern Californians.

Rich himself came in that day from Monterey. He was going up to Honey Lake with the Manolises that weekend, and I was invited, practically ordered, to go with them. It was important to my spiritual growth, they said, that I should bird Honey Lake. Besides, there were some birds in that area, notably the Sage

Grouse, that I would have to make a concerted effort to see sometime during the year.

Friday night we drove north in shifts. Rich and Georgianne and I left Sacramento in the evening, arriving near midnight at the temporary abode of the brothers Manolis — Tim and Bill — up in Chico. There we looked at Tim's recent drawings of birds, at photos of Flammulated Owls, and talked until two-thirty in the morning. In the meantime, Anne had arrived. We all started northeast from Chico — Rich, Georgianne, Bill, and Bill's girl-friend, Pooh, riding in Georgianne's Volkswagen, and Anne, Tim, and I, plus two large friendly dogs, in Anne's Datsun.

We had timed it to arrive before sunrise at Sage Grouse booming grounds near Honey Lake. The grouse would be performing their odd courtship ritual there at dawn, strutting and puffing out their white neck ruffs and making hollow booming noises. We would have made it in plenty of time — except that out in the empty miles northeast of Chico the Datsun developed engine trouble, overheating and losing power; finally, some thirty miles short of our destination, the car died altogether.

What to do? The other car pulled over and we discussed the problem, while the dogs romped about, glad for the break in the long drive. But the Californians were not to be stopped by mere mechanical difficulties. The Volkswagen was put into service as a taxi, shuttling the party over to and around the birding areas of Honey Lake, while a tow truck was summoned for the disabled Datsun. At the lake we ran into Gary Friedrichsen and some friends who had come over from Humboldt Bay, and they had some room in their car. Everything worked out all right, just as Rich Stallcup had insisted it would: everything would always work out if you just went forward boldly into every experience.

The people had been right: whether I had realized it or not, visiting Honey Lake was something I had really needed to do. Here under the wide skies at the edge of the Great Basin, birds were everywhere. There were Sage Grouse, of course; we arrived at the booming grounds in time to see a few late boomers and to watch them in excellent light. There was a stretch of road where we saw two or three Golden Eagles every mile, an amazing concentration. There was a large plowed field where Tim and I crawled across the furrows, stalking Lapland Longspurs, sometimes managing to get within yards of the birds. Out in treeless country we walked into an abandoned barn and found that it had a pair of Long-eared Owls living inside. And at first light Sunday morning there were Snow Geese feeding in stubble fields near the lake — thousands of white geese, with more skeins and flocks and lines coming in against a backdrop of sunrise colors, their cries blending into a single musical wild sound.

The weekend passed all too quickly. Various Manolises had to be home Monday, for school — Georgianne and Tim were taking classes, and Anne was teaching some; they went back in the Volkswagen. Rich and Bill elected to hang around Susanville, birding and partying while they waited for repairs to be completed on the Datsun. As for me, it was decided that I should ride over to Arcata on Humboldt Bay with Gary Friedrichsen and his friends. "This is a great time of year there," Gary told me. "The migration is just now really getting under way."

"Yeah, I know," I said, thinking uneasily of certain wintering birds in Washington State that might soon be moving out, migrating north beyond my reach. But it would be convenient to go up the coast from Arcata; and I might see some of the birds that my year list needed while I was there, perhaps even out behind the red house on the marsh. After all, Humboldt Bay was the gateway, the beginning of the great Northwest.

Shadow of Alaska, Shades of England

WHERE I SAT in the forest, overlooking the Anacortes ferry dock in a drizzling dawn, Winter Wrens were all around me. The tiny brown sprites seemed bubbling over with energy that morning. They chased each other among the dripping branches with the comic ferocity of mice; one hopped quizzically across the toe of my boot; another investigated a cavity in a stump, a possible nest site, a few yards away. From far and near, from higher in the trees, I could hear them singing their varied ringing trills: the Winter Wrens, belying their name, were announcing spring. Tomorrow would be the last day of March.

All the way north on the Pacific slope I had been feeling this same restlessness. All the way up the coast I had been noticing how the waterfowl, among the earliest of migrants, were beginning to move out. They had spent their winter on southern bays and estuaries and lakes, but now something had awakened in them. Now, it seemed, they remembered night passages over strange coastlines, remembered craggy Arctic ranges and the teeming tundra, remembered Alaska. And they were preparing to go there. At Humboldt Bay I had seen masses of the small dark geese called Black Brant, thousands of them, numbers building by the day; it appeared that soon the dam would burst and the Brant would flow north like a flood tide.

I had gone north ahead of them, arriving in the Pacific Northwest just in time to catch the last tag ends of winter. The winter birds would be leaving soon. But there were still Black Scoters around, and a Eurasian Wigeon, adding a couple of ducks to my year list. A Yellow-billed Loon, a scarce winter visitor, was still in the small-boat marina at Blaine, Washington. And just the previous afternoon I had caught up with a Gyrfalcon south of Vancouver. This Gyr had been my reward for hours of searching in a cold rain. The drizzle had soaked down endlessly, the gray wind had whistled Siberian dirges, and my Army-surplus poncho had alternately flapped in my face and swung wide to let in swaths of rainwater. But finally I'd seen the Gyrfalcon, the great Arctic predator — watched it haul past on powerful wings, watched it angle away into the curtains of falling rain. I'd felt then as if I'd found the Northwest Passage.

All of these birds would be moving on now, drawn to the north, but that wasn't my destination, not yet: I wouldn't be on my way to Alaska for another three months. Vancouver, B.C., had been the northern terminus of this run. There I'd turned around and headed back south against the tide. It was practically April, and I had to get to Florida, where the first waves of migrants would be arriving any day now. But before I made the long cross-country haul, I wanted to see the Sky Lark colony on San Juan Island.

It had been after dark the previous evening when I'd come back across the line from B.C., going through the usual hassle with U.S. Customs, and had arrived in Blaine, Washington. I was chilled, and still soaked from my Gyrfalcon search; so I'd walked to the local Denny's to have some coffee and dry out a little.

Sitting in a corner in Denny's, writing notes on my bird observations of the day, I had lingered for some time. It had been near midnight when I'd finally left the warm coffee counter and headed out into the night. This was not good timing. To get to San Juan Island — the major island in an archipelago collectively called the San Juans — required a ferry trip out of Anacortes, Washington. Anacortes was south of Blaine, and well off Interstate 5. While it seemed very unlikely that I could get to Anacortes in time for the ferry the next morning, I was wide awake, so I'd decided to try.

Driving from Blaine to Anacortes would take maybe an hour. Thumbing down in the dead half of the night, it had taken me six. The trip had involved a dozen long waits at freeway entrances, a dozen short rides, two questionings by the state police, three passing rain showers, and miles of walking on deserted State Highway 20. I'd gotten a final ride into Anacortes with a couple of young Native Americans from a nearby reservation. We had shared a few beers while they told me about the oppression they suffered under the government of the whites. "Right," I said. "So why did you give me a ride?"

"You?" One of them snorted. "Man, you got holes in your shoes, and you're all wet, and you're out here walking in the middle of the night . . . You don't look very white to me." We all laughed. I had to take it as a compliment.

Then more walking, on out of town, and here I was at the Anacortes ferry dock at first daylight. The watch in my pocket (the strap had broken long before) said it was only six-thirty. A printed schedule on the ticket-house window told me I had an hour and a half before the first ferry headed for Vancouver Island by way of Friday Harbor in the San Juans. Against all odds, I'd arrived so early that I had to wait.

So I had walked back up into the nearby trees and sat down to rest. Misty rain was falling again, but I was content to let it run into my eyes and trickle down my neck. This was a warm, comfortable rain, fit for the spring season that the Winter Wrens were proclaiming.

Eventually there was human activity in the scene below. I stood up and stretched. Time to get going. Tying up my backpack, I trudged down out of the woods.

Even with fog on the water I could make out islands offshore, evidently the nearest of the San Juans. The character of the islands did not seem to differ from that of the mainland. Shorelines were all black rock, with occasional gravel beaches below, and a solid skyline of evergreen forest above. Gulls of three or four types were flying back and forth, patrolling the shorelines, white wings against the dark trees.

The ferry was a large, multi-tiered craft, with more than enough room for the cars and trucks that were now being maneuvered noisily into the lower levels. Up above were observation decks, a passenger lounge, a cafeteria. I bought some coffee and, cradling the hot cup in my hands, walked up on the forward deck to look for birds.

Buffleheads, little black-and-white baby-faced ducks, were swimming and diving next to the ferry. Numbers of White-winged Scoters and Surf Scoters, dark sea ducks, were floating in the distance. Scanning still farther out, my binoculars picked up two bird silhouettes buzzing over the water on stubby wings: these were certainly alcids of some sort. Rich Stallcup had told me to expect a good variety of alcids on this ride.

At length I heard the muffled roar, felt the sudden vibration underfoot as the ferry's great engines came to life. A few more minutes passed. Then the horizon began to swing slowly around, before the feeling of motion had actually registered; and we were under way.

I was alone on the forward deck. The other passengers were all inside, hidden behind newspapers, looking like morning commuters anywhere. That was their problem; I was excited just to be here. The salty breeze in my face was just cold enough to make me wide awake. I could see a slight swell running in the gray seas, but I could not feel it — all I could feel was the deck throbbing underfoot with the power of the engines. The ferry plowed ahead on a level course, while the engines rolled with a pounding sound, like a train, like a seagoing train.

And as we moved out into open water, we entered a new domain. The waters were as gray as the skies above, but these waters were alive: alive with alcids.

Growing up in the Midwest, I had had little awareness of the birds in the alcid family. Strictly coastal and mostly northern, they were remote and mysterious from a Kansas perspective. I'd seen a few in California travels, and a few more on the boat trip off New Hampshire that January, but still I hardly knew them.

Now I was in a good place to see them and learn them. Almost as soon as we left the dock, I saw two Pigeon Guillemots on the water ahead. Evidently just molted into their summer feather, they were in perfect plumage, velvety black with bold white wing patches. As the ferry bore down, they craned their necks nervously and then took off, whirring away low over the water, their bright red-orange feet splayed out behind them.

As we went on, many more appeared. Pigeon Guillemots were the most conspicuous alcids of the day — we passed more than sixty. When we came too close, some would fly; some would simply dive underwater. Every one was in fresh summer plumage. By contrast, the Common Murres were still mostly in winter plumage, looking shopworn.

Out in the main channel we encountered Rhinoceros Auklets, bizarre alcids that were new to me. The first three were very close, on the water and then taking flight at the ferry's approach. Their dark gray faces were accented by staring pale eyes and long white plumes; they looked like caricatures of themselves. Each bird's orange bill was topped with a little "rhino horn," visible from quite a distance. With their strange faces, the Rhinos looked perpetually surprised, and I was surprised in turn each time I saw one well.

Many small alcids were flying about in the distance, in pairs or small groups, low over the water. These fast-moving midgets had me confused for a while. Some were gray-backed birds with the quaint name of Ancient Murrelet, but I finally decided that most were Marbled Murrelets. Often a pair of Marbleds on the water ahead would dive when we were still far away, then pop back to the surface like corks when we were close, taking off in a panic with their small wings beating furiously to get their plump little bodies off the water. They looked like pears or tiny footballs trying to learn to fly.

Now, stop, I chided myself. *Thou shalt not ridicule the children of the wild.* A Marbled Murrelet above the water was not at its best. Those little wings that made them so comical in the air were perfectly suited to flying *underwater,* and that was where these murrelets, like all alcids, were in their own element. Far from human eyes they navigated the depths, foraging freely beneath the waves, graceful as porpoises, mysterious as whales. And the Marbled Murrelet had a special mystery of its own. At that time, its nest was still unknown to science — a distinction shared with no other North American bird. Many searchers had hunted in vain along the rocky shores of the Pacific Northwest. Not until 1974 would it be revealed that these gnomes of the undersea world were building their nests and raising their young high in the trees in old-growth forest.

Marbled Murrelets

On this day I was thinking about another Marbled Murrelet mystery I'd heard from Rich Stallcup. Rich had taken this same ferry ride a few weeks earlier. He had seen many Marbled Murrelets, and he mentioned offhandedly that he'd seen two that "looked like they had white heads."

That took a minute to click. "Hey!" I said. "Wouldn't that be, uh, Kittlitz's Murrelet?" A northern bird, an Alaskan specialty, unknown in Washington.

Rich nodded agreeably. "Could have been."

"Well . . ." I sputtered. "Come on, Rich, didn't you . . . didn't you do anything about it?"

"Like what?" He looked at me in gentle amusement. "That's a big boat, Brother; are you going to tell The Man to turn it around, so you can chase a bird?" He had a point. And a brief sighting like that would not be enough to establish a first state record, even if the sighting were made by an expert like Rich; so what could he have done? What could I do, if I saw odd murrelets here? Nothing. That was okay; I expected to see Kittlitz's Murrelet in Alaska during the summer anyway.

Alaska! It loomed large in my mind, larger even than it was in life, like those flat map projections of the globe that shrink the lands at the equator while expanding Alaska and Greenland and Antarctica toward infinity. Alaska on my mental map towered above everything in the Pacific Northwest. It was the center of the world for the alcid clan, but Alaska was also the destination for many of the northbound migrant birds I'd been seeing: loons, scoters, geese, swans, eagles. So many of these waterbirds would be going there, to occupy the water and shoreline of summer.

Alaska had a million lakes and ponds above the permafrost in summer, a million miles of coastline if you measured it the right way, as well as thousands of islands. The whole southeastern arm of the state was fragmented by water, with Sitka and Ketchikan and Wrangell all situated on islands. From there down the coast of British Columbia extended the great chain of islands, large and small, finally trailing off in Washington State, in Puget Sound. It would not have been too far-fetched to say that the southernmost extension of Alaska was this group of islands, the San Juans, now rising out of the sea around the ferry.

I stood on the bow with the salt wind in my face, images of Alaska on all sides, and I thought: How strange that I should be coming here to look for a bird from England.

And then: How strange that I should be arriving by ship to look for a bird that had arrived in North America by ship.

How strange it must have seemed to the Sky Larks themselves, to be crammed into crates and shipped halfway around the world back in 1903, just because they were unlucky enough to be among the most celebrated songbirds in the world.

How strange it would seem to many of the bird-listers that I should make a major effort to see the Sky Lark, this alien bird, brought in and released here by humans. No matter that the larks had been surviving on their own here for seventy years now; no matter that their songs were the stuff of poetry and legend — for many birders, nothing could erase the stigma of a nonnative bird, a bird that was "introduced."

I roused myself from these thoughts as the ferry steamed into a natural harbor on the main island, where a town perched on the shore, and maneuvered toward a dock. Back in the interior of the craft there was a stir as people prepared to disembark. Although many passengers were going on across to Victoria, enough were getting off here to create a traffic jam when all those cars came out of the hold; for once I was lucky to be on foot. I walked down the ramp, onto the main street of Friday Harbor.

Now to go find the Sky Larks. The spot was the "American Camp," whatever that was, at the south end of the island. Shouldering my pack, I was out of town and into the country within minutes.

It was now midmorning. The gray sky overhead was rain-washed and fresh, and a light mist was still falling. The day was warm. It was hard to remember just how far north this place was: to reach this latitude on the Atlantic Coast, one would have to travel to Newfoundland, where the land would still be locked in hard winter. But the Pacific Northwest benefits from warm ocean currents, which keep the climate moderate all year. Rather like the situation in the British Isles. London lies even farther north than the San Juan Islands, but enjoys relatively mild winters, thanks to the moderating influence of the Gulf Stream current.

The road I walked on San Juan Island was partly paved, partly gravel, totally deserted, running through rural country. The landscape was a study in soft tawny yellows and browns, dark greens in the woodlots, occasional views of the steely sea, all the colors muted today under the gray sky.

Somehow it all reminded me of scenes from the writings of British naturalists.

I might have imagined whatever resemblance I pleased, since I had never been to England. But I had read so much about that country. So many of the great naturalists, ornithologists, and nature writers were from the British Isles. It seemed odd that they could love nature so much in a land that was so thoroughly tamed . . . but then, perhaps that explained it. Their land was civilized. They had no wilderness — no Grand Canyon, no rattlesnakes, no Mount McKinley, no mountain lions, no badlands. No wonder they could afford to think generously of their countryside. They had room, and reason, to appreciate those small elements of nature that would be overlooked entirely in the riproaring American frame of reference.

Haunting the library as a kid, reading poetry books when I was not reading bird books, I had been astonished at how often birds were mentioned in British poetry. Songsters like nightingales and Sky Larks appeared in literally dozens of works, going back beyond Shakespeare, back beyond Chaucer. Entire poems dedicated to such birds were written by Tennyson, Wordsworth, Shelley, Keats, and many lesser-known poets. I had run across half a dozen British poems just about Sky Larks; Thomas Hardy had even written a poem about Shelley's poem about the Sky Lark. The love of birds and of the English language were intermingled in British literary history.

Somehow we Americans had failed to import this English love of birds along with the language, except in a diluted form. But we had imported a few of the English birds themselves — along with birds from practically everywhere else.

The latter half of the nineteenth century was the heyday of the "acclimatization societies," which sought to "improve" the birdlife of North America by introducing new and different species. In that era, habitat requirements of wild birds were not well understood. Birds were shipped in by the crateloads, and many were released in places where they had no chance of survival. Naturally, most of these introductions failed. The exceptions were often birds like the House Sparrow and European Starling: tough, adaptable, aggressive birds that would carve their niches by pushing native birds out of the way.

Not surprisingly, a century after the "acclimatization societies" had done their worst, many birders detested introduced birds. A faction of the American Birding Association during the 1970s argued that all bird lists should be "N.I.B." — no introduced birds. Californians spoke derisively of all the exotic birds that had established feral populations in Florida, conveniently ignoring the fact that the Los Angeles basin was also full of escaped parrots and the like.

But in the talk about the evils of introductions, birders had few bad words for the Sky Lark. Unlike the English House Sparrow, the Sky Lark did not overrun North America: it failed almost everywhere it was tried. Unlike the starling, the Sky Lark did not seem to displace native birds. Unlike the Rock Dove (the common park pigeon), the Sky Lark did not bum around cities for handouts; it lived out in windswept fields, minding its own business. And its only business was to live and sing. This bird was not introduced for any practical purpose. The Ring-necked Pheasant, Chukar, and Gray Partridge were brought in as game birds; the House Sparrow was introduced in an ill-conceived scheme to control cankerworms; but the Sky Lark was brought because it had been loved by generations of Englishmen and had won a place in British literature and tradition.

So the larks were imported . . . but not successfully. Not at first.

Everywhere they were released on this continent, they vanished into the sky. Appropriately, it was in British Columbia that this British import finally took hold: in the open farmland around Victoria, on southern Vancouver Island.

After their original introduction at the turn of the century, the Sky Larks had gradually increased to a population of about a thousand, but no higher. This colony, at the southern tip of Vancouver Island, was surrounded on three sides by water; to the north, beyond the farmlands of Victoria, the remainder of the island was dominated by wild forests and mountains. The colony seemed to have no potential for expanding its range. For seventy years, Victoria had been the one place where birders could go to see Sky Larks in North America.

But sometime during those years, a few birds made it across the ten miles of water to San Juan Island and founded another colony. When the birds had actually arrived on San Juan was unknown, but they were discovered there around 1960. As late as 1973, many birders were still unaware of the San Juan Sky Larks.

For me their presence here was a major bonus. It meant I could save a couple of dollars by not taking the ferry all the way to Victoria. I did not have to face Canadian Customs once again. Sometime during the year, I was sure, Floyd Murdoch would stop in Victoria on his way to some other destination, ticking off the larks easily. Were it not for Murdoch, I might have elected to pass up this species, but in a direct competition I could not afford to skip any bird.

My thoughts were interrupted by the noise of a car growing out of the silent landscape behind me. By now I'd been walking an hour and a half, and figured I must be most of the way to the south end and the American Camp. I wasn't going to turn around and thumb for a ride. But the car stopped anyway.

It was a souped-up Chevy with a kid my age at the wheel — driving just to be driving, I guessed, and frustrated at owning a hot car on a chilly island with nowhere to go except a few miles of gravel roads. He wasn't used to seeing hikers out here. As we headed down the road, I asked him about the American Camp, and he shrugged: it was a historical site from a forgotten war, nothing to see there. Why did I want to go?

I told him about the Sky Larks.

"Far out," he said, not meaning it. "Yeah, there's a bird expert who lives down by there."

I was surprised that Rich Stallcup hadn't told me. "Really?" I said. "A bird expert?"

"Yeah," said the kid. "Knows all about 'em. Specially eagles. Has a coupla pet eagles, and he's doing some kind of experiment with them for the government. That's the American Camp down there," he added, putting on the brakes and gesturing to the right, where a meadow sloped down toward the sea. "There's a historical marker deal there. And I see the dude I was telling you about. The bird guy." Pointing to the left, where a solitary figure trudged across a field. "He can tell you where to go . . . tell him Tony said hello." I climbed out of the car, and it spun its wheels away down the road.

The lone man in the field had turned to face me. He had a shotgun in one hand and a dead rabbit in the other, and he did not look friendly. But I'd been dropped by the road in a most obvious way — sticking out like a sore thumber — so I couldn't just wander away casually. I picked up my backpack and walked out to greet him.

At close range his look was not hostile, just wary. I introduced myself and said he'd been pointed out as the bird expert. I'd already decided not to say anything about eagles — the story was too weird to be true. So I just asked about Sky Larks.

Yes, the man knew where they were, and he could show me. But first he wanted to know: had I seen an immature Bald Eagle around here?

I told him I hadn't. There had been one adult and a couple of immatures from the ferry, another immature near Friday Harbor, another white-headed adult on the way south on this road, plus a couple of Golden Eagles — actually adding up to quite a concentration of eagles. But I hadn't seen a young Bald Eagle near this spot.

The man swore under his breath. "I just released that bird two weeks ago, and I think something's happened to it already."

At that I must have looked as startled as I felt. The guy laughed shortly, and then he explained.

The man — whose name was Steve — had been a falconer for a while, but then he had wanted to do something more meaningful than just flying the birds for sport. So he had taken on an ambitious project.

Keeping eagles in captivity was generally prevented by federal law; but there were those who would illegally take young eagles from the nest and try to raise them as pets. Federal agents who intervened in such cases had a thorny problem: the captive-raised eagles were too well domesticated. If the birds were simply released into the wild, they might not know enough to hunt for themselves or to avoid humans. So Steve had decided to work on the problem. The feds had turned over to him several confiscated birds, Golden Eagles and Bald Eagles both, and he was attempting to train them for life in the wild.

Well, this is America, I said to myself; this is the West! I'd come looking for a diminutive creature, for a songbird celebrated in gentle verse, and I'd been sidetracked into this tale of lawmen and eagles. I asked the eagle-man if he were from here originally.

No, Steve said, he wasn't a native. He had settled on San Juan because he was impressed with the numbers of hawks and eagles present every winter. The raptors concentrated here partly because of the location, he said — and partly because of the rabbits. He held up the one in his hand, evidently one he'd shot. "They're European," he said. "They were introduced here, and they've sort of overrun the place. Or they would have, if there weren't so many birds of prey to keep them under control." Steve intended to leave this rabbit for the released bird, if he could find it, or feed it to a couple of other eagles that he still had at home. He was afraid that something had happened to the released one already. I gathered that the training-for-the-wild program was still in the experimental stage.

I wished the man luck, both in his search this day and in his quest to teach the American Eagle how to cope with freedom. He thanked me, then said, "Oh — you wanted to see the Sky Larks. Down there. Between the road and the beach, where the grass is taller." He paused. "Funny — I ran into a birdwatcher up in Friday Harbor, and he was sneering about the Sky Larks, saying they weren't 'real' birds because they weren't native here. Wonder what he'd think about the eagles I'm releasing? They're all introduced birds, now." Steve shook his head, laughed, and trudged away over the fields.

True enough, I thought. Where would the would-be "purists" draw the line between native and alien elements? This whole planet was altered by the hand of man.

A birder who scorned the alien Sky Larks might stand on San Juan and salute the native eagles . . . but some of those eagles had been released here; and they were living on an unnaturally high population of rabbits, from another continent, introduced here. The rabbits, in turn, were probably feeding on alien plants from other lands that were naturalized here — if the San Juan roadsides were anything like all the other roadsides in North America. And we birders of European descent were introduced here also, a few generations back. Even my American Indian friends of the night before could claim to be "native" in only a relative sense; their ancestors had come across the Bering land bridge from Asia. None of us is native here . . .

Pondering this, I had wandered down to the road and across it, to the edge of the tall grass, before I realized it. This was the place: somewhere in these fields, the Sky Larks lurked. Walking out across the fields might have been the fast way to flush them, but I was reluctant to cause such disturbance to a colony that was evidently small and vulnerable. So I put down my backpack and stood at the edge of the taller grass, and watched.

And I waited.

There was nothing there: only the dark earth and tawny grass, damp from late-winter rains, lying silent, awaiting spring. Beyond these fields the ocean grumbled ceaselessly. Away to the south I could see no further land — only gray waters stretching away to blend into gray mist and sky.

Spring had not yet begun here, I told myself; perhaps by the calendar, but not in reality. Spring might arrive here even tomorrow, but not on a day like this. Men might walk the empty fields on such a day, eagles might fly out to sea and not return, but the bird of the poets would not sing from that dark and wintry sky. Not today, I said.

. . . and then the song began.

It grew out of wave-noise and wind-sound, beginning in low trilled notes, soft but clear, one following rapidly on another. The sound arose from the fields somewhere between me and the shoreline, and it was at once so natural and so alien to the scene that it seemed to be a song without a singer. These first notes were identical in pitch, they did not ascend or descend the scale, but the source of the voice seemed to be rising; too late it occurred to me that the bird must be in the air. It was singing as it flew straight upward. Then the invisible singer seemed to reach a stationary peak in the sky, and the song burst into a cascade of clear notes. The sound grew louder and then softened again, broke into loud warbling passages and then receded through quiet chirring trills; and the song went on and on, without pause, from somewhere up above.

With a start, I realized that I was standing open-mouthed and staring at nothing. I began to look for the singer — wanting reassurance that it was a bird, not imagination or the spirits of the island. My eyes strained against the emptiness of the clouds.

There! So high above the earth that it was almost beyond vision, the Sky Lark hovered on the wind. Binoculars resolved this speck into the silhouette of a bird, suspended in the sky, its wings barely quivering to hold it aloft. It seemed incredible that any bird should have the strength to fly at the same time that it delivered this song: this amazing torrent of song, which came down so clearly and so continuously. On and on went the song. Finally the bird closed its wings slightly, and drifted lower; a few moments there, then it closed its wings further and began a series of steep glides toward the ground.

The song ceased abruptly.

I stood stunned, waiting for the performance to be repeated. And, in a few minutes, it was. Again the lark rose into the sky to deliver his flight-song, and again I stood listening, unbelieving. The beauty of the song went beyond any details of musical formula: it was the spirit that was so moving. The bird sang from a stage of immense proportions, sang as the soloist before the orchestral growling of the surf. I imagined a title: Concerto for Sky Lark and Pacific Ocean. The Sky Lark was the speck of life, the hope of spring, in a gray wilderness.

More, I wanted to hear more. For a couple of hours I wandered the edges of the fields, seeing and hearing other Sky Larks. A few times, singers coming down from the sky landed near me, and I was able to study them at close range. Visually they were designed for camouflage: streaky and brown. Gaudy hues would have been wasted, since the colors would not be visible from the ground when the bird performed his sky dance.

All the Sky Larks I found were along less than half a mile of the road. All were between the roadway and the beach. They appeared to occupy an area of a few hundred acres at best. What a small foothold it seemed, and what a vulnerable position; the whole population could be wiped out by one winter storm.

Even the Victoria Sky Larks were far from their native land. Their ancestors had been trapped out of the pastures of England and crated halfway around the world, to the shadow of Alaska. And the birds that had founded the San Juan Island group must have been lost themselves, storm-driven perhaps, from the population at Victoria. *This is really the lost colony,* I said to myself. *It's alone in the wilderness, an outpost cut off from the fatherland for eternity.*

Once more I walked down to the edge of the tall grass, to the border of the larks' world, and stood looking upward. A single Sky Lark was up there now, towering on quivered wings, high above the earth. The song that came rippling and running and trilling down spoke defiance: defiance to raging seas and rock-bound coasts, to the wintry cast of the sky, to the spirits of this northwestern island. It seemed then that even the elements must acknowledge this singer for the eloquence of his futile challenge. At length another Sky Lark came up to the west, and another off to the east; the voices rang down the sky, on and on, as if the song would go on forever.

Sky Lark

Dry Tortugas

IT'S A long way from Puget Sound to the Florida Keys. Travel by thumb, however, allows one to go on day and night. I could have arrived in Key West at three o'clock in the morning — but that seemed like a bad idea; so I asked the three longhairs I was riding with to drop me off on the Saddlebunch Keys, a few miles up the highway, and I camped out among the mosquitoes until daylight.

By the time I got rides into town, it was midmorning. It was also mid-April. Friday the thirteenth, in fact, but I was not superstitious; it felt like good luck just to be back in the exciting little island-city of Key West.

Walking toward the center of town, I was bemused again by a mix of impressions. Two-story, wooden frame houses, with shutters on the windows and wooden porches and balconies, stood close together along narrow streets. It could have been an older neighborhood in Anytown, USA. But in the main part of town, the houses were all surrounded by exotic trees: palms, filmy

Casuarinas, the flaming red-orange of Royal Poinciana. It struck me as a little like a New England town plopped down in the middle of a big tropical garden.

The people here were eclectic too. The first time I'd come, I had known only that Audubon and Hemingway had both worked in Key West (although in different centuries, of course). It still seemed an appropriate setting for artists and writers. Certainly everyone else was here: fishermen, musicians, retirees, sailors and soldiers on leave, Cubans, Chinese, Mexicans, African-Americans, Native Americans, tourists, cops, bikers, and hikers. I felt that I blended right in. A lot of hitchhikers wound up here simply because it was where the road ended.

Any time I looked up from the streets of Key West, I might see a Magnificent Frigatebird overhead. These lean, long-winged pirates were more common here than anywhere else in the States. Hunting must have been good in the warm waters around the Keys — the frigatebirds seemed to have a lot of time left over for drifting in the sky. I would see them sliding slowly past the radar towers at the west end of the island, or hanging motionless, high overhead, like black signatures on the clouds.

Once the previous year, crossing Tennessee, I had caught a ride with a guy who worked seasonally on shrimp boats out of Key West. He told me about that life: swimming in warm seas with tropical fish all around; watching pyrotechnic sunsets in the Gulf of Mexico; keeping an eye to the sky, and an ear to the radio, for indications of dangerous storms.

When I had asked about the birds, he had thought of the frigatebirds. He used the old name, Man-o'-war Bird. He liked them, he said — they were like reminders of the days when pirates sailed the Straits of Florida.

"Out at the Tortugas, you know, the Dry Tortugas," he said. "That's the best place to see them. And they make a storm warning too. Our captain told me about this — I saw it happen myself, once. It'll be a calm day around the Tortugas, but you'll notice how the Man-o'-wars start drifting in from all around.

They come around the fort there, 'til there's a couple hundred all hanging over the tower. Then they all fly away, a few at a time, all going the same way. You watch which way they go . . . within twenty-four hours there'll be a storm coming at you from that direction. The Man-o'-wars always know first."

Today I had reason to recall that conversation. I had come to Key West to take a boat out to the Dry Tortugas, and having arrived with plenty of time to spare, I spent several hours looking for birds along the shoreline and in the trees in town. By late afternoon, I was up at the public dock at the northwest end of Duval Street, where the boat was to depart.

Before long, other birders began arriving, and I was pleased to see Harold and Rachel Axtell drive up. A month earlier, during our unsuccessful Boreal Owl search in Ontario, Dr. Axtell and I had talked about this Tortugas trip — but at the time, neither of us had been sure we would be here for it.

Wally George, our trip leader, arrived with several other Florida birders, but most of the passengers were from elsewhere, and I talked with birders from a dozen states. Evidently, even in the early 1970s, news already was traveling fast in the birding subculture. People I'd never met were coming up to ask how my Big Year was coming along, and what I'd heard from the competition. I hadn't heard anything at all, actually, but a Tortugas trip was a virtual must for a year-lister. So it was no surprise when Floyd Murdoch showed up.

Floyd had loosened up since January, apparently no longer feeling self-conscious about our competition. Part of this change may have been because, at 440-plus species, I was now about fifty birds *ahead* of Floyd. "No big deal," I told him. "Those are fifty easy species. I've been mopping them up in the sunny South while you were sitting up in Michigan. You'll catch up, as soon as the migration catches up with you."

By midnight, when our boat arrived — the *Capt. Winner*, from halfway up the Keys at Marathon — about two dozen of us were gathered on the municipal dock. We made a strange sight under the glaring dock lights: heavily armed with binoculars, telescopes, cameras of all sorts, boarding this boat to sail away into the heart of the night. Wally George read down the list to make sure everyone was there, and then we were off — tunneling into the night, the lights of Key West receding behind us.

I should have tried to catch some sleep, but I was too excited. Floyd Murdoch and I spent a while talking to Harold Axtell, who told us how, in 1971, he had run up a year list of over 600, only to wind up in second place. One of us, Floyd or myself, probably would duplicate this act in 1973; so it was good to be reminded that second place would put one in good company. As usual, Axtell managed to amaze us. He had recently spent time watching flamingos, and he was going to describe them to us . . . Describe them? We knew what flamingos looked like. But we listened in fascination as Dr. Axtell enumerated those points of shape, posture, and behavior that would make it possible to pick out a flamingo miles away against the glare of the sun.

Late that night I crawled onto one of the benches near the stern and nodded off, rocked to sleep by the rolling of the boat and the throb of the engines. I awoke to the same motion and sound but with another element added, the sound and activity of birders arising. The sky was getting light. Getting up stiffly, rubbing the sleep from my eyes, I joined the cluster of birders at the bow. The Tortugas were already visible not far ahead.

Someone called out, "Hey! Shearwaters!" but the birds were terns; dark silhouettes of terns, flying past swiftly and low against the dark water. Their numbers increased as we approached the islands, as the light improved, as we closed in for our landing. It was as if our excitement level could be measured by the numbers and nearness of the terns.

If I go to the Dry Tortugas a hundred times — and I hope I do — I will never get over the feeling that this landfall is among the strangest in the world. Maneuvering up the channel toward the dock we were bracketed by a double spectacle, the big tern colony dominating Bush Key and the monstrous hulk of old Fort

Jefferson occupying Garden Key — abundance of Nature on one hand, ambitious folly of mankind on the other. Immediately to the east of us, almost in line with the brightness where the sun was about to break the glassy horizon, Bush Key throbbed with activity. Just above the tops of the shrubs covering the island, a mass of birds filled the air, literally thousands of milling, circling, swarming silhouettes, the famous Sooty Terns and Brown Noddies of the Tortugas. On the opposite side of the boat loomed the equally famous Fort Jefferson, a hexagon two stories high and a quarter mile wide, like a stripped-down castle lost at sea. The nasal cries of the Sooty Terns were echoing off the high walls as the *Capt. Winner* pulled in to the dock.

A ranger came out to welcome us to the Fort Jefferson National Monument, but our impatience must have been transparent. We were all eager to get ashore and look for birds. At that early hour, with the sun low in the east, the trees under the fortress walls were mysterious with shadows. The sight of small birds flashing between the trees spurred me on: they might be

Fort Jefferson

anything, in this exotic setting. But with the full rush of migration under way, they were likely to be warblers.

For many birders over the eastern two-thirds of this continent, warblers are the birds that symbolize springtime. Tiny birds, most warblers are no more than five inches long; what they lack in size, they make up for in variety and color. More than fifty species inhabit North America in summer. But almost all leave in winter, for these are insect-eaters who must go to the tropics to survive. (The Myrtle Warblers we had watched in North Carolina in February were exceptions.) When the warblers rush back northward in spring, the birders rush out to look for them, as we were doing in the Tortugas this morning.

Spring mornings like this are golden — afield at dawn, with the air cool and clear and a new flight of warblers in the trees. The first thing I saw that morning was a male Cape May Warbler in full spring plumage, every detail of its pattern sharply defined. It had probably made the hop from Cuba or Grand Cayman overnight. Seeing it glowing in the early sun, though, I could believe that it might have come from almost anywhere — it might have been cast by a goldsmith that very hour.

If so, the goldsmith had been busy. There were many warblers in the trees: several Cape Mays, several Blackpoll Warblers and Palm Warblers, a few Northern Parulas and Black-throated Blues, and a scatter of other migrant warblers. The birders from the boat were scattered, too, all over the crescent of land outside the fort on the southeast side, and we had covered the area thoroughly by the time the Park Service people opened the gates and let us into the fort.

Most of the landbird habitat on Garden Key is inside the great hollow hexagon of the fort on the parade ground, several acres of short-clipped grass. A few dozen short, gnarled trees with dense foliage are mostly concentrated toward the southwest edge of the parade ground, and most of the migrant birds concentrate there too. A small square fountain under the trees provides the only fresh water on the island for the birds. In the southwest corner a roofless maze of brick walls, once a storage area for gunpowder, is now overgrown with vines and serves as a hiding place for skulkers; this morning four or five Gray Catbirds lurked there, making nasal catcalls.

The open parklike setting made for easy birding, and we scoured the parade ground, turning up a random parade of migrants out of the Caribbean. There was one Blue-gray Gnatcatcher, one Blue Grosbeak, one Painted Bunting; no Northern Orioles, but at least a dozen Orchard Orioles. A lone Yellow-bellied Sapsucker tapped on trunks near the fountain, and a Grasshopper Sparrow rested in uncut weeds along one wall. Our tally of warblers for the morning grew to twenty-one species. The most numerous were those that wintered among the islands of the West Indies, like Black-throated Blue, Palm, Prairie, and Cape May warblers; Blackpoll Warbler, the long-distance champion of the tribe, up from wintering grounds in eastern South America; and others like American Redstart, Northern Parula, and Hooded Warbler, which could have been wintering either in the West Indies or in Yucatán. Warblers that generally migrate north through eastern Mexico or across the western part of the Gulf tend to be scarce in Florida, but strays land at the Tortugas, and we did pick out one Blue-winged Warbler.

Everyone was rarity-conscious. We all hoped for some rare stray from the West Indies. One swallow gave us some excitement for a minute: it was perched on the ground in a posture that hid the shape of its tail; could it be a Bahama Swallow? But when it finally flew, it was just a Tree Swallow. Then someone called me over to look at a nightjar perched on a tree limb. It was rather like a nighthawk, but "something about it looked funny." A lengthy discussion ensued, during which we determined that none of us knew enough about nightjars, but when the bird flew it showed the pattern of a nighthawk after all.

By ten in the morning I was certain I recognized many of the birds as individuals. By eleven we were already calculating, with confidence, the precise numbers of each migrant species present.

(On a small island, one can reasonably hope to see every landbird present on a given day.) By noon, I had not seen a new species for nearly two hours. By one in the afternoon, the enthusiasm of dawn had mostly waned; some birders who had not slept well on the boat were stretched out in the shade, asleep.

But this trip had cost me $35, an amount that would have sustained me for a month on the mainland, and I was determined to use the time well. At the southeast corner of the parade ground, I took a spiral stair that led up two stories to the roof of the fort.

The view was amazing. Around and beyond the seething bird metropolis of Bush Key, the colors of the water were intense: milky emerald in the shallows, cobalt in the deeper waters. Off to the northeast we could see a couple of white-sand shoals that barely broke the surface. Farther away to the west was Loggerhead Key, crowned with the thin feathery tops of Casuarina trees, with a lighthouse standing in the center. Beyond these fragments, there was nothing but the wide ocean horizon.

The fort was clearly being reclaimed by nature. Grass and prickly-pear cactus grew atop the walls where we stood. Water dripping through the lime cement in the upper walls over decades had begun to form stalactites in places. Some parts of the fort had been reinforced recently with concrete; more were crumbling, with signs warning visitors away. But if nature was going to retake the fort, it was going to take a while. The structure was huge: a great hollow hexagon with walls eight feet thick, two stories of endless corridors surrounding the open parade ground, tons and tons of bricks. A low wall circling the outside enclosed a narrow moat, an absurd extra touch for a fort already surrounded by the open sea. The whole thing might have been erected by a demented billionaire — which it was, I reflected, since it had been built by the U.S. government.

Fort Jefferson had been intended originally to guard the approaches to the Gulf of Mexico. Construction began in 1846 and continued off and on for thirty years, but was never completed.

By that time the introduction of rifled cannon had made the fort indefensible, obsolete; it never saw combat.

The fort's only long-term serious function was as a prison during the 1860s and 1870s. Its most famous inmate was Dr. Samuel Mudd, imprisoned for setting the broken leg of a wild-eyed man who pounded on his door one night in 1865. Mudd maintained he had not known that his patient, John Wilkes Booth, had just shot President Lincoln; but in the public hysteria for revenge, the doctor was branded as an accomplice. He spent four years in a Fort Jefferson cell. If only Dr. Mudd had been a birder, I thought, the stay here would not have seemed so bad . . .

I was brought back from these musings by a mysterious sensation I could not explain. It was a feeling that there must be a rare bird nearby.

This instinct sometimes comes on when the birder has not consciously seen or heard anything. The subconscious mind must pick up some sound, some glimpse that does not match any expected bird. This sixth sense has not always paid off for me, but I never ignore it. Now I began to examine the surroundings carefully.

Nothing to see near at hand: only a few swallows circling; some Brown Noddies were perched below us, but none looked different enough to be the rare Black Noddy. Farther out was the shore of crowded Bush Key. There'd be little chance of spotting anything among the terns there, unless it were really obvious. But there must be something around; what was it?

Nothing nearby but a few swallows, circling and gliding . . . birders don't look at swallows much. Only six or seven kinds are likely anywhere. Once you've learned them you can tell them all by shape, impressions of color, or mere assumptions in a split-second glance; so you cease to really *look* at them.

A chunky square-tailed swallow, a Cliff, came winging past. Yeah, Cliff Swallow . . . I've known the bird since I was ten years old. The swallow went on gliding down, circling in my binocular view, swinging around the corner of the fort and out of sight. Something about it was odd. I hadn't seen the head pattern, but the buffy patch above the tail had looked too dark. "Jeez," I blurted out. "I think I just saw a Cave Swallow."

"Oh, yeah?" said another birder nearby. Not that the Cave Swallow would have been a total novelty for a North American lister. One could find it any summer at Carlsbad Caverns, or at a few Texas caves. But at that time, it was still very rare in Florida, and very local anywhere north of the border.

"Think so," I said. "Funny-looking Cliff. Couldn't see much about the head pattern, though." That was supposed to be the definitive mark of Cave Swallow. "Wait a minute — this might be the bird again."

A swallow came up and circled, some distance out, below our level. Again it seemed to look a little unusual, but its head pattern was not obvious. The swallow swung away toward the far side of the island and was lost to view.

We lowered our binoculars and exchanged uncertain looks. Doubts and arguments ensued. What definite marks had we seen? Not one. But I had a growing sense that the bird was not a Cliff Swallow, so I ran off to find Dr. Axtell.

I had to run all over the fort to find him (spreading the rumor on the way), but finally, half an hour later, the majority of the group was gathered atop the east wall, with a definite Cave Swallow circling right overhead. Typically, Harold Axtell was the last person to make any statement about the bird. After everyone else had agreed on it, Axtell continued to study it, taking notes, taking his time. Later on, I knew, he would recite details about the bird that no one else had noticed.

We had no way of knowing, but the Cave Swallow at that point was just beginning a dramatic expansion of its range. It was destined to move out of the caves and begin nesting under bridges and culverts, becoming a common roadside bird over much of Texas; eventually it would even be found nesting under bridges in Florida. But in 1973 it was still a rare bird for all of us, and a life bird for many.

The excitement over, I wandered down out of the fort with Floyd Murdoch and his friend Chuck Turner, a Florida birder.

"Well, thanks," said Floyd. "You just saved me a big side trip to Carlsbad."

"Could've been better," I said. "It could have been a Golden Swallow, or a White-collared Swift . . ."

"That's all right," said Chuck. "This was a new state bird for me. Come on down to the ice chest, man, and have a cold one on us."

We sat in the shade, scanning the distant channel markers where odd birds were supposed occasionally to perch, and talking about birds we had not yet seen. No Black Noddy yet, although it was still considered both rare and hard to pick out among the Brown Noddies. No Roseate Terns, even though we thought they were supposed to nest here.

But now Floyd was looking thoughtful. "If there are any Roseate Terns here, or Black Noddies, we'd be more likely to see them if we got close to that island." Waving his arm in the general direction of Bush Key and the tern colony. "And one way to get close to it would be to take a ride in that glass-bottomed boat. What do you say?"

We looked down toward the beach, where a small boat was just landing. Park Service personnel had been taking people from our group, a few at a time, out in the glass-bottomed boat to look at the coral and other marine life. So far, the most hard-core among the birders had dismissed the idea, afraid we would miss some avian happening around Fort Jefferson. But now the boat seemed like a good idea.

No one was in line ahead of us, so Chuck and Floyd and I got to go out right away. The ranger, a confident young woman named Debbie, took us over close to Bush Key. Regulations (to protect the nesting terns) prevented our actually landing there. Debbie piloted the boat along slowly, parallel to the shore of Bush Key, while the three of us studied the terns.

All morning, all the birders had been running around looking for something rare. But the really important birds at the Tortugas are the most numerous ones: Sooty Tern and Brown Noddy. Nowhere else in the continental United States can they be seen in substantial numbers. A few of each can be seen on boat trips far offshore over the Gulf Stream, and Sooties have nested at a few other points in the southeastern states; but at Bush Key in the Dry Tortugas, the Brown Noddies nest by the thousands and Sooty Terns by the tens of thousands.

Most of the activity in the colony, and almost all the noise, was caused by the Sooty Terns. The sound that drifted over to the fort from Bush Key was a jumbled nasal cacophony, but every time a voice could be picked out clearly, it would be the *ker-wackawack* of a Sooty, perhaps calling in flight over the channel. Here in close proximity, in the boat, the noise of the Sooty Terns was so loud that we could converse only by shouting.

The Sooties looked surprisingly large in the air. Although they were a little larger than the average tern, their appearance of size was probably partly an illusion of their black-and-white contrast

Sooty Tern and Brown Noddy

and their brash, noisy behavior. A few times we had the chance to see them close, silent and alone on the sand, and in that setting they looked smaller and more vulnerable.

If the Sooties were the noisiest terns I'd ever encountered, the Brown Noddies were certainly the strangest. They looked like anti-terns: brown with white caps, the opposite of most terns, which are white with black caps. And unlike any terns I knew, these birds were nesting up in the bushes on Bush Key, leaving the traditional tern ground-nest sites to the Sooties. We scanned the Brown Noddies in the bushes and in flight as well as we could, hoping to spot something different enough that it might be a Black Noddy. Finally Chuck said, "This is neat, but if we want to study the noddies we could do it better back at the fort. At the old coaling dock."

At the northeast end of Garden Key, a line of rusted girders in the water marked the place where a coaling dock had once stood. These were favored perches for many birds. We never saw a Sooty Tern here, but Brown Noddies often lined the beams by the dozens. Somber brown with big eyes and droopy bills, the noddies seemed far more solemn and dignified than the Sooty Terns. We wondered if they came over to the rusted beams to get away from the rowdy-boy clamor of the Sooties in the colony.

Watching the noddies on the coaling dock, catching glimpses of the Cave Swallow, walking the perimeter of the island to stare out to sea, we passed the rest of the afternoon. In the evening, Captain Winner and his crew came back from their day of fishing and served up a dinner of fresh-caught Red Snapper. As the sun flamed down toward the golden horizon, we watched the frigate-birds, a hundred or more, hanging in the air above the tower on the fort and then drifting off, a few at a time, straight toward the east.

We were scheduled to start back toward Key West about nine Sunday morning. Checking around the island for birds, we felt that not many new migrants had come in, and apparently not many had left. I guessed the lack of turnover resulted from the weather overnight. The sky had remained clear, but now there was a gale blowing from the east. It had come up late in the evening and had blown all night, strongly enough to discourage small birds from setting out across open water.

Nine o'clock passed, and we wondered, When are we leaving? The answer came back: We're not. Those strong winds had discouraged more than just the birds. Small-craft warnings were up in Key West, the seas were very rough, and Captain Winner had decided not to chance it. "I'd go on back if it was just me and my crew," he told the assembled group. "But some of you folks ain't no spring chickens. Wouldn't want you to kick the bucket on *my* boat. You can watch your birds here for an extra day, and we won't charge you no extra for it."

Of course everyone was good-natured about it. Many had commitments or jobs on the mainland, but they could hardly be held accountable for getting marooned. So Sunday passed quietly, with more conversation and less birding than the previous day. Periodically, some of us would check around: examine the trees again, walk the beach, climb to the top of the fort to stare toward the tern colony. Sunday produced only four or five species we had not recorded Saturday. So Monday morning, as we gathered on the dock, people had no regrets about leaving.

A strong wind was still running from the east, and some members of the party were casting nervous glances out beyond Bush Key, where on distant shoals we could see big waves breaking. But the general feeling was that the captain knew best; so everyone downed their Dramamine and waited. And waited. And eventually the captain, who had been on the radio talking to Key West, announced that we would not be leaving today after all — conditions had not improved enough. This time the news was not taken with such good cheer, but of course we could do nothing about it. The group on the dock dispersed.

We did get a new bird that day. Off the northeast beach stood channel markers where boobies were supposed to perch at times. I had checked these regularly, without much optimism, but about noon Monday word went around that there was a Brown Booby on one of the markers. I ran out with the general stampede. The big seabird, surveying the scene with a comical expression, probably had just arrived. Boobies are strong fliers, easily covering the distances among the islands of the Caribbean.

Enthusiasm revived, everyone went out to walk the beach and to check, once again, every tree and shrub on the island. Someone thought they glimpsed a White-tailed Tropicbird flying over the fort, so we trekked to the top of the windswept walls to watch, but the tropicbird (if it was one) did not reappear.

After the other birders had gone below again, I stayed alone at the top of the fort, enjoying the exotic view and thinking. A new perspective was dawning on me. As a crass young bird-lister, I might have said: a trip to the Tortugas is good, because it adds species to the total. But a better viewpoint would be: working on a list is good, because it gives me an excuse to come to the Tortugas. After this Big Year was over, I hoped, I would be wise enough to come back to this place for its own sake.

Tuesday morning the weather had not changed perceptibly, but we returned to Key West anyway. The trip back was bad, very bad. The boat was pitching and rolling so violently that they wouldn't let us go anywhere near the bow, even if anyone had wanted to, so we all huddled at the stern.

For the first time (and, optimistically, the last) in my career, I got seasick on the way. I grimly stayed on deck as long as I could — thinking that if I left, and a surprising bird came past, Floyd would gain on me. Finally misery wiped out any such concerns. Down with competition, I murmured, and went to lie down on a cot below the forward deck. A few minutes later, Floyd — who had been looking a bit green himself — staggered in and collapsed onto another cot. Both of us were comatose for the remainder of the trip back. It was a relief to learn, on arriving at Key West, that we had not missed anything.

The Fall of a Sparrow

THE Cape Sable Sparrow was the last holdout.

It skulked in the marshes of southern Florida, unknown to science, until well into the twentieth century. When the bird was discovered, in 1918, ornithologists were amazed. The age of discovery on this continent was supposed to be over. Species new to science were to be sought in New Guinea or Bolivia, not in the United States. Yet here was this sparrow that had escaped the notice of all the earlier naturalists in Florida. It was predicted then that the Cape Sable Sparrow would be the last new bird species discovered in North America.

The prediction appeared to hold up through the following decades. New subspecies were still being described, but subspecies were different: mere local forms of species that were already known. In the 1940s there was brief excitement over an Appalachian find called "Sutton's Warbler," but it turned out to be just a well-marked hybrid. Evidently there were no new species of birds to be discovered north of Mexico.

So for a while, the Cape Sable Sparrow was a minor celebrity. It was not colorful: it looked like a greenish edition of the common Seaside Sparrow. It was not musical: its only song was a nasal buzz, a lot like the song of the regular Seaside Sparrow. But it was a rare bird, a Florida endemic, living in marshes miles from anywhere. For years it was distinguished as one of the few American birds that had not been seen by Roger Tory Peterson.

That notoriety came to an end in April 1973. I caught the news early that month, as I was hitchhiking from Washington State toward Florida. It had come out in the *Auk,* the journal of the American Ornithologists' Union, and the birders were all talking about it already. Not that the bird had become extinct — nothing so straightforward as that. An AOU committee had concluded that this bird, which looked and sounded so much like a Seaside Sparrow, *was* a Seaside Sparrow — just a local variety, or subspecies. In the jargon of the watchers, the Cape Sable Sparrow had been "lumped."

As humans with an interest in science, we crave precision. Looking at nature, we want to draw sharp lines to classify things, defining the limits of the species and the genus and the family. But nature does not work that way. Nature is fuzzy. Nature is all change and contradiction. The present moment is always just a snapshot, a freeze-frame of constant evolution in the works. No matter how we define what makes "a species," that basic building-block of classification, there always will be borderline cases: forms in transition, things that are more than mere races but less than full species. Classifying such forms often will be a matter of opinion.

To cut down on confusion, bird scientists in North America adopt one standard set of opinions: the decisions made by the Committee on Classification and Nomenclature of the American Ornithologists' Union. This group publishes the AOU Check-list of North American Birds, providing the classification that ornithologists follow in their work, or that birders follow in their birding games.

Because there are many borderline cases, and because new information comes to light, official opinion is subject to change. But at the beginning of 1973, the AOU committee had not had a public change of opinion in sixteen years. We were all happily using the 1957 list, and subconsciously we had come to regard it as permanent. But not anymore.

Birders were now talking about the "great April massacre of 1973." Since we counted only full species in our listing games, the action of the AOU had lowered everyone's lists. Cape Sable Sparrow had not been the only bird to lose its status as a species. Another Florida endemic, the Dusky Seaside, also had been merged with the regular Seaside Sparrow. The Eurasian Green-winged Teal, for which we had worked so hard in North Carolina, was to be considered just a variant of our own Green-wing. The Myrtle Warbler had been lumped with the western Audubon's Warbler under the uninspiring name of Yellow-rumped Warbler. Baltimore and Bullock's orioles had been merged into Northern Oriole. Blue Goose had been shown to be only a color variant of Snow Goose. The three flickers — Yellow-shafted, Red-shafted, and Gilded — were to be regarded as one. Slate-colored, White-winged, and Oregon juncos had been lumped, and there were hints that Gray-headed Junco might get it, too, in the next revision. The changes were made for good reasons, but many birders noticed only the side effects, as their life lists dropped by ten species or more.

However, the revision had not been all lumping. The new style of classification put less faith in outward appearances, and more in the biology of whole populations, and thus split some species as it lumped others. For example, the drab little birds called Traill's Flycatchers all looked the same, but there were two distinct types of them that lived in different habitats, built different nests, and sang different songs. Accordingly, the AOU had split Traill's into two species, Willow Flycatcher and Alder Flycatcher.

So the age of discovery goes on and on . . . but for the Cape Sable Sparrow, it was all over. The bird had been lumped.

Once a bird was lumped, as far as the listers were concerned, it might as well not exist. When the AOU had last updated their classification, in 1957, such distinctive forms as the Santa Cruz Jay and Bell's Sparrow had lost their designation as species — and the listers had promptly forgotten about them. Perhaps now the Cape Sable Sparrow would fall from the birders' field of view and skulk back into the oblivion from which it had arisen in 1918.

Whether it would count for my 1973 year list was unclear. The American Birding Association had no rules dealing with taxonomic changes made in midyear. But I did not care; whether or not it "counted," it was still an intriguing bird, an exile that lived in a rough place. Twice the year before I had tracked it down, once alone at the end of May and then again with Joel Greenberg in early June, after our Tortugas trip. Now I wanted to see it again, lumped or not.

That was why I was standing in downtown Miami, thumb out, hoping for a ride west toward Ochopee.

You might stand for hours in the neon circus of Miami (as we hitchhikers often did) and never know there was a real world out there. You might never guess there was another side to Florida, a land flat as the Plains, punctuated only by floods and alligators and mosquitoes and raging fires. You might not begin to realize it until after you had caught rides through downtown Miami and headed west. Past Coral Gables and West Miami, past the Palmetto Expressway, the sky would begin to get wider, and you would notice the horizon for the first time. The pavement beneath the wheels would become U.S. 41, the Tamiami Trail, the southernmost road to go all the way across the Florida peninsula. One hundred miles ahead, the Trail would strike the Gulf Coast at Naples, and U.S. 41 would swing north from there toward Tampa and St. Petersburg, running through towns and resorts near the coast. Between Miami and Naples, though, there was scarcely anything but the Everglades.

Coming out of busy Miami, dropping into the endless horizon of the 'Glades, I found the contrast just as startling as I had the year before. The two-lane Tamiami Trail ran straight as an arrow for mile after empty mile. To both sides lay the flat Everglades, the only Everglades in the world; there was not another water system like this anywhere. And that's what it was, a system, a flowing watercourse, even though it looked like level marsh or prairie (and was largely dry for half the year). The flow had been loused up by man-made dikes and canals — but the tradition of water here was to overflow the south shore of big Lake Okeechobee and seep southward, materially increased by rains, through the plain of sawgrass that stretched one hundred miles from Okeechobee to Florida Bay.

The 'Glades held treasures for birders. A tropical hawk, the Snail Kite, had its northernmost outpost here. The Limpkin, a cranelike brown bird with a banshee voice, was fairly common. There were also Wood Storks, herons, ibises, and many other creatures besides birds. This wet wilderness was a great place for wildlife. But not for man; the mucky soil was nearly impossible to build on, and the shallow waters formed one of the greatest mosquito nurseries on Earth.

For the first forty miles out of Miami, the Tamiami Trail traversed the great sawgrass plain, and hardly anything broke the horizon except a few palms. Then — at "Forty-mile Bend" — the Trail angled northwest for about ten miles before straightening westward again. Beyond this point the land was a little dryer, and there were stands of cypress trees. But the impression remained of a vast flatland. This was a quiet land, an empty land, the low edge of the flattest state in the country.

The five or six "towns" between Forty-mile Bend and Naples were merely wide places in the road then. Once the previous summer, Joel Greenberg and I had stopped at a roadside cafe in this part of the state and found ourselves cast back into rural America of the 1920s. The waitress who took our order was soon to graduate from high school; two days after graduation, she said, she was getting married — most of her friends were *already* married. Her intended came in: a crewcut boy about our age, who had his career lined up at the local gas station, and who bristled at the sight of two hippies talking to his woman. We were aliens here. The waitress and her boyfriend had never even been to Miami.

Ochopee was another wide spot in the road, a little wider than some, nearly seventy-five miles west of Miami, thirty miles from where the road came out on the Gulf in Naples. But for that last thirty miles the road angled northwest, closely paralleling the shoreline; from Ochopee, as the crow flies, the Gulf of Mexico was only five miles away. If you knew it was there you could feel it, you could see the brightness in the sky to the southwest, see how the coastline affected the cloud formations.

And that proximity to salt water was important.

Ordinary Seaside Sparrows hug the salt marsh more consistently than any other birds. As their direct descendants, the Cape Sable Sparrows hardly seem to belong in southern Florida. True salt marsh is in short supply there. The interior of the southern peninsula is nearly solid freshwater marsh, and the coast is mostly a great tangled forest of mangroves. The only extensive salt marsh in southern Florida is on the southwesternmost land of the peninsula, Cape Sable, where the sparrow of the same name was discovered in 1918.

During the decade after its discovery, the Cape Sable Sparrow was believed to occupy a patch of coastal prairie only six miles long by half a mile wide, and barely above sea level. Naturalists worried that one good hurricane could wipe out the population. They were right. The colony survived some storm damage in 1926 and 1929; but on September 2, 1935, a hurricane of incredible violence came out of the Caribbean and plowed right across Cape Sable. A wall of water eight feet high, driven by winds up to 200 miles per hour, rampaged across the area in the middle of the night. The sparrows were widely thought to have become extinct in that storm. It made good copy for nature magazines: the little birds awakening uneasily down in the long grass, hearing the shrieking winds, unaware of the huge storm wave that was bearing down on them out of the blackness . . .

By 1942, the Cape Sable Sparrow was officially back from the dead. Colonies were found up in the Ochopee region, and later Louis Stimson penetrated the interior south of the Tamiami Trail and found a number of them inland from the mangrove fringe. But it was more than thirty years before the bird was found again on Cape Sable itself.

This whole region of Florida, so beset by wind and water, was also strangely prone to fire. The Ochopee marsh itself had burned in 1959. Hurricane Donna came through a year later, bringing high water that flooded most of the southwest coast. Then drought set in, and during 1962, wildfires raged across much of the known range of the Cape Sable Sparrow. Yet the birds were still holding on.

I've said that Ochopee was only a wide spot in the road. But when I arrived that April afternoon in 1973, developers were busily making it wider. Perhaps someone figured this was close enough to Naples and the Gulf to be turned into a resort area. Yeah, I thought, Mosquito Manor. Building here on the west side of town was a difficult job, because the land was at least 50 percent water. The process had to begin with bucket dredges and bulldozers and other dirt-moving machines, to create some solid ground for a foundation. The machines were at work this afternoon all along the western flank of the main sparrow marsh.

There was a plot of naked fill dirt, nothing built on it yet, extending south into the marsh from the Tamiami Trail. I left my backpack at the far edge of that and walked on into the waist-high grass.

The water in the marsh today was about ankle-deep. I had seen it both wetter and drier. When I had come in May 1972, the marsh had been virtually dry. Hours of walking around the tract had barely gotten my feet wet. In June I had returned with Joel

Greenberg, telling him how easy it was to bird there; rain had fallen in the meantime, and we found ourselves slogging in knee-deep water. So today's level was only average.

Trudging south from the Trail, my idea was just to get out there, out in the middle of the marsh, and wait for one of the sparrows to sing. Which could take a while. Midafternoon was not a great time to seek sparrows. Most small birds are quiet in the heat of afternoon, and marsh birds especially so, maybe because their habitat is so open to the sun. In the cool dawn, probably there would have been a few singing immediately. Had I been covering Florida by car, it would have been logical to make a run out here from Miami early one morning; but this was another time when hitching was different. Waiting on rides, counting on luck, I'd reached Ochopee at the worst time of day.

No matter: if the sparrows didn't show this afternoon, I'd still be here in the evening, when activity ought to pick up. If they didn't show this evening, I'd dig in at the edge of this mosquito paradise, camp overnight, and be here to see them in the morning. *If* the sparrows were here at all, this year.

At least it was a pleasant afternoon to be out on the marsh. The sun was warm, and a light breeze from the west was pushing a slow parade of white cumulus clouds across the sky. As I walked farther the Tamiami Trail grew small and distant behind me, a picture without sound, and looking away to the south I could imagine myself in the Florida of 1492: no sign of civilization disturbed the wild landscape there.

For my first two hours out in the marsh, I saw or heard no trace of the sparrows. But there were plenty of other birds around. I saw eleven species of herons, and several times I was startled by Least Bitterns, the smallest of herons, that flew up from the grass at my feet.

There were vultures patrolling the horizon, as there always seem to be in Florida. When a shadow crossed in front of me I looked up, expecting to see one of these dark scavengers. But the shadow was cast by a beautiful creature, the Swallow-tailed

Kite, swooping and planing overhead on pointed wings and long, forked tail. It circled overhead for a while and then was joined by a second. These kites, the most graceful birds of prey in North America, hardly seem to be hawks at all; their elegant shape and buoyant flight suggest some kind of seabird.

Down at my level were smaller predators: dragonflies. Some I recognized. Here were many *Celithemis,* unstable and fluttery, their patterned wings marking them at any distance; amber-winged *Perithemis,* small dragonflies, keeping low; many skimmers, *Libellula,* coursing over the marsh. The attraction for these dragonflies was obvious: they were feasting on mosquitoes. I had soaked myself with repellent before starting out here, so I was getting few bites, but the whining horde of mosquitoes around my head was more than a little annoying. I thought about the rugged biologists who had explored Florida before the advent of repellents. Perhaps they had missed the Cape Sable Sparrow because they were too busy swatting mosquitoes.

After two hours, I was wondering if I would miss the sparrow myself this time. I kept stopping to listen every time a Red-winged Blackbird sang in the distance. There were Red-wings all over the Ochopee marsh, and their song had about the same pattern as that of the sparrows. As I recalled from the previous summer, the tone was different — but memory had blurred in ten months, and I kept wondering, just how different was it?

But of course, the subconscious mind is a better authority than the plodding conscious mind in such cases. When the real sparrow sounded off, out at the limit of hearing, I knew it immediately.

Standing in the sun-soaked marsh, I strained my ears to catch the sound a second time. A minute later the bird sang again. It seemed to be a little west and north of me. I walked in that direction and the sound became more distinct. Finally, I spotted the bird itself, perched at the top of a stem, dark against the surrounding marsh.

It stayed while I made a cautious approach. The bird had the flat-headed, long-billed look of a typical Seaside Sparrow. At close range I could see the greenish tinge on the back and the whiter look below — field marks which had set it apart, but which had not been enough to impress the AOU. Occasionally it would tilt its head back and sing again. Its voice was only a long, nasal buzz, but it had no need to be more musical. The song was a claim to territory, a message heeded only by other Cape Sable Sparrows — and by birders.

But as I watched the bird, I wondered: How many more birders would see the sparrows here? How long would the colony last? It looked as if the developers meant to fill in the entire marsh. Some of the Florida birdwatchers had been pushing for a sanctuary here, to protect this colony, but I guessed that impetus would fade now that the AOU had lumped this bird with the common Seaside Sparrow. Even as an endangered species, the Cape Sable

Cape Sable Sparrow

Sparrow had not aroused much local interest. What was it worth as a mere endangered subspecies?

On that same trip I stopped to look at a related bird, the Dusky Seaside Sparrow. Like the Cape Sable Sparrow, it was a Florida specialty: the Dusky was found only in a small area of marsh near Titusville. Like the Cape Sable, the Dusky had been "lumped" in the latest revision by the American Ornithologists' Union. It was now just the Dusky race of the Seaside Sparrow, and already the birders were losing interest, writing it off.

At the time, we all assumed that these decisions on taxonomy were permanent. They seemed to carry the finality of What We Know Now, as opposed to What People Used to Think, and we assumed that this was how birds would be classified forever into the future. We did not realize that the pendulum of scientific opinion could, and would, swing the other way.

Within a decade, the very definitions of species and subspecies would be opened up to question. By the early 1990s, some respected biologists would be suggesting that these localized forms were full species, after all. But by that time, the Dusky Seaside Sparrow would be extinct.

Legions in the Sky

B Y April, the plodding progress of travel-by-thumb had taken me to the four corners of the Lower 48 States, but there were still many common birds that I had not seen — especially long-distance migrants. There were dozens of species in that category, birds that nested in North America every summer but left the continent entirely every winter, flying to the gentler climates of the tropics. No amount of searching in the States would have produced most of these before the end of March.

But now winter was over, and the birds were coming back. In another month or two, all these migrants would be established on their summer territories. In theory it would be possible, then, to go and visit them all on their nesting grounds. In theory, but not in practice: their nesting grounds were too widely scattered. Some birds would go to the southern swamps, others to the central prairies; some to the eastern hardwoods, some to the northern spruce bogs, and some to the tundra. It would simply take too much time to track down all these birds in their summer homes, one by one. No, spring was the time to see them: in April, when all the migrants, regardless of their destinations, would be piled up in the southern tier of states.

Florida had produced many migrants for me, especially birds that wintered on Caribbean islands, like Cape May Warbler and Black-throated Blue Warbler. But I was pinning my greatest hopes on Texas. Birds coming north out of Mexico and Central America might fly straight across the Gulf of Mexico, or they might follow its coastline north, but either way they would concentrate on the upper Texas coast. So I must make a concentrated effort there as well. Late April in Texas might dictate the success or failure of my Big Year.

I reached Houston on a hazy, humid Friday evening. The musicians I was riding with dropped me off on the eastern outskirts, and their van went rattling on into the city. I walked to a pay phone on the corner and called a local birder.

Birding was good now, he told me. The migration was on. Reports from coastal woodlots, particularly from High Island, suggested that the northward flood of migrants was approaching its zenith, with a whole galaxy of warblers, vireos, thrushes, orioles, tanagers, a treasure trove for birders. Unfortunately something had come up, so he wouldn't be birding much himself this weekend. "Why don't you call Victor Emanuel?" he suggested. "He and some others are doing a Big Day run on Sunday. If you could join them, that would be an ideal way for you to see a lot of species in a short time."

Sure, I thought, Why not? I called Victor Emanuel. This was a person I already knew well by reputation — the organizer of the big Christmas Bird Count at Freeport, Texas, the biggest count in the nation — but we had never met, and he undoubtedly had never heard of me. Without thinking of that, I started by asking if I could join his birding group for their Big Day on Sunday.

There was a long pause.

"Well," said Victor, "realistically, I couldn't just invite you myself, without consulting the other people involved. There are already four of us, with Jim Tucker, Benton Basham, Noel Pettingell, and myself, and adding a fifth person would make things a little crowded in the car . . ."

He sounded naturally friendly, but I had put him in the position of having to either turn down a stranger, or impose an unknown person on his companions for Sunday. For all Victor knew, I might be a rank beginner, blithely inviting myself along on an intensive day with four of America's top birders.

"Yeah, I understand," I said, embarrassed, wishing I could retract the phone call. "I don't want to crash the party. Benton Basham is the only one of you guys that I know, anyway."

"Oh, you know Benton?" Another thoughtful pause from Victor. "I'll be talking to the others tonight," he said. "Why don't you call me back tomorrow, say around three o'clock. It will have to be a group decision, of course, so I wouldn't count on anything."

In the meantime, of course, I would go birding on my own. The first birder I'd called had mentioned High Island as the place to look for migrants. When Emanuel suggested it also, I decided that this was serious advice. "So, do I need a boat to get there?"

"No," said Victor. "It's not that kind of island."

It was not. I could see that as I headed south from Interstate 10 early on Saturday morning, going down narrow Highway 124 about sixty miles east of Houston. The land grew flatter, the trees grew smaller and scarcer, and rice fields gave way to broad, flat marshes. Then up ahead, beyond the bridge over the Intracoastal Waterway, appeared an obvious rise — an island of higher ground above the marsh. This feature clearly had geological significance, because the rise was surrounded by a wide perimeter of oil well pumps, nodding in rhythm, sucking out the black gold from underneath. But something more precious than oil stood on top of the mound: trees. Covering the mound, surrounding the houses of the small town, stood a virtual forest, the only big trees for miles around. For birds coming in off the Gulf of Mexico, High Island would provide the first refuge.

The fishermen who had given me a ride dropped me off at a little store in town. In the store, the plump, friendly woman behind the counter gave me directions to the local hot spots for birding. The nearest one, which she said was "real good," was a place called Smith Woods. I had hardly stepped from the store when a carload of birders stopped and offered me a ride over to Smith Woods.

I rode over with them. Arriving, we found a dozen cars parked in front of the woodlot; my companions said that they all probably belonged to birders. I spent the rest of the morning in Smith Woods, marveling at the variety of migrants present.

The woods were not tall, but they were dense, with heavy-trunked live oaks interspersed with ashes and elms. Narrow trails ran through the woods at odd angles. Down the center of the woodlot was a muddy seep, where Northern Waterthrushes lurked; in the denser thickets nearby, Hooded Warblers and Ovenbirds played hide-and-seek with the birders. In a big mulberry, Scarlet Tanagers and Summer Tanagers were quietly feeding on the ripe fruit, while Gray Catbirds and Swainson's Thrushes made nervous forays into the tree. Here and there among the sturdy oak branches were little foraging flocks of brightly colored warblers. I quickly picked up about ten new birds for my year list, including such uncommon migrants as Cerulean Warbler, Philadelphia Vireo, and Gray-cheeked Thrush.

About midmorning, talking to a birder from Houston, I mentioned that this was my first visit to High Island. "Really?" he said. "It's unfortunate you had to hit it on such a bad day."

What? I protested. Bad day? But the experienced Texans felt that it was. A really colossal day at High Island, they said, resulted when a north wind or rain or a cold front centered on the upper Texas coast. Trans-Gulf migrants arriving against such opposition would be "socked in" at the first patch of cover they hit on the coast; birds would pile up, and it would be one of those spectacular days with warblers dripping from the trees. But yesterday and today the weather had been mild. On days like these, the Texans said, many migrants coming over the Gulf would keep flying, not coming to earth until they were miles inland. That was why there were not more birders here: there would have been three times as many, if conditions had looked right for a migrant fallout.

Late in the morning I teamed up with two birders from Ontario reveling in their first trip to Texas. We brought each other luck, for we found a Swainson's Warbler — a new bird for them — and managed to follow its wanderings in the undergrowth for fifteen minutes, getting great views of this elusive little hermit. Inspired by success, we went to look at shorebirds in the flooded rice fields near town. Then, since we were so close, we decided to drive over to the Anahuac National Wildlife Refuge.

As we found out, there was nothing "so close" about Anahuac. It was a long drive down deserted roads, a long way across the flat and empty coastal plain. A wooden shelter at the entrance amounted to little more than a roofed-over bulletin board, on which there was a map of the place, a list of recent sightings (not many), and a doleful message about how many miles one would have to walk to call a tow truck in case of difficulties. There seemed to be no other birders around. But we figured we should look around while we were there, just in case we never took the trouble to come back.

And about three-thirty in the afternoon — somewhere out on the long muddy roads in the middle of the refuge, the middle of nowhere — I remembered that I was supposed to call Victor Emanuel at three o'clock.

We were probably an hour's drive away from the nearest telephone, and I doubted that the Canadians would want to give up the rest of the afternoon's birding to get me to a phone — just so I could be informed that I was not going birding with the heavies the next day. Maybe things had turned out for the best, I told myself. Victor would be spared from having to tell me I was not invited. I could just call him the next week, to ask how their day had been. Resigning myself to the situation, I concentrated on birding Anahuac.

Late in the afternoon, far ahead of us on the road across the refuge, the low sun glinted on the windshield of a moving car. This was the first sign of human life we'd seen all afternoon. The car seemed to be coming our way. After about five minutes, the other car pulled up even with where we were standing. The guy in the passenger seat started to give us a friendly hello, and then he did a double-take and jumped out of the car to shake my hand. It was Benton Basham.

The driver of the car, a thin man with quick, alert eyes, was promptly introduced as Jim Tucker, founder of the American Birding Association. "We hear you wanted to go on our Big Day tomorrow," he said.

"Yeah, well, I ought to apologize for that," I said. "For trying to crash the party. I should have known better. Anyway, I'll be interested to hear how you make out."

"What?" said Benton. "Haven't you talked to Victor yet? Hey, Kenny, we voted you in! You're going with us!" So I said goodbye to my Canadian friends and rode into Houston with Tucker and Basham.

Having fallen into this Big Day event through such a string of coincidences, I felt mentally unprepared for it. But the celebrity birders and I had a great day in the field, running up a day's total of 203 species, apparently a new record for the state of Texas.

So I had something exciting to tell Rose Ann and Pelican when I came into Austin later that week.

I had not seen these two since the preceding June, when I'd met them on the Tortugas trip and then visited them briefly in Austin. In the time since, I'd dropped them a few postcards from distant points, but I didn't know whether they'd be receptive to visitors. Pelican's warm greeting on the phone dispelled any doubts. "You're just in time," she told me. Dear Peli, with her fine understanding of what was important in life; in time for what? Why, in time to watch the sunset from the hills, the Balcones Escarpment, west of town. So we sat in her car on the edge of the hills watching the sunset, watching the heat lightning, listening to the first Chuck-will's-widows calling, and sharing the latest news.

Peli told me that Rose Ann was temporarily down at the Welder Wildlife Refuge, doing environmental checking for the Texas General Land Office. She would be back the following night. Pelican herself was doing editorial work on the Texas bird book project now being shepherded to completion by Edgar Kincaid. It was a privilege to work with Edgar, she said. A scholar of great erudition, Kincaid also had a wry sense of humor. It was he who had started the Texas tradition of applying bird names to the birders, nicknaming all his friends.

Peli and I went out Thursday morning to hunt up the Golden-cheeked Warbler, the bird that had made Austin famous.

The Golden-cheek belonged to a distinctive group of four warbler species with black throats and yellow faces. There was the Black-throated Green Warbler in the Northeast and East, Townsend's Warbler in the Northwest, and Hermit Warbler in the Far West, all of them nesting in tall evergreen forests. A thousand miles from any of them, in the heart of Texas, the Golden-cheeked Warbler lived on dry juniper hillsides of the Edwards Plateau. Austin, just below the eastern edge of the Plateau, was the traditional starting point for trips after the bird.

"Are we going to look the same place as last summer?" I asked Peli. ". . . up at Bearcat Mountain?" The actual name of the place was Cat Mountain, but I couldn't keep it straight; it looked like a spot for bears, or mountain cats, or bearcats, a land of dry rocky ravines with scraggly junipers and dense low oak tangles.

At Cat Mountain, Peli told me, houses were gradually taking over. Before long, she predicted, birders would have to range farther afield from Austin to find Golden-cheeks. So far as I could tell on arriving, though, the houses had not yet completely taken over the hill — they merely lurked there, and the construction vehicles lurked, and the rough new scars of dirt roads went snaking away among the junipers as if searching for bearcats. It still appeared a wild enough spot for Golden-cheeked Warblers.

We hiked the hillsides for a while. At length we heard a warbler song, a series of husky notes, ascending the scale — "That's it," said Peli; "that's the Golden-cheek." A dry sound, hazy with distance, but carrying well across the slopes.

It didn't take long to track down the singer. Flitting through the dark juniper branches was a study in crisp black-and-white pattern, with black cap and throat framing the brilliant golden-yellow cheeks. The warbler was active, and we had to keep moving to keep up with him, but he seemed unconcerned by our presence. We guessed that he already had a mate, and that she was likely on the nest already, sitting on eggs. Related warblers were still on the move, heading north, but here in warm central Texas the birds could start nesting early.

We went on to an area known as Four Corners to look at another Austin specialty, Black-capped Vireo, a nervous gnome that stuttered in the thickets. Then Peli had to go to work. I took off on my own, to bird around a series of ponds east of town. Numbers of shorebirds were in, including Great Plains migrants like Baird's Sandpipers. Occasionally a small flock of Franklin's

Golden-cheeked Warbler

Gulls would come drifting over the fields. Late in the afternoon, as I was starting back toward Austin, a graceful long-legged bird flew in to alight near the road, giving a rippling callnote as it dropped into the grass. I recognized the bird as Rose Ann's namesake, the Upland Sandpiper, or by its more poetic earlier name, Upland Plover.

The Plover herself got back from the Welder refuge that evening. Rose Ann glowed — with a fresh suntan, and with happiness at watching another springtime spreading across her home state. There had been migrant birds everywhere, she said, at Welder and down on the coast, and wildflowers on all the roadsides. This was the high time of the year for Texans.

It was arranged that we should go to the upper coast that weekend, to the High Island/Anahuac area, to join Victor Emanuel for two days of looking at migrants. As soon as Rose Ann and Pelican got off work Friday we were away, driving east, leaving Austin behind us in the flaming colors of a Texas sunset.

Rose Ann had brought along something to read on the drive to Houston: a copy of the *Auk*, the journal of the American Ornithologists' Union. This issue had a piece by Sydney Gauthreaux, the great investigator of migration, about the arrival of migrants coming across the Gulf to the coast of Louisiana in spring. The situation in coastal Louisiana was like that at High Island, Rose Ann said, so this article would be a good primer for our weekend. Pelican took the wheel while Rose Ann read aloud to us; I sat in the back seat and listened.

In my brief acquaintance with these two I had unconsciously made assumptions about their approach to birds. Rose Ann had been birding since childhood and now had a good understanding of ornithology in general. Pelican's avocations were artistic and literary, and she had come to her interest in birds more recently. So I had categorized them: Rose Ann as having a scientific interest in birds, Peli as having a poetic interest.

But as I watched their reactions to this technical article, I knew I had been wrong. It was pointless to make this distinction between science and art, because there was no real difference. The two came together in the story that Rose Ann was reading to us now.

Dr. Gauthreaux had carried out his migration study through direct observation and also through the use of radar, which proved quite effective in detecting numbers of flying birds and could give him approximate data from as much as a hundred miles away. His findings, of course, had great scientific import. But in this reading of them, we were struck more by the dramatic aspects of what they revealed.

Here were the migrants, thousands of small birds, streaming north from the coast of Yucatán — taking off at nightfall for an overwater flight of twelve to eighteen hours, a flight that could even take twenty-four hours if they were slowed by weather over the Gulf. Here were the radar stations at Lake Charles and New Orleans, the sweep of the radar detecting the incoming migrants as they approached the coast, picking up their echoes as much as fifty to seventy-five miles offshore. Here were the migrants again, arriving at midday over the coast of Louisiana; some would come down to the first patches of cover, but most (if the weather were good) would continue to fly for miles inland, crossing the coastal prairie to the forests of the interior. Here was evidence that the migrants, after this bold flight, were not arriving totally exhausted: after an eighteen-hour flight, after landing on the Louisiana coast at noon, they might depart again at dusk that very night to continue northward. Here, among all the numbers, was a hint of the awesome scope and magnitude of the migration.

"Listen to this," said Rose Ann. "He says: 'On 8 May 1967 the trans-Gulf flight was delayed by adverse winds, and many migrants landed south and southwest of New Orleans late in the afternoon. After dark, when birds were still moving inland from over the Gulf, the grounded migrants started their nocturnal migration.'" Rose Ann paused. "'That night a peak radar density equivalent to a migration traffic rate of fifty thousand birds occurred . . . This is the highest density I recorded during the study, and is probably representative of the magnitude of an entire trans-Gulf flight for a given date in late April and in early May.'"

"Wow," said Peli, quietly.

Rose Ann flipped back a couple of pages. "The migration traffic rate . . . he's talking about the number of birds crossing a mile of front at a given time. So that's fifty thousand birds per mile of coastline . . ."

"So," I said, "for each twenty miles of the Gulf Coast, you'd have a million birds coming over on a peak night."

"Evidently," said Rose Ann. "How long is the coast of Louisiana?" We both gave her blank looks, so she went on. "Let's say Louisiana is about two hundred miles across. That would be ten million birds arriving from over the Gulf, just in the state of Louisiana, on a big flight."

"And another three or four million between Port Arthur and Houston," said Peli, steering the discussion back to Texas. "So it's no wonder that the woods at High Island are filled with birds when the weather turns bad."

It staggered the imagination. Even as the three of us were driving east, hundreds of thousands of small birds, even millions of them, were vaulting up from the woods of Yucatán to stream northward across the Gulf of Mexico. Tomorrow we would see a few of those birds. But if the weather stayed clear and calm, the majority of those migrants would keep flying inland, to disappear into the vast area inland from the Gulf.

Two more things happened that evening that would make me remember forever that drive to Houston.

The first was a change in plans. It came about when Rose Ann decided to stop at a pay phone to let Victor Emanuel know what time we'd be arriving. After a minute on the phone, she put down the receiver and came over to talk to me.

"Did you know about the Big Day that Jim Tucker was planning to run this weekend?"

"Sure," I said. "Jim Tucker, Stuart Keith, Joe Taylor. Just the three hottest birders in the American Birding Association. We should stay out of their way, for safety's sake."

"That may not be your only option," Rosie told me. "They're going tomorrow. And they want a fourth person for the team, but everyone in Houston already has plans for the weekend. Jim was talking to Victor earlier this evening, and they thought maybe you'd be willing to skip birding with us at High Island and go on the Big Day instead. What do you think?"

"What do you think I think? Jeez, Plover, I'd hate to miss a weekend of birding with you guys, but . . ."

"That's what I thought." She smiled. "I'll tell Victor. He'll pass the word along to Jim that you'll do it."

The second big thing that happened that evening was that I was christened with an official Texas bird name.

It came about pretty simply. We had been talking about our early birding experiences, and I had mentioned my childhood fascination with Western Kingbird. Rose Ann and Peli put their heads together and then announced that that would be a perfectly good bird name for me. The Western Kingbird often lived along roadsides, just as a hitchhiker might. It was common in Kansas, but it wandered widely, all over the continent. Peli, knowing that I liked to argue, pointed out with a wink that the Western Kingbird's voice often was described as a "bickering" sound.

Nothing regal was implied by the name, but I took inspiration from it anyway. Now I had the bird name of a bird that I admired, and I was about to go on an exceptional field trip with three of the top birders on the continent. No matter what happened, it was certain to be a memorable day.

A Day As Big As Texas

So it was decided: once more into that curious mania that grips a birder on a Big Day. Once more into that heightened awareness of the distant and the hidden, that straining for faint sounds and subtle movements, while shutting out anything that is not a potential New Bird. Once more into that mode in which views of birds are measured in milliseconds, in which bird songs are classified instantly and then ignored, in which no precious moment of daylight could be wasted on aesthetics. Once more to prove that this kind of birding was the furthest thing in the world from bird *watching*.

It was past midnight when Rose Ann and Pelican dropped me at the Holiday Inn in Houston where the Big Day team was staying. Jim Tucker got up long enough to let me in — and to endure some affectionate ribbing from the women, who had a standing joke about his baby blue eyes — and then he dropped right off again. As I was rolling out my sleeping bag on the floor, Jim opened one baby blue eye and pointed at the motionless form in the other bed. "That's the world's top lister," he said. "You'll be introduced in a couple of hours. Get some sleep while you can."

Only a couple of months earlier, G. Stuart Keith had hit a major bird-listing milestone — "getting to half." Under the classification used then, the world's total bird list was considered to be 8,600 species, and Stuart Keith had become the first person ever to see 4,300 of those in the wild. I was impressed by that, and more impressed by the fact that he really knew something about those birds, having done significant field research in Africa and elsewhere. Besides, since Stuart had held the North American year-list record for fifteen years, and I was going for the record now, I already felt that we had something in common.

The other member of the Big Day team, Joseph W. Taylor, had also hit a milestone not long before. In June 1972, he had become the first birder ever to list 700 species in North America. Of course, the "lumping" of species that had been announced in the April 1973 issue of the *Auk* was going to set him back a little, but it seemed likely that Joe would track down a few more and break 700 again.

Both of these milestones had been predicted in 1970 by Jim Tucker. So the guys I was joining for this day all had major credentials in bird listing. We were going to have a major day today, too. I knew that, having been over the route just the week before. The route was a mind-blower.

It had long been recognized that the Texas coast held lots of birds in April, when the resident species were augmented by hordes of migrants. The Texas birders over the years had settled on three general routes for Big Day runs. One was on the upper coast, the Houston region, featuring residents of the southeastern forests and sometimes great numbers of across-the-Gulf migrants. A second route covered the central coast around Rockport and Corpus Christi, great for waterbirds and around-the-Gulf migrants. A third, in far southern Texas, was not as hot for migrants, but picked up species from Mexico that just got across the line in the Rio Grande Valley. Any one of these routes, worked intensively on the right spring day, might produce a list approaching 200.

But to hit all three of these sections in one day — to even consider it, one would have to be crazy.

That was where we came in.

That was where Jim Tucker came in, mainly, and you must understand that this is a compliment. Tucker, the energetic founder of the American Birding Association, was the natural guy to tackle the full-coast run; he had worked out a route and schedule and could make them almost work. I'd seen him do it the weekend before, when I had arrived in Houston and gotten myself invited on a Big Day with the Texas elite corps. We had scored 203 on that run, the first "official" 200-plus Big Day in Texas. But that was nowhere near the North American record of 227, set by Guy McCaskie's team in California the year before. There was still that to shoot for. With Keith and Taylor coming down for an ABA officers' meeting, Jim wanted to try it again, and by a fluke I had been invited along . . .

I was still lying there thinking about it, it seemed, when someone shook me awake. Stiff and groggy, I got my things together. Outside under the parking-lot lights, the chilly air in my face brought me around, and it was 3:00 A.M. in Houston.

I don't recall being introduced to Taylor and Keith, though I suppose I was. We were all in the car promptly, and moving — and lost. It was easy: an exit blocked by construction, a wrong turn . . . We needed to get reoriented. A Denny's restaurant beckoned ahead. Inside, Friday night revelers were getting sobered up for Saturday. We elbowed our way to the counter and gulped hot coffee. Jim Tucker, visibly irritated that Denny's did not carry his standard birding drink, Dr. Pepper, kept checking his watch. We had arisen early on purpose and still had plenty of time to get to our first stop. After that, "plenty of time" would be an alien idea for the rest of the day. We had to hold to our impossible schedule;

we had to reach the Santa Ana refuge, on the Rio Grande, with enough daylight left to find the easy Mexican birds there — otherwise, the last two hundred miles of driving would be wasted. So the inexorable timetable would push us all day, forcing us to leave many of our stops before we had picked up every possible bird. Such was the strategy.

Precisely at 3:45 A.M. we pulled up to a tree-lined square in front of Houston City Hall. From the branches came the squealing din of an unseen horde of birds: a restless roosting flock of starlings and grackles. The sound echoed eerily from the glass and steel of the buildings that towered on all sides. It was an appropriate setting for a science-fiction movie, or for the start of a Big Day.

At a fast pace, we tramped through the ornamental plantings. "For some reason," Jim explained to the others, "migrants sometimes concentrate in here. Had a Whip-poor-will here last week — only one of the day." A small bird flew up from underfoot, and Jim nailed it in the flashlight beam as it clung to a twig in a sapling overhead. It was an Ovenbird — a migrant, good for starters.

By four o'clock, Jim was piloting the station wagon up a straight empty road northeast out of Houston, racing to reach the woods near Lake Houston before first light. Two night birds there, Chuck-will's-widow and Barred Owl, would stop calling at the approach of dawn.

Unexpectedly, these gave us trouble. Neither was calling where we had heard it the week before. "I can't believe this spot is the only place to hear them," said Joe Taylor. "All this habitat looks perfectly fine for those birds."

"You're right," said Tucker. "They could be anywhere in these woods. This wind is our problem — it's keeping the birds quiet." We drove on, stopping every half-mile or so to listen. The Chuck-will's-widow sounded off within a few minutes, but there was already a hint of light in the east before we heard, off in the dark forest, the baritone barking of a Barred Owl.

At the same time, from the other side of the road, a series of clear bell-like notes was dropped experimentally into the darkness: a Cardinal was tuning up. It was five o'clock, and day was about to break.

On a typical Big Day, the most productive period is a two-hour span centered on sunrise. That is when most of the small birds are most vocal. The emphasis is on listening rather than looking, since a bird heard counts the same as a bird seen. But to recognize all the birds by voice alone is a challenge. Taylor and Keith were both skilled at naming birds by sound, and Tucker had been dubbed "The Golden Ear." In such company, I was very glad I'd been over the route a week earlier: it gave me an idea of what to expect at each stop. "Pine Warbler," I said quickly, as the musical trill came out of the pines behind us at Deussen Park. The wind had died, and dawn was painting the eastern sky. Wide awake now and straining to hear, we named each new bird as it sounded off. A distant Wood Thrush fluted, Blue-gray Gnatcatchers whined, and a Summer Tanager gave a snappy crackle from nearby. A Yellow-crowned Night-Heron flapped overhead, in gray silhouette, clinching our identification of it with a decisive *wack!*

Jim Tucker checked his watch. "Come on," he said. "We have some ground to cover."

Stopping by an arm of Sheldon Reservoir, with full daylight now, we quickly picked up Prothonotary Warbler, Double-crested Cormorant, and Little Blue Heron. "All essentials," Jim pointed out. "We won't get those farther south."

Moving back toward the city, we stopped briefly at a wooded corner and ticked off Swainson's Warbler and Acadian Flycatcher by voice. A Pileated Woodpecker flashed across the road, and a Kentucky Warbler rolled out a ringing chant as we passed. Another quick stop, at woods beside the Bell plant, produced the expected Yellow-throated Vireo in short order. But other birds were moving in the trees, too, and we spread out to look at them.

"Hey," called Jim, "come on. We can't get behind schedule." But just then I heard a Scarlet Tanager, an unexpected bonus;

the other guys listened and nodded in agreement. We were getting into the car when Joe said, "I hear a Pine Siskin." Jim was astonished — but there they were, five siskins, flying overhead.

It was now six o'clock, and we had covered all our stops northeast of Houston. Now we had to get around the city, through the sprawl of satellite suburbs, south to the Texas City/Galveston area. Jim Tucker took us through the growing morning traffic with finesse — dodging in and out of lanes, whipping through yellow lights. "That Pine Siskin," he said, wheeling through a parking lot to avoid stopping at a corner, "that's a very good find this late in spring. There were lots this past winter, but usually they leave before this." We rumbled through the tunnel below the Houston ship channel. "This past winter was the coldest of the century, so far, on the Texas coast. It brought down a lot of northern birds, and some are lingering. That's to our advantage; normally the twenty-eighth would be a little late for a Big Day here." He turned to me. "How are we doing?"

I'd been going over the checklist on which we checked off the day's birds. "Sixty-four species," I said.

Stuart Keith asked, "How does that compare with your total at this time last week?"

"Don't recall," I said. "Noel Pettingell was keeping the list then. He could probably reel off hourly totals and tell you exactly what we saw where."

"Noel's got every birding record in history in his mental file," Jim added. "He probably knows your 1956 year list better than you do, Stuart."

We headed out the Gulf Freeway toward Texas City. The day's first Turkey Vulture circled over the road, and we saw a flock of Purple Martins. At Texas City we worked through a woodlot at a half-jog. Few birds were there, but we did locate a towhee, another lingering winterer. Pulling up to the Texas City Dike, we leaped out of the car like gunslingers, binoculars blazing. In a matter of moments we had checked off two dozen new birds. Two Common Loons floated low in the water, like enemy submarines. Several White Pelicans and a flock of Eared Grebes were valuable bonuses. Among the Ring-billed Gulls and Royal Terns we picked out two Herring Gulls, a Caspian Tern, and a Sandwich Tern. In less than five minutes we were back in the car driving away. "No time for aesthetics!" laughed Stuart Keith.

Heading for the Galveston causeway, we made a few quick roadside stops. We were scanning a field for plovers when Joe, behind the telescope, announced: "Greater Prairie-Chicken!"

"Good Lord," said Stuart. "Is that supposed to be here?"

Tucker was momentarily stunned. "There's a colony not too far from here," he said. "I didn't include it in the route because it would take too much time to get to them. But if they want to come to us, that's all right!"

We all had a quick look at the prairie-chicken, who was performing his courtship dance near an uninterested audience of Whimbrels, and then we headed for Galveston Island. I made a quick tally. "One hundred and fourteen species so far."

"Not a bad start," said Stuart. "It's only eight o'clock." Joe commented that in the old days in New York, the goal had been to break a hundred for the day.

"I don't know if we're doing all that well," I said. "That woodlot back in Texas City — last week we had a bunch of migrants there, a good percentage of our songbirds. Today, the place was dead. If we don't run into a wave pretty soon, we're going to be hurting for warblers and things."

Luck plays a big hand in Big Days on the Texas coast, because concentrations of migrant songbirds can be so scattered and unpredictable; failure to connect with such flocks could lower the list by twenty species. But Tucker had worked several likely spots into the route, to increase the odds that we would hit migrants somewhere. The strategy paid off two stops later.

The place was Kempner Park, a little square of good habitat in the heart of residential Galveston. We were stopping there mainly to see Red-headed Woodpecker, and incidentally to see if there might be a few migrants around.

There were, as it turned out, a few migrants around.

I knew it as soon as we jumped out of the car. There is subtle excitement in a woodlot where a wave of migrating warblers has come in. Light lisps and chips in the treetops, almost too soft to be heard; constant movements, almost too quick and delicate and distant to be seen — the presence of the warblers is detected more as a feeling than as a sight or sound. That feeling hit all of us when we stepped out at Kempner Park.

The best habitat in Kempner, with ornamental plantings and heavy undergrowth, was surrounded by a high fence. All we could do was to stalk along the fence and peer in. The park was alive with warblers — and with vireos, thrushes, and other tran-

Texas spring migrants:
Swainson's Thrush, Solitary Vireo, Magnolia Warbler

sients on their way to the north woods. Lining up at the fence, a few yards apart, we began calling off the new birds as they appeared. A Magnolia Warbler chased a Bay-breasted Warbler through the branches. A Swainson's Thrush ran across a gravel walkway. A Ruby-crowned Kinglet, which should have left for the north already, went dithering nervously through the bushes. Rose-breasted Grosbeak, Solitary Vireo, and Orchard Oriole each put in their appearances, before being swept on by the tide of warblers that flowed through the treetops.

The four of us were not far apart — Big Day rules said we had to stay within "conversational distance." Even so, from our vantage points at the fence, we weren't seeing the same birds at the same time. Stuart called out, "Black-and-white Warbler"; a minute later, it was in front of me. Joe and I spotted a Nashville Warbler at the same moment, but it was five minutes before it worked its way over to Stuart and Jim. Tensely we circled the park, straining to see or hear every bird.

At last, Jim said reluctantly, "Let's go — I'm seeing some of these birds for the second time." He grimaced at his watch. "The schedule didn't allow us nearly that much time here."

We drove out of the city and south, discussing strategy. Our stop at Kempner Park had eaten up nearly half an hour. Inevitably that would cost us a few species at the far end of the route; we hoped those lost birds were more than compensated for by all the migrants at Kempner. Such tradeoffs were typical of the adjustments made en route during a Big Day. "We still need Wilson's Plover," said Jim. "What else?"

I scanned the checklist. "Golden Plover," I said. "Black Skimmer. Dunlin." Jim looked thoughtful, then slammed on the brakes and turned down a side road. His detailed local knowledge paid off: over a detour with several odd shortcuts, Tucker produced the target birds that the list required. By 10:30 A.M. we were off Galveston Island.

And racing southward. Keeping one eye on the roadside wires, I counted up the checklist. "We've got a hundred sixty-one species now."

"Looks like we have a good chance of breaking last week's new Texas record," Jim said.

"Then I suppose anything over two hundred three would be a new national second-place, wouldn't it?" asked Stuart. "Or a national record, if we could break two twenty-seven."

"Well, the record's out," said Jim. "I sat down with Noel and Victor and worked it out, based on last week's count. We figured that to break McCaskie's two twenty-seven we'd have to be leaving Galveston Island at ten o'clock sharp, with a solid one hundred seventy-five species."

We digested that thought in silence, but there was no sense of letdown. A Big Day is like any other sport: until the game is over, you do your best, regardless of the score.

As we drove down the flat coastal plain at well over seventy miles an hour, our eyes strained to pick birds out of the scenery flashing past the windows. Each new bird was announced with a shout: *"Eastern Bluebird!"* and it was about time; this bird would become less likely as we went south. *"Yellow-headed Blackbird!"* A good find. We stopped — actually stopped, for about thirty seconds — by a farm pond, to look at a Brewer's Blackbird, and spotted a White-crowned Sparrow on a fence.

Tucker was still at the wheel. It made him nervous for anyone else to drive his car, he said. The rest of us watched for birds, although "watching" seemed too mild a verb. Our eyes were starting to feel the strain of constantly shifting from powerline to fences to fields to sky to treetops to powerline . . . eight hours, and the day wasn't even half over. "We still need shorebirds, Jim," I said. "Wasn't it near here we had good flooded fields last week?"

He nodded. "Right. I'm looking for those." We reached them a minute later and pulled onto the shoulder. Water from recent rains had flooded the furrows of a plowed field, a bonanza for a flock of migrant shorebirds. Among them were twenty big Hudsonian Godwits and several Wilson's Phalaropes, new for our list. The godwits were in bright spring plumage, a treat for Taylor and Keith, who usually saw these birds only as drab fall migrants on the Atlantic coast. "No time for aesthetics, though," we said, and we were off again.

It was one o'clock and we were steaming into Rockport, forty-five minutes behind schedule, when we had a flat tire.

Almost had it, actually. We were just entering town when Tucker suddenly looked down at the dashboard with an expression of horror. He'd caught the vibration through the steering wheel. "My left front tire is losing air," he announced.

An instant of dismay: No! This could be the delay that kicked the guts out of the Superschedule. Suddenly the Rio Grande Valley seemed to be dwindling away from us. There was no telling how long it would take to get the tire changed, the flat fixed or replaced.

There was a gas station just ahead so we pulled in, the car wobbling noticeably by now. The guy manning the pumps informed us that, Yup, he could fix the tire, but there was no need to take it off the car; he'd plug it where it stood. At the time, I guess, this was a new concept to all of us. We watched, dumbfounded, while the man located the leak, pulled some sleight-of-hand with a rubber plug and a fast-sealing compound, and gave the tire a shot of air. In five minutes, we were gone.

And racing cheerfully down the road, again crowing with triumph. "Whatever total we wind up with," said Joe, "we can say, 'and that was even though we had a flat, right in the middle of the day!'" "That's right," echoed Jim, "just wait until I tell Victor that! He knows this route — he won't believe it!"

We'd been very lucky. But five minutes lost was still five minutes lost, and we were now fifty minutes behind schedule. Our list for the day was now up over 180; we were doing well, but we simply had to get to Santa Ana in daylight. Approaching two o'clock, we still had three hours' drive to the Valley, and we'd intended a number of stops on the way.

The weather had been calm all morning, but about noon a southeast breeze had come up. I'd ignored it, assuming it would fade after we passed Corpus and moved inland. It didn't, though.

Gradually the wind increased. Cloud banks built up and scudded across the sky. By the time we hit Kingsville, half an hour beyond Corpus Christi, a gale was whistling out of the southeast.

That afternoon was rough birding. Crossing the brushlands of the King Ranch, en route to the Valley, we would have expected a number of easy birds on a normal day: Curve-billed Thrashers and Pyrrhuloxias perched on bushtops, Cassin's Sparrows singing from grassy patches, and several others. But the wind today was keeping everything down, making it tough to hear birdsong. We stopped, too many times, to try to squeak birds up out of the mesquite. Finally Jim stated flatly that we could not stop for anything else. We still didn't have a Curve-billed Thrasher, and that was ridiculous; but there simply was no more time.

We pulled into the Santa Ana refuge at 6:10 P.M., an hour and ten minutes behind schedule.

The wind had begun to diminish about the time we had passed Harlingen, making the final jog up the Valley toward the refuge. By the time we reached Santa Ana, only fitful gusts moved the branches of the big trees.

These were the first big trees we'd seen for hours. We had gone through so many different regions this day, enough diversity for half a dozen normal-sized states. From the pine woods and swamps above Houston, to the flat land and white sand beaches of the Rockport region, to the mesquite brush of the King Ranch, and now to the subtropical forest of the Rio Grande Valley . . . where, at the moment, golden rays of evening sun were filtering among the trees. The soft light glowed on branches hung with Spanish moss. Nearby in the woods, chachalacas were making quiet conversational mutterings. Into this peaceful scene staggered our Big Day team, tired and wind-blown and bleary-eyed, but still determined to do the best we could with the time remaining.

Miraculously, we all seemed to rebound at the same time. It must have been the awareness of all the new species that were possible in this new habitat. We double-timed it down the trails, picking up a surprising number of those possibilities. Long-billed Thrashers and Olive Sparrows skulked in the brush. Two Groove-billed Anis flew from the trees. Joe squeaked a Verdin up into view, and Stuart spotted a Red-billed Pigeon as it hurtled by overhead. There was a Least Grebe on the West Pond, Audubon's Oriole and Buff-bellied Hummingbird near the river. With daylight fading, we birded like madmen around Santa Ana.

And finally, on the bank of the Rio Grande, we all paused. It was almost over. We had birded the place out, and the sun was setting; nothing remained for us but a few night birds.

While there was still enough light, I began tallying our list. I'd lost track of the total in the furious pace of the last hour, when it had been far more important to look for new birds than to keep a running tally. Now I checked off the new species and counted the checkmarks, but when I was finished, I did not believe the total. Something seemed to be wrong. Again I counted, more carefully, but the number came out the same.

"Holy rats," I said, quietly. "We're within inches of the *record,* man. We've got two hundred twenty-three."

We were stunned. Ever since ten-thirty that morning we had assumed that the national record was out of reach, so we hadn't even thought about it; we had just been doing our best because that was the way you played this game. Suddenly, it seemed we might have a shot after all.

"What other birds can we expect?" asked Joe.

"Pauraque," said Jim. "We'll be hearing Pauraques any minute now. Eastern Screech-Owl, up by refuge headquarters. There's a dependable Elf Owl over at Bentsen, and we had Barn Owl there last week. That's four. That would tie the record."

There was a fifth possibility, I suddenly realized. From this very spot, earlier in the week, I had seen my first Lesser Nighthawk for the year; and here it was again! We stared at the bird as it coursed, batlike, above the river. "That could do it for us," said Stuart. "Let's go."

In single file, we hurried back along the trail toward the car, while Pauraques wheezed hoarsely in the dusk. Number 225. After several minutes of anxious searching around refuge headquarters, we finally heard the screech-owl's quavering trill. Species number 226.

We were keyed up and impatient as we drove the short distance west from Santa Ana toward Bentsen State Park. It was nearly nine when we rolled into Bentsen and pulled up to our stakeout from the previous week. The Elf Owl was calling even as we jumped out of the car: our 227th species of the day. All we needed now was the Barn Owl.

So we waited, listening.

The night was quiet. Insects chirred in the trees; the Elf Owl went through several bouts of chattering, and then subsided again. We could hear a beer party going on in a distant campsite. But there was no hint of a Barn Owl in the woods.

It was frustrating. Six days earlier, finishing the day with barely over 200 species, we had heard the Barn Owl time after time. It had seemed a guaranteed bird, so we had not even thought of having a backup location. All we could do was wait.

So we waited, listening. Half an hour passed, forty-five minutes. I walked to the edge of the trees and tried imitating a Barn Owl, with an explosive hissing sound. I'd seen Bob Witzeman call them up that way in Arizona. But tonight no response came out of the woods.

And finally, after we had waited more than an hour, it appeared that our Big Day was over. We were really about to leave. It was well past ten o'clock, and Tucker was dead tired: he had been driving for nineteen hours and 550 miles. But it felt awful to abandon the chance for setting such a record. We might never come so close to the biggest Big Day again.

Dragging our feet, we headed for the car. We took our time about getting in, closing the doors, feeling dreadfully let down. Jim started the car . . .

And as the engine kicked to life, I thought I heard it. The Barn Owl. It would not have been possible to hear that rasping hiss over the sound of the motor, but I thought I heard it anyway. *"There it is!!"* I yelled.

Jim cut the ignition. The engine died. In the sudden silence we all froze, listening.

Nothing.

Had I imagined the sound? Was it just my subconscious mind stalling for time, stalling for one more minute?

I'll never know, actually. But at that moment, we really did hear it. From far away over the trees, distant but unmistakable, came the rasp of a Barn Owl.

"That's it, by Jove," said Stuart. We all jumped out of the car. The Barn Owl called again. And again. And again.

And we raised a ragged cheer, there in the dark in the state park, whooping and yelling and punching each other. We had done it, we had broken the record. At that moment we were the four proudest guys in Texas.

The few other patrons in the all-night coffee shop in McAllen seemed mystified by these four dusty, disheveled, red-eyed, red-faced, windblown men who stumbled in, crowing with triumph. "You know," Stuart announced, his cultured British tones contrasting oddly with our appearance, "that Ovenbird at Houston City Hall before dawn was the only one we saw all day." The waitress stared at him in alarm and fled.

Pulling out the checklist, we tallied up the number that each of us had seen out of the day's total. Jim Tucker and Joe Taylor had each seen 210 species. Stuart Keith had 211. To my surprise, I came out with 214.

Joe Taylor offered me hearty congratulations for picking up a record one-man, one-day list. "Just luck," I said. "I mean, it could have been any one of us. It's Jim Tucker's route that deserves the credit."

"Oh, forget the modesty," said Stuart. "Enjoy the success. We'll be modest tomorrow."

But the modesty of the next day did not prevent the guys from stopping at Falfurrias on the drive north, to brag about the Big Day to a friend there. Jim, Stuart, and Joe went into the hospital where the man worked, while I stayed in the car, reading.

A few minutes later I looked up to see Tucker striding out of the hospital. He was waving our checklist in the air and scowling like a thundercloud. Reaching the car, he shoved the list at me and announced melodramatically, "You goofed!"

Instantly, with a sick feeling inside, I knew what he meant. The night before at Santa Ana, squinting at the checklist in the fading light, I'd felt certain that something was not quite right. Of course: I must have miscounted. We were only tied with the record, or perhaps had missed it completely.

Tucker was watching my face. "What did I do?" I asked.

"Did we get an Olive Sparrow at Santa Ana?"

"What?!" I exploded. "Jim, you know we did! They were calling all over the place! We saw two right out in the road over by West Pond . . ."

Jim Tucker smiled. "Yes," he said, "I know; but you forgot to mark it on the list. That's two hundred twenty-nine, Kenn! We're two over the record!"

"Then . . ." I said, "all that time we spent at the end, waiting for the Barn Owl . . ."

". . . was worth it," Jim concluded. "It was the right way to finish a Big Day — we gave it everything we had."

Springtime Fades Away

WHEN THE breakneck speed of Big Day birding came to an end, I went back to my normal pace of birding for the year. The stopwatch was off. In a way, however, all year I could hear the ticking of a stopwatch that was more subtle but no less inexorable. My year-list attempt had to be completed within 365 days, and those days were passing.

Any bird-listing attempt limited by time — a Big Day, a Big Year, even a life list — was like a reminder of mortality. The day ends, the year will end, everything will end. *Time is short,* reads the underlying message; *make the most of it.*

When April ended and May began, I had exactly 500 species for the year. Finished with Texas, I headed for northern California, where a boat trip out of Humboldt was scheduled for the sixth. As it happened, Joel Greenberg also had arranged to go on this trip. I had regaled the guys with tales of the northern California birders, of Rich Stallcup And His Merrie Men, and it had appealed to Joel's imagination — he'd always wanted to find a birding youth culture. So I hitched to Sacramento and rode to Arcata with Rich and the Manolises; Joel flew to San Francisco and rode up with birders from there; and we all got together, along with everyone else, in the red house by the marsh at Humboldt Bay.

Joel should have been impressed. There were even more free-wheeling friendly birders around than there had been the previous October. After a long afternoon birding around the bay, we spent the evening at Mona's Bar before the party moved back to the red house. At sea the following morning, spirits were just as high, and I felt as if we weren't just observing the birds, but celebrating them — the shearwaters passing in lines and squadrons, the great albatrosses that came gliding close past the rail, watching us as we watched them.

When the Kansas Kid rode into Tucson a few days later, under the sun of high noon, he thought he was ready to take on the Parker Gang at last . . .

After all, I had had many adventures — finding rare birds, going afield with top birders, breaking records, running up my lists. I figured I had enough news to impress the rest of the Tucson Five.

Big deal. I might have known. While I'd been trying to do well in the States, Ted Parker and the guys had made an incredible expedition into southernmost Mexico.

In Chiapas they had hired a guide and pack horses for a trek into the mountains. There they had seen Barred Parakeets and Resplendent Quetzals, and other fine highland birds. They had observed the rare Azure-rumped Tanager; up to that time, probably fewer than a dozen naturalists had seen one alive. "Mark spotted it first," Ted admitted. "He swung around — nearly knocked my head off with his binoculars — then he started yelling, 'It's the Azure-cabbed . . . the blue-rumped . . . the rump-winged . . .' and I ran back up the trail to find Joel and Dave."

And, most impressively, they had encountered the Horned Guan: an almost mythical fowl, a large and spectacular but elusive guan of the remote cloud forests. Deep in the forest near the highland village of El Triunfo they had stared, awed, at this big black-and-white bird with the red "horn" on its head, this fowl that perched in the ridgetop trees, craning its neck and clacking its bill at them. Two nights later, having started back down the mountain, reliving the scene in their dreams, they were kicked awake by some local Indians who asked whether the *gringos* would like to buy a couple of baby birds. The guys stared, awed, again: the baby birds were obviously Horned Guans!

"Ted lost his cool," Joel told me. "We could've bought those birds for fifty pesos — but Ted had to jump up, all excited, and start babbling about how the young bird wasn't known to science." That had sharpened the Indians' bargaining instincts; perhaps, they said, they should eat the young guans instead of selling them. But the guys had managed to purchase the birds by trading off money, a sleeping bag, a flashlight, and other goods ("Thank God the *car* was forty miles away," said Dave). One of the young guans promptly died; the other was taken back to civilization and presented to the Mexican biologist Miguel Alvarez del Toro, who put it in a cage to raise it and study its growth and behavior.

Now the guys were back . . . back to the mundane States, to dull classes and college routine. Ted paced back and forth in his dorm room, as if caged himself. Just as he had found, a few years back, that Lancaster County was too small for him, now he was finding the North Temperate Zone too small, too predictable. In the American tropics, by contrast, there were Horned Guans and other amazing sights waiting around every corner. Ted Parker was burning up with frustration in the States, he had to get back to the tropics.

But since he happened to be still in Arizona at the moment, he would go out in the field with us and demonstrate, in passing, that he knew these temperate-zone birds quite well.

The station wagon came to a halt at a dirt crossroads in the pre-dawn dimness, while Ted and Mark argued briefly about which way to turn. A decision was made, we drove on, and I dozed off; when I came fully awake it was sunrise, and we were pulling into Scotia Canyon.

The car crawled up the bumpy track at the canyon mouth on the south face of the Huachuca Mountains, a stone's throw from the Mexican boundary. This canyon was, at that time, considered the only reliable place to find Buff-breasted Flycatchers north of the border. Once fairly common in southern Arizona and New Mexico, the bird had receded from most of its U.S. range.

Scotia Canyon had meadows interspersed with open stands of oak and pine, and a few white-trunked sycamores grew along the stream that meandered down the canyon floor. Climbing from the car, we heard Buff-breasted Flycatchers almost immediately: a sharp *chee-wip!* with the explosive quality of many small fly-catchers' calls. Two of the birds were moving about in trees up the hillside above the stream, but they were flighty. We had to stalk after them for a while before they settled down to give us a decent look.

A few minutes later we found another pair building a nest on a pine branch not far above the ground. Every couple of minutes, one of the birds would return with a billful of fine grasses to work into the nest cup. These Buff-breasteds were tiny flycatch-ers, small even for the pint-sized *Empidonax* group, but their wash of cinnamon-buff color made them more distinctive than most. They displayed all the spunk typical of the family: one member of the pair harassed and finally chased away a Grace's Warbler that had ventured into the nest tree.

Satisfied with the flycatchers, we went exploring for other spe-cies. A quarter mile up the canyon we found an abandoned farm-stead, and Mark, a reptile man before he got into birding, said there should be some interesting lizards or snakes around the old foundation. He went in and began poking around. Within about a minute, he suddenly yelled "Hey!" and made an excited pounce, flinging an upturned board to one side — and held up a striking large lizard, the Arizona alligator lizard, a handsome creature with a banded pattern of chestnut and gray.

Inspired, the rest of us joined the hunt. Carefully turning over boards and rocks, we soon found a couple of bunch grass lizards, a tree lizard of some sort, and a few things that got away unidentified. While we were engaged in the search, an old man wandered up and stood watching us — surprising us a little; we had thought the canyon was deserted. But the man lived nearby in the small village of Sunnyside, and after spending a few minutes telling us about the history of the place, he gave each of us a booklet of Bible quotations and wandered on down the canyon.

Leaving Scotia around 9:00 A.M., we continued around the south end of the Huachucas and up the east side to Ramsey Canyon. In many respects, Ramsey was similar to several other canyons in the border ranges — but here, for years, hummingbird feeding had been practiced on a grand scale by the owners of the Mile Hi lodge. With twenty or thirty sugar-water feeders up in a small area, there was an incredible concentration of artificial food for hummingbirds. Several notable species, hummers from Mexico, had been recorded here. Violet-crowned and White-eared hummingbirds were now almost regular, Lucifer Hummingbird had been observed, and the first Berylline Hummingbird for the United States had been photographed at the feeders here in 1967.

Today, Ramsey seemed quiet. Carroll Peabody at the Mile Hi

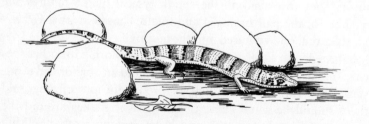

Arizona Alligator Lizard

told us that it was a slow spring — the main concentration of hummers had not built up yet. After watching the feeders for a while we walked up the canyon, seeing Scott's Orioles, Painted Redstarts, and other predictable birds, but nothing unusual.

Leaving Ramsey, we stopped for lunch at a restaurant in Sierra Vista. The place was crammed. We spotted an empty table, apparently the only one in the house; it hadn't been cleared off yet, but the occupants clearly had departed. We pulled up a fifth chair and sat down to wait.

With no birds to keep them occupied, Joel and Dave started kidding around. "Tell me, Inspector," Dave was asking, "what brings you to Sierra Vista?"

"What brings me here?" Joel echoed, staring blankly around the restaurant. "I'm investigating a very strange case. The Rowlett's Owlet Slayings: there was no evidence of any crime."

"Oh, no," said Parker. "Not that Owlet stuff again."

"Are you against freedom of speechlessness?" demanded Joel. "Listen, if Rowlett's Owlets are outlawed, only outlaws will have Rowlett's Owlets!"

"Serves 'em right," Mark yawned. "Wonder when this table's going to get cleared? Wonder when they're going to take our order? I'm starved."

Admittedly, the restaurant was busy. But after we'd been there twenty minutes, they still had not even cleared off our table. We couldn't sit there all day; we had other birds to seek. So we got up and walked out.

We were driving out of the parking lot when Joel said, "Wonder what *her* problem is?" We looked: the crone who had been presiding over the cash register inside was now peering out the door at us.

"She's writing something down," Ted observed. "Writing down the license number?! What for?"

"Oh, man," I said. "We better go back." Mark agreed. We wheeled around the block, and Mark and I walked inside.

Obviously, the woman had seen us get up from the table and

walk out without paying. Now she couldn't seem to comprehend our explanation. To our dismay, a waitress insisted that she had served Mark and me. ("Get Joel in here," said Mark. "She'll *know* she's never seen *him* before.") Finally it was determined that the check from that table had been paid. The mystery still loomed in the cashier's mind, but the monetary angle had been settled; "I guess it's all right," she said.

Back out in the car, Joel was indignant: "She *guessed* it was *all right?*" "Forget it," said Parker. "Let's grab a hamburger someplace and get out of here. We've got to get to Sonoita Creek."

It was well past noon when we pulled through the town of Patagonia and arrived at the Nature Conservancy sanctuary on Sonoita Creek. The magnificent stands of huge old cottonwoods were fully leafed out, and upstream from the main gate, a Common Black-Hawk circled low over the trees, uttering hoarse whistles.

The five of us split up to see what birds were around. Summer Tanagers gave their snappy crackling calls high overhead, the males glowing rose red against the green of the cottonwood foliage. Those clowns of the bird world, the Yellow-breasted Chats, hooted and snarled and gurgled from deep in the thickets. We saw a few birds that were still clearly on their way north, like Townsend's Warbler, although at this latitude the main part of the migration was over by mid-May.

We had planned to stop only briefly there, but several hours had passed before we got everyone back into the car and headed down Highway 82 toward the most famous roadside rest stop in the United States — most famous among birders, anyway. It was only a small turnoff, with a few picnic tables, across the road from Sonoita Creek. But in the 1960s a birder from Nogales, Bill Harrison, had discovered that this rest area was a reliable place to find Rose-throated Becard, a rare bird north of the border. So he had begun visiting more often and had found more exciting birds, including the first United States colony of Five-striped Sparrows and the second colony of Thick-billed Kingbirds. Before long, birders from all over were flocking to the area and discovering state records like Yellow Grosbeak, Black-capped Gnatcatcher, and Yellow-green Vireo, plus a host of lesser rarities. This phenomenon — of rare birds attracting more birders, who then find more rare birds, attracting more birders, and so on — was soon given a name: "The Patagonia Picnic Table Effect."

The final stage of the Picnic Table Effect would be to attract so many birders that the landowner would put up big fences and "No Trespassing" signs between the highway and the creek; but in 1973, you could still walk in. We left the station wagon parked at the picnic tables and hurried across to Sonoita Creek.

It was late in the afternoon. In the shadows of the tall trees, in the groves along the stream, birds were already becoming quiet. We tracked up and down the creekbed for a while. "Listen," Parker said, finally; "there it is." A slurred whining whistle, the call of the Rose-throated Becard. It took us another ten minutes of carefully scanning the leafy branches overhead before we actually saw the becard — an inconspicuous bird, patterned in somber grays except for the rose red throat.

We wandered on up the stream, listening for Thick-billed Kingbirds, but heard none. "That's okay," said Parker. "We'll see them next week at Guadalupe Canyon. Right now, we'd better try for the sparrows."

The Five-striped Sparrow was a bird of brushy desert hills; the only known colony in the United States at that time was in a dry ravine that opened onto Sonoita Creek opposite the roadside rest. We hiked past a series of red rock cliffs to an old broken-down railroad trestle that marked the entrance to the "Five-striped Sparrow Canyon."

After fourteen hours in the field, our zeal was diminished, and we hoped the sparrows would be easy to find. They were not. We searched for half an hour, while our concentration gradually ebbed away. The end of that time found the five of us merely sitting on the hillside, halfway up the east side of the canyon.

By now the sun had slipped behind the western hills, casting the scene below us into shadow. Not a bird was calling from the Sparrow Canyon. We were silent as well. I was depressed, knowing I would have to make a special trip back here for the sparrows later in the season, when time might be running short. But today was almost over . . .

Then Ted Parker shook his head slightly and got to his feet. For a long minute he stood looking up and down the canyon, frowning in concentration. Then — "Come on," he said to me, and I followed. We hiked all the way down the canyon without seeing or hearing a single bird. At the mouth of the draw, by the old railway trestle, Ted paused and then started up the slope again, a little to the west of the way we'd come down.

Halfway up the hill we found one of the sparrows foraging under some dense brush, silently, inconspicuously. We called the other guys down, and we all watched the Five-striped Sparrow for fifteen minutes.

If some cartographer had hiccuped at the wrong moment during the delineation of the Gadsden Purchase, Guadalupe Canyon might have ended up completely outside the United States. The canyon was barely within the boundary. It started in the absolute southwestern corner of New Mexico, rimmed the edge of Arizona for a few miles, and then dropped into Mexico. It was such a minor feature, relative to the vast distances in the Southwest, that the canyon and the road to it were not even shown on most highway maps.

But this insignificant sliver of geography had produced many significant bird records. It had been the first place in the U.S. where the Violet-crowned Hummingbird was seen regularly, and it was where the first U.S. colony of Thick-billed Kingbirds was found, several years before that species began to appear along Sonoita Creek and elsewhere. In the early 1970s, Guadalupe was still the only place north of the border where that mysterious

Mexican night bird, the Buff-collared Nightjar, had ever been found. That was why the approach of dawn on May 17 found Ted and Mark and me driving along the rough dirt road that ran east from Douglas, Arizona, toward the canyon.

Mark drove cautiously on the bumpy road because his car was loaded down; he was going to take off directly from the canyon to go back to Missouri for the summer. We were going to stay over tonight, and then the next day Joel and Dave would stop in, and I would go on with them through New Mexico and Texas. Ted had arranged for a ride back to Tucson with someone the following weekend. Joel had kidded him about that — suppose the ride didn't come through? — and invented a legend in which Ted became the Abominable Birdman and wandered forever in the canyon. Ted was not worried though. He would not mind being stranded there a while, he said, because Guadalupe Canyon had potential for some new discoveries.

At sunrise we reached the mouth of the canyon, where groves of tall cottonwoods and sycamores stood in sharp contrast against the surrounding dry hills. The brash and noisy Thick-billed Kingbirds were back for the summer, and we could hear their staccato metallic bursts and their ringing *karreeep!* calls

*Thick-billed
Kingbirds*

from the trees. One pair was building a nest, and we watched as they made repeated trips with nest material, punctuating each visit with loud calls and much wing-fluttering. Also nest-building was the kingbirds' opposite-number among the flycatcher family, the tiny and inconspicuous Northern Beardless-Tyrannulet. A mile up the canyon we saw a pair of Zone-tailed Hawks at a nest, a large stick platform high in a huge cottonwood. Most of the birds present on this date were on their nesting territories, with only a few migrants still on their way north.

About halfway up the road stood the house of the McGoffin family, the only people living in the Arizona section of the canyon at that time. We stopped out in front and waited while the McGoffins' mongrel horde of watchdogs raged about the car. Eventually Mrs. McGoffin came out to shoo the dogs away and say hello to us. We asked, cautiously and diplomatically, whether they'd heard any Buff-collared Nightjars this spring.

Because they were cordial to visiting birders, the McGoffins had been caught in the middle of a debate over whether there were still any Buff-collared Nightjars in Guadalupe Canyon. The species definitely had been there in 1958, when scientists had collected specimens up in the New Mexico part of the canyon. Two years later, one had been shot on the Arizona side of the line. But since 1960, Arizona experts had been unable to find any nightjars in the canyon — while, oddly enough, novices or out-of-state visitors often did. If a person desperately wanted to hear the odd song of the nightjar, there were plenty of things that could sound somewhat like it. There was, for example, the full song of the Vermilion Flycatcher, often given at dusk or dawn, when one might expect a night bird to be calling. There was the odd dawn song of Cassin's Kingbird. Sometimes there were birders elsewhere in the canyon, playing nightjar tape recordings made in Mexico. There were mockingbirds imitating the tape recordings. Maybe some of the visitors heard the genuine nightjar, but there had been no confirmed records since 1960.

So Mrs. McGoffin phrased her reply carefully. As in preceding years, she said, they had heard some calls this spring that might have been the sought-after bird. And some visitors had stopped by to say they'd heard nightjars "all over the place" at the upper end of the canyon. She didn't want to pass judgment. We were welcome, she said, to try for the bird ourselves.

We tried for the bird ourselves that night. For hours, Ted and Mark and I wandered the road, playing our tape recording of Buff-collared Nightjar, hoping for a response. We played the tape out beyond the canyon mouth, where Poorwills called mournfully from the dry slopes; we played it in the lower canyon, where tiny Elf Owls chattered and chuckled from the sycamores; we played it in the upper canyon, next to stark cliffs where silence had reigned until our arrival. Full moonlight framed the cliffs. The nightjar's odd, unbirdlike song, made tinny and shrill by the tape machine, came echoing back from the rocks. In that setting we easily could have believed there were nightjars around, could have believed anything . . . but no response ever came back from the moonlit hillsides.

Of course we had no way of knowing it then, but just four years later, in June 1977, I was to find a pair of Buff-collared Nightjars on territory in the lower canyon. Just a couple of years after that, they started showing up in other spots around southern Arizona. Eventually they would become regular summer residents in a dozen areas.

By the time that happened, the Tucson Five would be only a memory. Ironically, it was I, the transient, who was the only one to wind up living in Tucson later. The other four scattered to four different states, and after that May of 1973, never again would all five of us get together. But the brief life span of our little gang was a golden time — a time of discovery and wonder, a time when so many of the birds were still elusive and mysterious to us, a time that would never come again.

We left Ted at Guadalupe Canyon. Joel and Dave and I were going on east to Carlsbad and then to Big Bend, where we would search for (among other things) the rare Lucifer Hummingbird.

Two days after we left, Ted — just because he was Ted Parker — would find a Lucifer Hummingbird in lower Guadalupe, and even find its nest, the first known nest of the species for Arizona. But we would not learn that until a couple of months later. We were driving east, just three kids on the verge of being kids no longer, but trying to hold on to these teenage years that were coming to an end . . . joking a little too hard, driving a little too fast, trying to outrun time.

The Kenmare Convention

UPLAND Sandpipers were performing flight-songs overhead as I waited beside Highway 52. When I looked hard enough, one hand up to block the sun, I could usually find one: small and dark against the Dakota sky, a sandpiper floating on quivering wings as it breathed out haunting vibrato whistles that echoed across the prairies. But of course the birds were not up there for the sake of music. Each singing sandpiper was a male staking its claim to land below, warning other males to stay away, inviting females to stay and mate. It was ownership and territorial defense. The birds sang in flight because that was the only way, in this treeless terrain, to broadcast their claims across their chosen pieces of land.

I was trying to hitch a ride to Kenmare, North Dakota, where the very first convention of the American Birding Association was beginning that day. At the time it was an ambitious move for the Association to try to hold a meeting. The ABA was in its fifth year and had 1,500 members, but it had no professional staff, no real budget, no experience with conventions. However, it had the energy of Jim Tucker and the goodwill of a growing corps of birders. That was enough.

When convention plans were first announced, some ABA members wondered: Why North Dakota? No one regarded it as a birding hotspot. But it was. In June the prairie sloughs of North Dakota would be alive with grebes and phalaropes and ducks and other waterbirds. The grasslands would ring with songs of birds, including several specialties that would be new for birders from either coast. North Dakota was a fine state for a birding convention. Even if it was proving, for me, to be a slow state for hitching rides.

Northwest past Minot, I had very long waits punctuated by short rides. Several cars that passed me had ABA decals. I considered holding up a sign saying "ABA member," but if my binoculars were not badge enough, I would get there without the birders' help. As it happened, my binoculars caught the eye of a local guy. When he stopped and I got into his pickup, he asked, "You're going to that birdwatchers' convention, right?"

Kenmare was a small town, he told me, and everyone there knew that the birders were coming. This man worked on a local dairy farm; the farmer's wife was one of the volunteers helping out with the ABA meeting.

From upland prairie and farmland we dropped into the lightly wooded valley of the Des Lacs River, and after about thirty miles we came rather suddenly into Kenmare. I had just enough time to gain the impression of tidy yards along quiet streets before we pulled up in front of the school building: this, the guy said, was where the convention was headquartered. I was glad he knew, because I did not. I had not gotten around to registering for the convention, since I had not been sure I would have time to stop here before going to Alaska. Thanking the man, I shouldered my pack and started up the walk toward the school.

The building looked brand-new and modern, large for the size of the town, probably serving not only Kenmare but also a considerable outlying area. Stepping from the sunlit sidewalk to the dim interior of the lobby, I found there were already several dozen birders milling about in conversation. Near at hand was a row of tables where local women were dispensing information to the conventioneers.

As I approached, one of the women pleasantly asked who I was, preparing to consult her list of registered attendees. I mumbled some sort of apology. "Listen," I said, "I'm not registered for the convention, and I can't afford the field trips or anything. Do you mind if I just sort of stick around and watch?"

The woman frowned. Evidently she had not anticipated that bearded teenagers with backpacks would come to lurk around the edges of the otherwise orderly group. She paused, apparently marshaling her thoughts to deal with me in a fair-but-firm manner. But at that moment, Jim Tucker, Benton Basham, and Joe Taylor came over to greet me, not guessing that there was trouble brewing. "How's it going?" they asked. "How's the Big Year?" Surrounded by three of the top ABA brass, I was hustled away into the school auditorium for the Elective Members' meeting, leaving the poor volunteer nonplussed. I knew I would have to seek her out later and apologize.

In the auditorium I saw from a distance my new friend from the Texas Big Day, Stuart Keith. Here, instead of being the intrepid fieldman, he was cast in the more formal role of President of the Association. In running the meeting he had poise, quick wit, precise delivery. He set the tone that characterized the best of the ABA: dignified but fun, civilized but adventurous.

Emerging later from the Elective Members' meeting, I found that my friend Paul Lehman had arrived. Paul was the young New Yorker I'd met on the New Hampshire boat trip in January, and who had caused a stir by discovering a rare Fieldfare in New York in February. Later in the afternoon a group from the Lancaster County Bird Club showed up, including a kid younger than me, Eric Witmer. Some friends of the Lancastrians, birders from Baltimore, showed up in the evening: Doug and Joan Cook, and their teenage daughter Elaine. And I met a couple of very young birders, Kevin and Barry Zimmer, who lived in North Dakota. I was glad there were other kids present besides me.

Most of the time I wouldn't be able to hobnob with the celebrity birders, but I could run around with a gang of young kindred spirits.

After dinner that night there was a social mixer at a local pub, the Midget Bar. There were dozens of new people to meet, new faces to be connected with familiar names. Scanning the room, I spotted a familiar face, but one I'd seen before only in photographs. It was my hero, Roger Tory Peterson.

I admired Peterson intensely for both his accomplishments and his approach. He had come into his world eminence in birding via his own route, without going through channels. He had been just the kid from Jamestown, New York, many years ago — the kid who would not become a professional ornithologist, and who was told that he could not make a living as a bird painter . . . until in 1934 he brought out his first *Field Guide to the Birds* and launched a legendary career. In the years since then he had been acclaimed as the great painter, great writer, great photographer, great fieldman, great man; he was, without a doubt, the world's best-known ornithologist.

At a distance, Peterson looked his age, about sixty-five — the face was developing lines, the hair was turning white. But at closer range I noticed his eyes. Those eyes blazed with a fiery blue intensity. The eyes had the same burning gaze they must have had fifty years before, when he had first sought birds in the hills of western New York. His eyes had never lost their youthful keenness for birds.

I don't know how late the social mixer lasted; I left early. After several nights on the road, I was tired. Fortunately, here I would not camp on roadsides: the town of Kenmare was taking care of us all. Since the one hotel and one motel in town could not begin to accommodate all two hundred birders, many were staying as guests in local homes. The rest of us were sleeping on the floor of the school gymnasium — so I had a roof over my head, and a shower! As far as I was concerned, this was luxury.

Early Friday morning I was awakened by the alarm clocks of the other sleepers in the gym. In the adjacent cafeteria, breakfast was being served. I dug into my backpack for my own breakfast — a can of vegetable beef soup, spooned straight from the can. While everyone else piled into six yellow school buses for a field trip to the Lostwood National Wildlife Refuge, I set out on foot for the Des Lacs refuge on the outskirts of Kenmare.

The refuge was a long narrow tract, aligned north and south along the course of the Des Lacs River. Through much of the refuge this river was dammed to form a lake, managed to provide marsh habitat for waterfowl. Kenmare lay near the south end of the lake, on the east side; on the opposite shore was refuge head-quarters. I headed in that direction first.

As I crossed the lake on the road out of town, I stopped to watch the Western Grebes. Their reedy calls carried as far as the town when the wind was right, providing background music for summer in Kenmare. Here at the edge of the lake, some sat on floating nests out in plain sight, others swam and dove in the shallows; occasionally a pair would go into an active courtship display, bowing in an exaggerated way and then rearing up to go pattering away side by side across the surface of the water.

On the far side of the lake I followed the road up onto the prairie. It was prairie birds, after all, that were the specialties here. The grasslands and farmlands were green at this season; thickets of wild rose were blooming, and masses of yellow sweet clover blanketed the road shoulders. Around many of the thickets were Clay-colored Sparrows, singing flat, buzzy songs. Yellow-throats were also common. The local Yellowthroats seemed to have an unusual propensity for flight-song: the little bird would bop up into the air — and then, as if surprised to find itself out in the open, it would rap out a fast *wichy-wichy-wichy* while it scooted back into the brush.

In a damp field I found a new bird for my year list, a Le Conte's Sparrow. This was a weak-voiced but colorful little sparrow, one I did not know well, and I watched it for quite a while. But by the end of the morning, to my surprise, I still had not found the bird I wanted most at Kenmare: Baird's Sparrow. This was the most localized of the Dakota specialties; it was the one that would be hardest to pick up later in the year if I missed it here.

During the afternoon I planned to look for Baird's in new fields south of Kenmare; but shortly past noon a strong wind came up, keeping most small birds under cover. Even the Red-winged Blackbirds seemed to disappear. I was annoyed about the wind at first, but it created a different birding spectacle: a flock of American White Pelicans came soaring overhead, huge ponderous birds wheeling slowly in formation on the wind.

Back at the school in late afternoon, young Eric Witmer and I were sitting around back by the gym and talking about lists. By this time — with my tally up to 575 — I was willing to agree that I would have a decent score for 1973. But the really spectacular year list, I felt, was still out in the future, not to be glimpsed this year. Eric and I were discussing the higher theoretical planes of year listing when we noticed that a stranger had stopped to listen. We broke off and greeted him.

The guy sat down and introduced himself. He was a bearded, quiet man in his thirties, from Columbus, Ohio; his name was Tom Thomson. Our conversation had caught his attention, he said, because he himself was doing a Big Year this year. Obviously he had heard only the latter part of our discussion, and did not realize my interest in the subject. Keeping a straight face, I asked Thomson how many species he had for the year so far.

Thomson paused, adding figures in his head. He had just returned from Churchill, Manitoba, and the birds he'd seen there would put him up to 469.

I'm not sure what I would have said. But Eric, usually a courteous kid, was surprised enough to laugh out loud. "That's nothing," he said. "Kaufman's a hundred species ahead of you."

Thomson was nonplussed, and I was embarrassed, but I was surprised, too. Thomson had been traveling and birding widely this year, yet up to now he had not known of Floyd or myself, and we had not heard of him.

Eric and I had planned to go owling around the edge of town after the dinner and program that night. The girl from Baltimore, Elaine, had decided to come with us. We were getting ready to leave when Tom Thomson and his friend Frank Bader came over and invited me out for a drink . . . showing that there were no hard feelings among competitors; and I saw that I, to be an equally good sport, should accept. I turned to ask Eric and Elaine if they would excuse me, and Thomson invited them as well. Eric declined — after briefly considering his chances of passing for drinking age, whatever that was, here — but Elaine, who looked closer to my age, accepted. So four of us went over to the Midget Bar.

We settled in at a table and I started asking Thomson and Bader about their just-completed trip to Churchill, Manitoba, the outpost town on Hudson Bay. They were telling us about the things they'd seen there when the waitress came over to take our order. Thomson and Bader ordered mixed drinks. I asked for a beer. Elaine ordered a scotch and water.

The waitress paused and looked more closely at Elaine. "How old are you?" she asked.

"Eighteen," said Elaine, an uncertain look starting to play around the corners of her eyes. I was beginning to notice what her eyes were like: smoky hazel, and reserved, but with an occasional unsettling directness.

The waitress frowned. "I'm sorry," she said; "legal age here is twenty-one. Really, you shouldn't be in here at all."

At this Elaine bit her lip and looked down at the table, trying to control her expression. I was afraid she might start crying. "Listen," I said to the waitress, "you won't get in trouble. I'll vouch for the kid. We can claim that she forgot her I.D., or something." Elaine shot an angry look at me; possibly she realized that I, behind my beard and my sunburn, was only nineteen and therefore just as illegal as she was. At least now she wasn't going to cry, because now she was mad instead.

As it worked out, we didn't have to leave. Evidently word had been handed down that the ABA convention-goers were not to be hassled. So Elaine sipped a lime juice and tonic water and pointedly ignored me while I watched her, slightly amused, from behind my beer.

The conversation eventually came around to rare birds and the impact they could have on an attempted Big Year. At that time, in the early 1970s, there was nothing like a national Rare Bird Alert. Finding out about rarities while they were still around was largely a matter of luck. Neither Thomson nor I had heard about the Fieldfare in New York before it had disappeared, so we could write that one off for the year.

That reminded me of an earlier stakeout. "Did you get the Loggerhead Kingbird?" I asked Thomson. At this, Elaine looked up from her lime and tonic. "That's a Caribbean bird," I said, explaining it to her. "There was one staked out in Florida this winter, and . . ."

"I know," she interrupted, coolly. "I saw it."

Something stirred in my memory. "Oh, yeah," I said. "I guess your folks hang out with the Lancaster crowd. Did you go down for the kingbird with Ted and Harold, when they made that fast trip in early January?"

"No," she said. "We *told* Ted and Harold about the kingbird, and that's *why* they made that trip in January." Elaine and her parents had heard about the bird only through coincidence, she explained. They had gone to Florida over Christmas, and while they were eating dinner in an Italian restaurant in Homestead, they heard some birders at the next table talking about the kingbird they had seen that day.

As she talked, Tom had raised his eyebrows in surprise. Now he laughed. "I thought you looked familiar," he told her.

Elaine stared at him blankly for a second, before laughing herself. "Oh, that's right. You were one of them! The one who got a speeding ticket on the way to Florida. Wasn't that you?"

Thomson winced. "Yes, that was me. But I'd rather you remembered me for giving you the directions to the Loggerhead Kingbird."

It was late when Elaine and I got back to the school. Eric was already asleep, but he'd left a note — "Wake me up if you want to go owling" — so we did. The three of us went out and wandered the quiet streets of Kenmare for a while. With Eric half asleep, and me slightly drunk, our owling was not a success. The only birds we heard were grebes and coots, their calls drifting up from the lake.

After our owling attempt, I was still too keyed up to sleep, so Elaine and I sat and talked for a while. Although she was only eighteen, she had already finished a year at Cornell University. And she actually knew a lot about birds. In spite of myself, I was beginning to be impressed.

Saturday morning I joined everyone else on the yellow school buses, as much to see the phenomenon of the field trip as for the birds we might encounter. I expected something of a circus, but it actually was not bad at all. The open marshes and prairies of North Dakota could accommodate a lot of birders. At our first stop, we were on a hillside overlooking the south end of Middle Des Lacs Lake. A hundred and eighty pairs of binoculars, and scores of scopes, scanned the lake and the shoreline. Somebody picked out a Wood Duck, locally uncommon, and a singing Sedge Wren popped up into view in the field between us and the lake. White Pelicans came over, Yellow-headed Blackbirds appeared, and each new bird was seen by virtually everyone.

Late in the morning we were dispersed along a roadside by a marshy field. This was the stronghold of the Sharp-tailed Sparrow — the prairie race, Nelson's Sharp-tail, more colorful than the Sharp-tails on the Atlantic coast. At length, one sparrow perched up in the open to sing for close to twenty minutes, while all the birders converged to watch it.

I moved back a little to look at the birders and noticed that Jim Tucker was doing the same. "Think about it," I told him. "As founder of this organization, you were the one who brought all these people together. You deserve to be proud."

Jim shrugged and smiled. "Mostly," he said, "I'm just amazed. Five years ago, when we started the ABA, I never thought I'd see anything like this."

At the approach of noon the buses wound around to Tasker's Coulee, a wooded draw west of Kenmare. I was surprised at how numerous the Veeries were here, in what seemed a slim habitat for these shy forest thrushes. From up and down the ravine we could hear the Veeries singing: clear airy whistles, descending golden spirals, easily the most ethereal of thrush voices.

After we'd box-lunched at Tasker's Coulee, and after a brief sortie into Kenmare for a staked-out Orchard Oriole, the buses took us back to the school. Most of the others were through birding for the day, but I was keenly aware that my year list still lacked the most specialized of the Dakota specialty birds.

For most of the morning I'd been more or less hanging around with Elaine . . . "Listen," I told her, "I'm going to take off. You people had Baird's Sparrows yesterday, didn't you, on that bus trip? Over by Lostwood? If you'll give me directions, I can hitch over there. I'll be back before the banquet tonight."

Elaine regarded me doubtfully. As far back as March, the Lancaster birders had been telling her stories of my supposedly amazing ability to hitchhike fast and far, but she was unconvinced. "I can give you directions," she said. "But it must be ten miles from here, and it's not on a major road. You might be out there all night."

"This is the West."

"No, it isn't, you dummy. Don't you know anything about birds? Most of the bird species here are eastern ones. Anyway, why don't I ask my father if he'll take us?"

Her dad said he wouldn't mind seeing the birds again, and Eric Witmer decided to come too, so four of us drove over to the sparrow stakeout. It was a section of upland prairie sloping down to a lake, a plot known as the Longspur Pasture.

Elaine wandered down to the lake to watch the Wilson's Phalaropes — she liked phalaropes, she said, because the females were brighter than the males — but Doug Cook and Eric and I tracked off across the pasture in search of Baird's Sparrows. I had imagined the sparrows might be elusive at this hour, since it was siesta time; but we heard several singing and managed to stalk a couple for close views. The Baird's were not colorful, with no more than a pale wash of mustard-yellow on the head, but their simple song was surprisingly musical.

The Baird's Sparrows were not the only birds in this field. Chestnut-collared Longspurs were everywhere, rising into the air in little warbling song-flights and then fluttering down again like butterflies. The males were spectacular in black, white, and chestnut. As we human intruders advanced across the pasture, a pair of big, long-billed, cinnamon-tan birds flew up ahead of us, calling in protest. These Marbled Godwits must have had a nest nearby. We detoured to avoid upsetting them further, but until we were several hundred yards away the godwits continued to circle overhead, their cries ringing across the prairie.

And somewhere high above the godwits, a Sprague's Pipit was singing in aerial display. At first I missed its song completely — perhaps, subconsciously, I thought my ears were still picking up echoes of the Veeries at Tasker's Coulee. Like the Veery, this pipit

Baird's Sparrow

sang with a breezy quality, in a descending pattern, a wheeling spiral of sound. I had seen Sprague's Pipit before only on the wintering grounds, where it was a furtive skulker in tall grass. Here it was the highest of singers, pouring out its song while hovering far above the earth. For a moment I was transported back to the San Juan Islands in Washington, where, in March, I had seen the Sky Larks performing their song-flight from a similar towering height.

With all due respect for tradition, and for the Sky Lark's place in literature, I found the song of the pipit no less stirring. Perhaps it was not quite so musical, not quite so varied, but it floated down from the prairie sky with a clarity to match its surroundings. If the poet Shelley had lived in North Dakota rather than in nineteenth-century England, his "To a Skylark" might well have been dedicated to a Sprague's Pipit.

For the convention banquet that night, the school cafeteria was transformed into some degree of elegance, and the people were transformed as well. The lady birders and the wives and daughters, who had been just friendly gals in blue jeans, appeared in jewelry and makeup and dresses . . . reminding me uneasily of another plane of existence, beyond the birding scene.

As Master of Ceremonies, Stuart Keith made the room seem less a cafeteria and more convincingly a banquet hall, as he thanked the local volunteers and introduced the officers and guests at the head table. But the introduction of the main speaker was what he was leading up to, and there was sincere enthusiasm in his voice as he turned to "present . . . the greatest birder of them all: Roger Tory Peterson!"

Walking to the podium, Peterson looked slightly embarrassed by the laudatory introduction and the applause. But the self-conscious look vanished as soon as he began to speak.

He didn't have slides to back him up, and he followed no obvious outline. He just talked — a rambling series of impressions, reflections, and memories about birding and birds.

It was fantastic.

Listening, I realized he might have been any kind of artist. He might have been a composer: the great composer who began as a youth and learned to play all the instruments, who studied the intricacies of music theory, searching for musical perfection . . . until he could sit down at the piano and improvise so brilliantly that every measure of music rolling forth from the keys would be an inspiration to the listener. So it was with Peterson, only it was birds, not music. Since his boyhood he had been watching birds, painting them, photographing them, writing of them, letting his quest for birds take him to all parts of the globe; now he could hold a room full of birders spellbound simply by reminiscing, by improvising. When it was over we would all be on our feet, rocking the room with applause — but while he spoke, no one made a sound.

On Sunday, the last field trip of the convention was to Teddy Roosevelt National Park, in far western North Dakota. I took my backpack along on the long bus trip down, intending to hitch on from there rather than returning to Kenmare with the field trip.

On the bus I sat next to Elaine. It was logical to talk to her some more, I told myself, because her school — Cornell University — was well known as a center for bird studies. The famous Cornell Laboratory of Ornithology was located there. Elaine knew a lot of the ornithologists. Sometime, she said, I should come to visit her at school.

That day I also had the chance to go birding for a while with Roger Tory Peterson. Although I'd noticed the intensity of his eyes when we'd first met, I found his ears were equally keen; he picked out every birdsong instantly. I was quiet, listening to whatever Peterson said, wanting to learn from him. Stuart Keith joined us for a while and then insisted on getting a photograph of me birding with Peterson.

"If that photo comes out," said Jim Tucker, "I'm going to use it on the cover of *Birding* and caption it 'The teacher and the beginner.' Or, maybe, 'The master and the future.'"

The future, I said to myself. *What does that mean? Do I really have a future?*

I was still asking myself the same question two days later, as I waited by the highway in Alberta. Once again, Upland Sandpipers were performing flight-songs overhead. My thoughts were up in the air, too.

Even though my thumb was pointed north toward Alaska, my mind was busily going over (and over and over) every word of conversation I'd had with Elaine. But what was I doing getting involved, even mentally, with a woman?

I knew something about relationships. Not from experience so much as from those drivers, dozens of them, who had talked about their failed marriages and broken dreams. Bitter or angry or just mystified, these people had talked on and on, spilling it all, telling me everything because I was an anonymous listener who meant nothing. Listening hard, I'd learned at least one thing: every relationship had heavy costs.

The spark for a relationship might come for free — a look, a word. But the fuel to keep it going would always be expensive. Money might not buy happiness, but the lack of money could buy endless unhappiness for any two people. And lack of money was my hallmark, from the holes in my shoes to the scratches in the lenses of my twenty-dollar binoculars. I had no income, no savings, no prospects, no right to be interested in a girl from an Ivy League school.

No prospects. That was true, wasn't it? I was working so hard on my year list this year, but what was it going to bring me in the real world? Nothing. Even if I won the year-list "contest," at year's end I would still be an unemployed high-school dropout with no prospects for the future.

I had nothing to offer Elaine. I might have been some male bird singing in the sky, but a deceptive one, a bird that held no territory on the ground below — no land down there, no nest, nothing at all.

A Thousand Miles of Gravel

THE BORDER between the United States and Canada may have been the friendliest in the world in 1973, but still it could be an obstacle for hitchhikers. Canadian Customs officials were understandably unwilling to admit foreign kids with little or no money. I had been turned back at the border more than once, and I had also resorted to sneaking across it. But in June 1973 I walked up to the border station at Coutts, Alberta, confident that they would let me in: I was carrying almost five hundred dollars. I did not tell the officials that this money, scraped and borrowed over the preceding months, represented half my total budget for the year. I did not tell them that I might as well have been penniless, because I was hoarding practically every cent for a couple of essential plane flights. When they asked about my destination, I mentioned a nearby city. The truth was that I was going to traverse most of western Canada, aiming for the heart of Alaska.

I had traveled this route the summer before. The trip had been a major adventure, and I was excited to be going back. As I stood by the roadside, reliving memories from the preceding year, I found I was not just excited about my destination. Much of the anticipation, and the apprehension as well, focused on the road that I would follow to get there.

Hitching rides in southern Canada was not too different from hitching in the northern edge of the Lower 48. The roads were about the same, amount of traffic was about the same. The "schedule" was identical: you stand a while, and then you ride.

But if you were heading north, you would notice gradual changes. Civilization and traffic would begin to thin out. Most of Canada's population was concentrated along the southern edge of the country. By the time you had hitched north for a day, the majority of Canadians would be to the south of you. Get up around Grande Prairie or Prince George and you would notice how the summer twilight lingered through the night and the dawn arrived early, and you would feel how you were rising up over the curve of the earth.

And then at Dawson Creek, British Columbia, you would find something new: after a whole continent of roads, that was where the roads started to run out. Two routes came in from the south, but the map showed only one road — one long, wavering line — striking out toward the north. If you ventured up this road (and you would), you could throw away the map because all the confusing crossroads would be behind you.

Up the pavement for about fifty miles from Dawson Creek, the road ran through open country, with many farms and small settlements of the fertile Peace River district. But north of Fort St. John, the forest would close in. A sign by the road would announce "Pavement Ends," which it would, with bone-jarring suddenness. As clouds of dust enveloped the vehicle, as the driver began to curse the sharp gravel bouncing off the windshield, you would realize that you were on the notorious Alaska Highway.

The Alaska Highway! The *only* road to Alaska. Variously called the Alaska-Canada Highway, or the AlCan; called worse things, frequently, by those who traveled upon it. It is fifteen hundred miles long. In 1973, a thousand of those miles were still unpaved.

I wrote down my impressions of the AlCan as soon as I had the time, shortly after my Big Year ended, but by that time I was already writing history: the road would never be that bad again. Construction of the Alaska oil pipeline from Prudhoe Bay began in 1974, workers poured northward, and with increased traffic came the need to improve the highway. It was a shock to hear just a few years later that the AlCan was mostly paved and largely straightened out. In some perverse way, I felt lucky to have experienced the AlCan when I did.

People who traveled the road then, as drivers or as hitchhikers, all shared stories about this highway. It was said that this road was built during the Second World War, when somebody realized that Alaska was more accessible from Japan than it was from the Lower 48 States. The military wanted a land link, so they built it. The road wound back and forth, around and around, even where it crossed perfectly level ground. People said the military built it that way so that Japanese planes wouldn't be able to strafe long sections of the road in a single run. It worked, too; you hardly ever saw Japanese planes strafing the Alaska Highway in 1973. Another story: this road was built in such a hurry that when a bulldozer started to sink in the boggy ground, they would let it sink, and lay the roadbed over it. In places there were supposedly bulldozers stacked six deep, supporting the road. Whether the stories were true or not, they helped to build the legend of the AlCan.

One thing was certainly true of this road: it was often the toughest hitchhiking on the continent. They said that one guy had been stuck at Teslin, in the Yukon Territory, for forty-six days before he got a ride out. That might have been an exaggeration, but it was common for thumbers to get stuck for three days, four days without a ride.

On my trip north the previous year, 1972, I had thought I was doing well when I reached Fort Nelson, three hundred miles up the road. That, I thought, was a significant stop. It sure was: there were already about twenty thumbers stuck in Fort Nelson, thirteen going north and five or six going south, and some had been around for three days or more.

Arriving at the historic Klondike town of Whitehorse, which passed for a city in the Yukon Territory, I'd thought I had it made. After all, I was over halfway. But I got stuck there for two days anyway.

I didn't think things could get any worse, and then I came to Tok Junction, Alaska, the "Graveyard of the North" for hitchhikers. Tok was where the road forked, going northwest to Fairbanks and southwest to Anchorage, so lots of hitchers got dropped off there. It seemed there was a perpetual revolving commune of thumbers all summer long at Tok, with some headed for Anchorage, some headed for Fairbanks, and many chucking it all and going back to the Lower 48.

Being stuck at Tok wasn't so bad for a birder. Bohemian Waxwings and Pine Grosbeaks were around, and there was always the ghost of a chance of seeing a Boreal Owl. But for young travelers who were not birders — and, obviously, most of them were not — Tok could be a very dull place. Nothing to do but keep out of the way of drunken gold miners and natives, flirt with the too-young local girls, wander over to the Tourist Information Center ten or twelve times a day for free coffee, and watch the hordes of tourists.

Wait a minute. Hordes of tourists? If there were so many people coming through on these roads, why was it so tough to get a ride?

The reason was rooted in another legend of the North, a tradition etched into the AlCan's dust: the Curse of the Winnebago. On this road, a great many of the tourists were driving huge, luxurious, everything-including-the-kitchen-sink motorhomes. These came in many brands, but the various sizes of Winnebago seemed to be most popular with tourists on the AlCan — hence most unpopular with the hitchers there. Standing by the road on any dusty July afternoon, we would watch the Winnebagos roll past; the old men driving them would glance over and shrug: "Sorry, no room!"

The curse fell upon both great and small along the Alaska Highway, not only the luckless thumbers but also on the truck drivers, the kings of the road. Once in the Yukon Territory I got a ride with a trucker who spent a hundred miles swearing non-stop at the Winnebagos and their drivers. "Americans drive bad enough without giving 'em something the size of a *battleship* to fool around in. I mean, cheezus . . . They oughta at least have to get a special *license* to drive one of them things. It ain't like driving a car. Not on *this* little dirt road." Each time we encountered one of the motorhomes he would watch it moodily, taking obvious satisfaction in any erratic driving moves. "Cheezus," he'd say, "look at how this greenhorn is drifting from side to side." Or again, triumphantly: "Look at that! Parked just below that hill . . . That'd be a real problem for us, if we was coming the other way." And he'd hit the horn, shake his fist at them as we rumbled past.

This driver blamed the motorhomes for the loss of a friend not long before, a trucker who had been sent on the final ride. "There was another trucker some distance behind," he said; "saw it happen. Johnny was coming around this curve, and suddenly there's a couple of them sonsabitches trying to *pass* each other — on a *curve,* dammit, a blind curve! Johnny went off the road to miss hitting 'em — why, I'll never know — got a whole hillside full of tree branches through the windshield, and when he hit bottom a whole trailerload of pipe come through the back of his cab. I tell you, not enough left of him to feed a squirrel."

So though other travelers might curse them back, the Winnebagos rolled on, bringing latter-day adventurers who wanted to traverse the wilderness with all the comforts of home. And over and over, on most of these luxurious motorhomes, you saw the same crudely lettered signs: "Alaska or bust."

Despite the invasion of rolling civilization, this area was still basically wilderness in 1973. The narrow ribbon of the AlCan was overwhelmed by the vast land that it crossed. The province of British Columbia, after all, was larger than Texas and Oklahoma combined; the Yukon Territory, just a sliver of the Canadian map, was twice the size of Colorado; and of course Alaska was immense. Many were the lakes and canyons and mountains here that would have been designated as national parks, automatically, had they existed farther south; but in this wilderness, these features might not even have names yet, unless they lay close to the road. And the land seemed all the more wild for the lack of names.

The people who lived up here did have an all-inclusive name for this whole huge region of forest and lakes and mountains and muskeg. They called it "the Bush" — a term used, in several different parts of the world, to describe country that was too big for description.

The civilizing influence of the AlCan hardly extended more than a hundred yards back from the road shoulder. The influence of the Bush flowed across the highway from either direction, like a tide. True, the bears around the outpost towns on the road might get their meals from the local garbage dumps. But back in the surrounding Bush were wilder bears, bears that would live long and never see white men. True, some of the locals might bag any game-sized animal they saw along the road. But the surrounding Bush still held plenty of animals — plenty of moose, for example, wandering into the road, to cast a shaggy stubborn glare upon the approaching driver.

Sometimes in the endless forest there were Northern Hawk Owls perched on spruce-tops near the road. Sometimes there was strange music overhead as wild swans flew above the AlCan. One unforgettable morning I saw a lynx, a wild and graceful Canada lynx, that bounded across the road and then paused to look back before vanishing into the trees.

Once, along with four other thumbers, I caught a ride in the back of a pickup truck — a very windblown and dusty ride for eighty miles in the Yukon Territory. We were rolling through the trackless Bush, miles from any town or side road, when an old Native American woman stepped from the trees, flagged down the truck, and climbed in the back with the rest of us hitchhikers. Her back bent with age, her hair as gray as a glacial stream, her face as brown and wrinkled as tree bark, this woman seemed old as the Earth. She rode with us for twenty miles and then rapped on the cab to be let out at another remote spot in the forest. Turning to my companions as we rolled away, I said: "You know — she was beautiful. I don't know why, but she was really beautiful." In any other setting, I'm sure they would have laughed. But they had been traveling in the North, too, and had come under its influence; they nodded their heads solemnly, agreeing.

In June 1973, as soon as the ABA convention was over, I set out to hitch the AlCan Highway for a second year in a row. But this time the feeling was different. In '72 I had been buoyed up and

Canadian Lynx

carried along by the sheer novelty of it. This year, knowing already that the trip was at least possible, I was impatient to get on with it.

Based on my previous trip, I calculated it would take me ten days or more to get from North Dakota to Fairbanks. I had no time to lose: early summer was best for finding birds in Alaska, and in late summer I hoped to be back in the Lower 48 with time for several birding destinations. Sunday afternoon, the day the convention ended, I was on the road.

I followed Interstate 94 southwest to Billings and then took I-90 west. In the higher country of western Montana it was still just the edge of summer, chilly and damp, and I was dodging heavy rains as I headed north through Helena and Great Falls. By the time I crossed into Alberta on Tuesday morning I had left the bad weather behind, and I made good progress north through the center of the province, reaching Edmonton late that night.

Going up Highway 43 the next morning, up the long road that ran northwest across the prairies from Edmonton to Dawson Creek, I was surprised at how sparse the traffic was. Motorhomes and trailers were virtually absent. Evidently mid-June was too early in the season for the rush of AlCan vacationers. I did not mind the lack of Winnebagos, but the lack of traffic in general was not a good omen.

Late Wednesday afternoon I made it to Dawson Creek, the jumping-off point for the road north. The town was quiet; there was no traffic jam in front of the Tourist Information Centre, as there had been the summer before. After walking through town I got a ride with some local kids for the fifty-mile stretch up to Fort St. John. The sparse traffic on the road all looked like local traffic. From the turnoff into Fort St. John I walked on up the road a mile or so, put down my pack, and waited.

And waited.

Everything was quiet. At this latitude the sun was still out, but it was late evening, and the birds in the forest had fallen silent. No breeze moved the treetops. I waited, watching the pastel colors fade from the sky. After I had been standing for over an hour without a single vehicle coming past, I heard a sound growing out of the distance, coming up the road from the south. The sound resolved itself into a Volkswagen van. The van pulled up even with me and stopped.

The driver was headed for a job in the north country and was in a hurry to get there. If I would help drive, he said, I was welcome to come along. It would get me as far as Haines Junction, a hundred miles beyond Whitehorse — well over halfway to Fairbanks. Let's go, I said, and jumped in.

The van's owner (his name was Bob) and I took turns driving all night, pushing over the hills and around the curves of the deserted AlCan, through the semidarkness of midnight and the long hours of dawn. In the 250 miles between Fort St. John and Fort Nelson we encountered only one car and two trucks. Bob was not surprised, initially, by the lack of traffic; this was his first trip. When I described the mob scene I'd seen here the previous July and August, he was inclined to agree that the road was more pleasant in its current condition.

We passed through Fort Nelson before anyone was awake and into the Yukon Territory by midafternoon. We drove at sixty or sixty-five miles an hour when we could, but in places we were forced to slow down to thirty or even slower. Maintenance crews had not had time to fix all the damage to the road from snowmelt and spring rains. I could hardly complain about being slowed down though; I had fully expected to spend this whole day standing just outside Fort St. John.

I'd been very lucky to get this ride . . . but it might have used up my quota of luck. Bob would be turning off at Haines Junction, five hundred miles short of Fairbanks. Thumbers could be stuck at Haines Junction for days, even at the height of the tourist season; there was no telling how long I might be stranded on this nearly deserted road.

We pulled into Whitehorse that evening on the tail end of a heavy shower. The electric lights of the town glared oddly against a sky rolling with dark clouds; Cliff Swallows and Violet-green Swallows flew low over the streets, a sign that more rain was imminent. Bob wanted dinner, so we made a stop (at a Kentucky Fried Chicken stand, seeming out of place here) before starting on the last hundred miles to Haines Junction.

On this stretch I was driving again. Through another rain shower and around a corner we came to a spot where the surface was wet clay, slick as glass; and the van, without any warning or fanfare, skidded neatly sideways into the ditch.

I felt awful, but Bob told me not to worry, we'd just drive it out. That proved somewhat easier said than done. Bob took the wheel and wrestled the van up out of the ditch, only to have it slide right across the road and into the ditch on the other side. While we were absorbed in the challenge a truck came up behind us, a large four-wheel-drive pickup camper driven by a large bearded man. The stranger stopped and asked if we needed help. About this time, Bob finally got the VW back up on the road. We told the man No, thanks for stopping anyway; and he drove on.

I took the wheel of the van once more. ("Go ahead," Bob said, cheerfully; "let's see you do that again.") We had ridden in silence for five or ten minutes when a thought hit me. "Hey! That guy who stopped — I wonder where he's going?"

Bob considered the question. "His truck was fitted out for distance. Chances are, he's turning off at Haines Junction or going on straight into Alaska."

"You don't mind if I speed up and try to catch him, do you?" I stepped on the gas, driving as fast as I dared, clutching the steering wheel grimly across some more slick spots. After about fifteen anxious minutes, the truck came into view ahead.

"Pull up alongside of him," Bob suggested. "I'll ask him." I maneuvered up to a position beside the truck. Side by side, the two vehicles occupied nearly the entire road; I hoped we wouldn't round the next corner and meet a Winnebago. Bob rolled down his window and called across: "Hey, Pardner! You got room for a passenger?"

"Which way you want to go?" the man called back.

"Huh?" said Bob. "Oh, it ain't me . . . it's him," gesturing in my direction. "He's been good company for me so far, but he's going to Fairbanks, and I ain't."

"Sure," the stranger said gruffly, "as long as he don't mind driving straight on through. I got to get to Fairbanks in a hurry."

Of course, nothing could have sounded better. We pulled over and stopped, and I changed vehicles.

When the stranger and I passed through Haines Junction an hour later, dark thunderheads were pounding down torrents of rain. Looking out through rain-streaked windows at the desolate roadside where I could have been stranded, I murmured silent thanks to the capricious spirits of the Bush as we rolled on toward the northwest, toward Alaska.

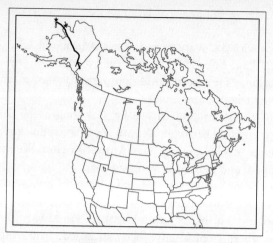

The Edge of the World

WHEN WE crossed the border into Alaska the highway surface turned to pavement again, and we rolled on without incident for the final four hundred miles into Fairbanks.

My first destination in Fairbanks was the post office, where I expected a note from Harold Morrin. Harold had arrived in Alaska three weeks earlier for a Bird Bonanzas tour of the state; always helpful, he had offered to send me notes on what birds they saw, and where. Of course, I already knew where I was going: hitchhiking to Denali, and then flying to Nome and to the Pribilof Islands. Choosing where to go was not difficult. There were only three categories of "specialty" birds in Alaska, and their whereabouts were predictable.

First, there were the birds of the northern forest, like Bohemian Waxwing and White-winged Crossbill. They were possible anywhere in the boreal zones across Canada, but the forested interior of Alaska was a logical place to look for them.

Second, there were the seabirds. These, a variety of auklets, puffins, cormorants, and others, nested on many islands, but the Pribilofs had regular air service — and birding tradition: that was where Peterson and Fisher had gone to wrap up their grand tour of Wild America twenty years earlier.

Third, there were the Asian birds. The mainland of Alaska and the mainland of Siberia were so close that a few species of birds made the jump every spring: a very few, like Bar-tailed Godwit and Yellow Wagtail, would nest on North American soil. Come autumn, these same birds would fly back across the Bering Strait before turning south, to spend the winter in southern Asia. Only about five species fit this category, but that was reason enough for a year-lister to visit Nome, in western Alaska.

And if my imagination went wild, I could dream about other Asian birds. Siberia was so close. Migrant birds did make mistakes at times. Over the decades, a variety of stray birds from the Asian side had turned up here and there in Alaska — on the coast, on the islands, in the interior. The possibilities were amazing, but the odds were slim. A birder could hope for such rarities, but actively seeking them was out of the question.

Or so I thought, until I read Harold Morrin's letter. In the time it took to read that letter, my whole viewpoint changed, and I saw the future of birding trips to Alaska.

The Bird Bonanzas group had been led by the energetic expert Dan Gibson, who was not satisfied with merely checking off the usual birds. From the start, as Harold described it, the tour had been actively seeking strays from the Asian side.

Adak: They had gone to Adak Island, in the Aleutian chain. Halfway to Asia, the only one of the Aleutians that was birded regularly (because a naval station and refuge headquarters were there), Adak had produced several Siberian strays in the past. Harold wrote that the Bird Bonanzas group had been somewhat disappointed: an Old World duck, the Common Pochard, was the only real rarity they had found.

Pribilofs: They had gone to St. Paul in the Pribilof Islands, a place that I intended to go also. They had been pleased with the numbers of nesting birds, but Asian vagrants had not turned up the way Dan Gibson had hoped. Again, a single Common Pochard had been the only rarity discovered.

Nome: The group had advanced to Nome, halfway up the west side of the Alaska mainland. Here the birders' luck had picked up a little. In addition to seeing the uncommon White Wagtail, they had found a Great Knot — among the very few North American records for this Siberian sandpiper.

Gambell:

... where on earth was Gambell?

I stared at the name for a minute, my mind a blank, and then began to recollect. Gambell was a village on some island, St. Lawrence Island, out in the Bering Sea west of Nome. I'd seen ads for "Eskimoland Tours" to Gambell, promoting it as the place to see an untouched native way of life — as if the Eskimos would have been able to maintain native ways with tourists bopping in and out. There had been interesting bird records from St. Lawrence Island, years in the past, but I didn't recall seeing it mentioned in recent *American Birds* reports. Now I read on, to see what Harold had to say about it.

The group had gone to Gambell and had found the best birding of their entire trip. In addition to the expected swarms of alcids and flocks of eiders, at the eleventh hour of their tour, they had found enough rarities to make up for all their other stops! They had seen Red-throated Pipits in numbers, and McKay's Bunting. They had seen Brambling and Rustic Bunting, two Asian songbirds, very rare on U.S. soil. They had seen a Common Rosefinch — only the second one ever for North America. To top it off, they had seen the legendary Ross's Gull — the petite pink gull of the Siberian high Arctic — one of the least-known and most-wanted gulls in the world.

When the results of that Bird Bonanzas tour became widely known, the birding community at large would begin to see Alaska differently. Within just a few years, the burgeoning bird-tour business in the forty-ninth state would be focusing on a search for Asian strays on the outer islands. As for me, Harold Morrin's letter altered my plans for Alaska birding immediately. By that afternoon I was down at the Fairbanks airport, searching for the quickest and cheapest way to get to Gambell.

I took the first available flight to Nome, midmorning Sunday; from Nome I hoped to catch a flight on to Gambell. Going west from Fairbanks, a couple of hours' worth of wilderness passed beneath our wings before we approached the coast. No place in the Lower 48, I reminded myself, could one fly so far in a straight line without crossing a single road. We landed at the village of Kotzebue and then flew southwest across Kotzebue Sound and the rugged interior of the Seward Peninsula. As we approached Norton Sound, an arm of the Bering Sea, the plane began descending toward the Nome airfield.

Even from the air, it was obvious that Nome was a rough-cut gem. It had been the largest city in Alaska, briefly, at the turn of the century, when news of gold had brought in twenty thousand prospectors and profiteers practically overnight. Although that invasion had peaked seventy years earlier, Nome still wore a temporary look, as if the town had been hastily patched onto the land.

Stepping from the plane, I took in the scene: the big pale sky; the muted greens and grays of the tundra to either side of the airfield; starting up to the north, the dark and barren hills, with their patches of remaining snow; and just to the south, beyond a gravel ridge and gravel beach, the Bering Sea, from which a cold fresh wind was blowing. The airfield here had no central terminal at all, just a scatter of sheds and hangars, and between them runways of bulldozed gravel. *This,* I said to myself, *really looks like Alaska!*

There were no scheduled flights to Gambell for two days, but the guy at the Munz Northern hangar told me to check back tomorrow: they frequently made unscheduled flights. Shouldering my pack, I walked down through the dusty streets of Nome and out the east side of town.

The road east from Nome paralleled the beach. As I walked off the road onto the springy, spongy tundra, with the first stirrings of a mosquito swarm around me, two birds I did not know fluttered up from the ground to circle overhead, calling a loud *tseeap!* Silhouetted against the sun they looked small, with rather long tails; their bodies seemed hinged or bent at the midpoint, so that the whole bird undulated oddly in flight. Finally one landed and began walking about, giving me views to confirm what I suspected: the birds were Yellow Wagtails. Common over Europe and Asia, the Yellow Wagtail spilled across the Bering Strait in summer to reach the northwest rim of Alaska.

Singly or in pairs, Whimbrels would fly out to meet me, circling overhead with loud calls before landing again. I paid a lot of attention to these big shorebirds — hoping one would turn out to be the rare, almost mythical, Bristle-thighed Curlew — but all proved to be the familiar Whimbrel. I did find a Bar-tailed Godwit, however. This big cinnamon-colored shorebird was another Eurasian species which, like the Yellow Wagtail, extended its range just far enough to take in the west coast of Alaska.

Jaegers, those predatory seabirds, were here cast in a different role as predators over land. A few Parasitic Jaegers flew by near the beach, but Long-tailed Jaegers were the common ones here. Often I would notice one coursing low over the tundra, perhaps seeking a scurrying lemming; less often I would see two or more flying higher, calling to each other in shrill voices. The Long-tails were buoyant in the air. With each wingstroke, their long central tail feathers would undulate up and down, seeming almost independent of the bird itself.

After a fitful night of camping among the mosquitoes, I went back to the airport in the morning to find a twin-engine, ten-passenger plane being loaded with cargo for an unscheduled flight to Gambell. I paid my ticket and climbed aboard.

This was no tourist flight. The rear of the plane was crammed with freight, and the other four passengers were all natives of the island. The pilot told me that heavy cloud cover was frequent in this region, but today the sky was clear; after a calm forty-five-minute flight across the blue-gray Bering, we began to descend toward St. Lawrence Island.

We landed at Savoonga, a village halfway along the north shore of the island, to drop off one passenger and a few boxes of goods. Then we flew west, following the shoreline. Looking out the window I could see the gray beach broken by a few coastal lagoons, and behind them the flat interior of the island, mostly tawny tundra with the occasional pond or patch of snow and with a tinge of green that suggested summer was just arriving. There was no sign that humans had ever been there. Offshore, under our right wingtip, stretched a wide band of floating ice. I heard the Eskimos in front of me saying that there was far more ice than usual for late June.

A long, low, flat-topped mountain came up ahead of us. The other passengers leaned forward to stare intently out the windows, and I stared too, not knowing what to expect.

As we passed the north end of the mountain, where slopes dropped sharply to the sea, the pilot swung the plane into a wide turn. I had the impression of hordes of birds in the air below us. Beyond the mountain, flat gray land stretched off to a broad point a mile away. On the water's edge was the ramshackle wood and rusted metal of the village, and far beyond that across the water I caught a glimpse of snow-capped mountains on the horizon — it had to be the Siberian mainland! Then the plane leveled out of its wide turn and there was an airstrip ahead between a frozen lake and the ocean, and within moments we were bouncing down the airstrip. As we taxied to a crawl, a cloud of dust kept pace with us just off the runway; at the center of the dust-cloud was a smiling Eskimo in mirrored sunglasses, riding an all-terrain vehicle.

Climbing from the plane, a little unsteadily, I stood looking around.

Nome had looked like Alaska to me. But this place was something different, beyond any preconceptions. The landscape was stark, almost bleak, etched in monochrome: gray and white. Off to the east was the flat-topped mountain we had flown past, the near side still bearing great banks of snow. Nearer at hand, a low area held a huge sheet of ice, with only a little open water; if it melted before the end of summer it would form a sizeable lake. On the opposite side of the runway was the edge of the Bering Sea. This was the same sea that lapped the shore at Nome, but the wind from the ocean here was much colder than at Nome.

From the direction of the village, a brigade of Eskimos was bearing down on us. Leading the charge, engines blaring, were several all-terrain vehicles. With hardly a glance for the onslaught of ATVs, the pilot turned his attention to the cargo in the plane.

The first wave of Eskimos reached us, and, given that planes arrived here every day or so, their greeting seemed a bit over-enthusiastic. A few were expecting cargo or visitors, but many seemed to have come just for the excitement.

I was the only nonnative in the crowd, but it seemed I was not novel enough to attract any attention. Not at first. But as I was walking north from the airstrip in the direction of the village, one of the Eskimo men stopped to talk to me. He clearly was someone important; he had the biggest and loudest ATV, and much of the cargo had been for him. Now he was greeting me effusively. It took me a minute to figure out that he was speaking English, and that he was offering me a place to stay.

"Thanks," I said, "but I had figured on just camping out."

No, he insisted, not good; very cold at night; much better at his house, and with low daily rates. I thanked him again and said I couldn't afford to pay for a room. At this, his smile went out like an electric light. He revved up his ATV and chugged away.

A minute later at the edge of the village I was surprised to be greeted by a young white woman, who was walking the same direction I was going. "You look a little disoriented," she said, probably an understatement. "Can I help you find something?"

Grateful, I fell in step beside her. She told me she was here with her husband, an anthropology student from the University of

Alaska, who was studying the Eskimos' walrus-skin boats, or umiaks. There was also a team of Swiss archaeologists camped on the flats, digging for clues to Gambell's past, as well as a preacher of some sort, and a couple of guys from Anchorage at the National Guard armory. The rest of the village was pure Eskimo — "At least the people are," she said. "The culture isn't. Not any more. But you'll see that for yourself."

She was right. Everything about Gambell suggested transition, a culture caught up in change. The few dozen dwellings in the village were mostly wooden frame houses, some brightly painted in blue or green or white, incongruous in this wild setting. Other houses were smaller, made of weathered wood or rusted tin, but there was nothing constructed of local material. The houses were arranged in even rows, but between them was nothing resembling streets or yards, just stacks of debris and a flat plain of gravel. Wires strung among the houses, and the hum of a generator, told

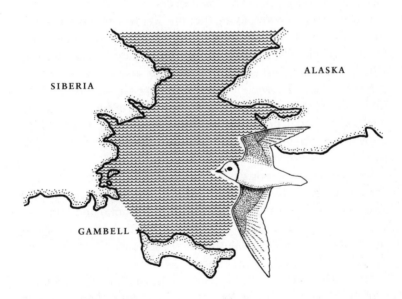

Ross's Gull over the Bering Sea

me that the people here had electricity — and of course they had gasoline for their ATVs. They also had teams of sled dogs, apparently idled for the summer; some of the Huskies barked at us from the ends of their chains as we walked past.

My temporary guide pointed out a corrugated metal building as the local store. Peering in the door, I saw loaves of bread, cans of beans, packages of Oreo cookies. But several of the nearby houses had large racks out in back, on which strips of seal meat were drying. Clearly the people did not depend solely on the store for their sustenance.

"That's right," the woman said. "The people of Gambell can get all the food they need from the sea and the island, if they have to." She pointed toward the north, where their boats were lined up inverted on the shore. Some of these were wooden boats, but most were the traditional umiaks: deep open boats, twenty feet long, made of walrus hide stretched over driftwood frames, appropriate craft for bold seagoing hunters.

Harold Morrin had told me that the best way to see eiders and some other birds was on a boat trip along the north shore east from Gambell. The man to contact, according to Harold, was Vernon Slwooko. I asked the woman if she knew him.

She laughed. "I saw you talking to him just a minute ago," she said. "I'm sure he'd take you out, if you can afford it. But you might get a better price out of Winnie James . . . and I think he knows more about birds, too." Since she was going to that end of the village, she took me over and introduced me.

Winfred James Senior, despite his Anglicized name, looked 100 percent native. His English, however, was much better than Slwooko's. I sensed some rivalry between Slwooko and James — a rivalry in which Slwooko would have the edge, because he was the local agent for Wien Consolidated and other air carriers, and thus always got to the tourists first.

James had had his triumphs, though. In 1968, when the American Ornithologists' Union had met in Fairbanks, there had been an organized field trip to Gambell; Winnie James had taken several ornithologists out birding in his boat. As evidence of the occasion, he pulled out a copy of the *Field Guide to Western Birds* — autographed by Roger Tory Peterson!

That evening I went out along the shore with Winnie James in his boat — not in the big umiak, but in a smaller wooden job ("Use less gas that way," James explained, logically). We headed east from Gambell, so that the sun, riding low on the northwestern horizon, illuminated everything before us in a brilliant white light.

Out on the water, we were surrounded by thousands of birds. The low boat plowed through rafts of resting Common Eiders, bringing us within yards of the big sea ducks before they could take to the air. King Eiders were there in lesser numbers, and we passed several flocks of the smartly patterned Steller's Eiders. Most exciting of all were four Spectacled Eiders. Rare specialties of the Bering Sea region, these big goggle-eyed ducks had an unearthly, strangely beautiful appearance.

Great flights of alcids coming our way would split, veer off, and pass us on both sides. The air was filled with auklets, puffins, and murres. Most of them, thousands, were flying from east to west, so that we seemed to be traveling upstream in a river of birds. Later I was to learn that this mass alcid exodus occurred every evening; James had timed this boat trip to coincide with the main flight. Nine species of alcids passed within yards of our bow, and six of these were birds I had never seen before.

Late in the evening we pulled into a salt lagoon along the shoreline, many miles east of Gambell. A big Yellow-billed Loon swam away before us, but James was looking for something else: down toward the end of the lagoon, a group of five silhouettes on the water. With the outboard cut to a low speed we were able to approach these quite closely. They were Emperor Geese, another specialty of the Bering Sea region, small and elegant geese that I had barely dared to hope for.

The wealth of birds that evening was so dazzling that I forgot all about list-chasing for the moment. During that evening boat

ride, my year list passed the landmark figure of six hundred —
but I was so captivated by the birds themselves that I did not
realize that, or even think about year listing, until sometime the
following day.

One of the things that struck me about Gambell was the scarcity
of songbirds. In this harsh environment, it seemed, only a few
songbirds were tough enough to survive.

A few White Wagtails lived in the vicinity of the village. Like
the Yellow Wagtails I had seen at Nome, these were birds that just
spilled across from Asia. Flighty and hard to approach, the White
Wagtails would flush ahead of me, to undulate away into the
distance. I guessed that they must be nesting in piles of debris
around the village.

To see other songbirds, I had to make the long trudge across
the gravel plain to the base of Sevuokuk Mountain, a mile east of
the village. Where the slope began, the gravel gave way to tawny
grass and mats of tundra moss. Here Lapland Longspurs were
conspicuous with their short warbling songs, delivered from a
boulder-top or while in flight; conspicuous, too, for their bright
summer plumage of black and white and chestnut.

Snow Buntings were also common on the mountain — the females white and brown, the males white and black. And high on
the slope among great banks of snow I encountered an ultimate
snowbird, the McKay's Bunting. Its plumage was almost solid
white, except for black tips on some of the wing and tail feathers.
When it flew, the black wingtips were all that showed of the white
bird against white snowfields. It seemed to bound and flutter like
a white butterfly dancing across the slopes.

The second time I searched the mountainside, I found a bird
that was not even pictured in my bird guide: Red-throated Pipit.
Streaky and brown, walking among the boulders, the pipit was
inconspicuous until it turned and showed the salmon pink of its
throat. In the dozen years since the 1961 edition of Peterson's

western guide, this Asian pipit had been showing up more frequently, but it still had the aura of a new discovery.

But Gambell was exciting enough without a few lost stragglers. And there were plenty of birds on the mountain. Dunlins, little sandpipers with red backs and black bellies, were everywhere on the slopes. There were also a few Rock Sandpipers, looking like big faded Dunlins, as well as Western Sandpipers, Ruddy Turnstones, and Common Snipes. The tundra was the nesting ground for these birds, and many of the males were performing songflights above the mountainside. The songs of the sandpipers made up for the scarcity of genuine songbirds.

I went exploring near the north end of the mountain, where the boulders gathered into rockpiles and rockslides. Clambering uphill, looking toward the sunlight, I was confronted by mystery creatures — little things that sat up in silhouette, barking in small voices: *Ow! Ow!* Maneuvering to get better light, I saw that these were Crested Auklets. Evidently they were nesting among the rocks. These slaty-gray alcids looked comical at close range, with their waxy red bills frozen into permanent "smiles" and their loose crests flopping down in front of their faces.

Also nesting in the rockpiles were Least Auklets. Their whirring and chirring callnotes reminded me of the flock notes of young starlings. In flight, they also looked somewhat like starlings, compact and chunky and short-tailed. Perched, they looked like nothing at all familiar: the tiniest of the alcid clan, they looked like pale-eyed, stubby-billed gnomes.

Various other alcids were nesting on the mountain, more and more toward the north, where the slopes became steeper until they turned into the cliffs at the north end. Seen on the ground, any of the alcids looked somewhat comical. There came a time each evening, however, when the alcids became instead a spectacular sight, as they poured down from the mountain to take part in the great evening flight.

Some birds could be seen flying along the shoreline near Gambell at any time of day. The evening flight, however, was remarkable. At this northern latitude the sun did not set until after midnight, and ·throughout the long evening hours the birds would stream past the Gambell shoreline, the northwesternmost point of St. Lawrence Island. At their peak, I estimated that they were passing at a rate of thousands *per minute* — thousands of birds of more than a dozen species.

Flocks of eiders took part in this mass movement, and there were always a few small parties of Harlequin Ducks and larger flocks of those long-tailed sea ducks, the Oldsquaws. Loons would pass as well: lots of Pacific Loons, smaller numbers of two or three other species. There were gulls in the flight, and Pelagic Cormorants. But without question the alcids dominated, by their diversity and their sheer numbers.

Each of the alcid species tended to flock only with its own kind, giving a sort of orderly look to the flight. Orderly, but overpowering in its abundance. The alcids that flew past Gambell each evening seemed vastly too numerous to have come from just the cliffs at the north end of Sevuokuk Mountain. I guessed that there must be other bird cliffs along the north shore of the island.

Most numerous at most hours were the Crested Auklets. Occasionally I would see some diving and surfacing in the gentle swells just offshore. But usually they were flying, a score or more at a time in flock after densely packed flock. Late in the evening, after about ten o'clock, I estimated that several thousand Crested Auklets were passing every minute. Parakeet Auklets, dark above and white below, were far less numerous. Mostly they appeared in pairs, and a minute or two might pass before the next pair came by.

Tight-packed bunches of Least Auklets would buzz past, tiny dusky brown birds barely clearing the surface of the water. Sometimes they were close enough that I could hear their little chirring callnotes. Usually they were in packs of no more than about twenty birds, but sometimes there were dozens of such flocks passing at the same time.

Pairs and small parties of puffins came past the point regularly: chunky birds, like footballs with colorful bills. The two species of puffins here would mix, but only with each other. Most numerous was the Horned Puffin, a white-faced, white-bellied bird similar to the Atlantic Puffins I had seen in New England. Often Tufted Puffins would be conspicuous as the one or two black-bodied birds in a flock of eight or ten Horned Puffins.

At some hours, murres outnumbered even the Crested Auklets. Both kinds of murres were here, Thick-billed and Common, and they seemed to travel in freely mixed flocks. The largest alcids of the Bering Sea, as big as ducks, they would come flapping sturdily past the point in flocks of up to a hundred at a time. While the auklets and puffins had conspicuous face patterns, the murres did not: their dark eyes in dark faces gave them an impersonal look. Anonymous and businesslike, the murres would sweep past on their way out to their fishing grounds.

When the wind was from the west, the alcids would all fly low,

The evening flight, Gambell, Alaska

beating into the headwind. But I was on the beach one evening when the wind was from the east; with the wind behind them, birds were flying at all levels, from just above the water to more than fifty feet up. Some were in over the shoreline, so that I had to rock back and look up to see them. On this evening there were thin layers of cloud overhead but the western horizon was clear, pale pink sky showing beneath the cloud strata, and sunlight gleaming on the distant Siberian mountains. In this setting the abundant alcids made an unforgettable sight: with tightly bunched flocks, long single files, disciplined chevrons, wavering streams, isolated pairs, the swift fliers passing the slow and being passed by the even swifter, weaving a dizzying web of patterns against the calm sea and the sky.

The spectacle put me in mind of imagined scenes from the past, from lost America. I thought of clouds of Passenger Pigeons darkening the sky, armies of bison stampeding down the plains and shaking the earth. But the vision before me was no dream from the past: this was real, this was today.

As I got to know the Gambell Eskimos a little, I developed a tremendous respect for them. Proud, self-sufficient, they were balancing modern conveniences against ancient customs.

There was nothing primitive about these people. Most had been to school on the mainland, and several had traveled in the Lower 48. They had their ATVs and they knew how to maintain and repair them; they had a jukebox in the cafe that played almost-current hits; they had at least one plane a day coming in when the weather allowed. But always there was the sense that their center of reality was this village, the site where their families had lived for centuries. The rest of the United States (and Russia too) could disappear, and when the fuel ran out, the Gambell Eskimos would park their ATVs forever in the ancient bone middens and go on surviving as they always had: fishing in the Bering Sea, hunting seal and walrus on the ice floes, stalking geese and eiders on the lakes, harvesting the eggs of murres from the cliffs.

On my evening boat ride with Winnie James, I had been impressed at how well he knew the local birds. But everyone here seemed aware of all aspects of nature.

The Bird Bonanzas group had been surprised to see Ross's Gulls at Gambell. As I learned from discussions here, the locals were surprised, too. Several people commented on the "red gulls." They had seen them before, but not like this year, not in such numbers. The older hunters thought that the persistence of so much ice offshore so late in the season accounted for the presence of these birds.

Ross's Gull was like a fantasy for most birders then, rare and beautiful, a distinctive bird with a narrow black neck ring and with a pink tinge to the plumage. It was in the North American bird guides only because it showed up regularly in late fall at Point Barrow, in high arctic Alaska. But since I had read Harold Morrin's letter, I had begun to hope that I might have a chance of seeing Ross's Gull myself.

On my third day at Gambell, watching along the shoreline, I was seeing scores of Black-legged Kittiwakes. These small gulls were abundant here, and their flocks included a few one-year-old birds, marked by dark diagonal stripes on the wings. During a lull, a lone bird came winging along, and I glanced at it: another young Kittiwake. But something made me look again. It had the dark wing stripe, but its shape was odd, with narrow wings and a very short bill. As it passed me I saw that it had a partial ring around its neck. Could this be some plumage of a young Ross's Gull? Desperately I followed it with my binoculars, but it flew on down the beach and out of sight.

For a couple of hours I agonized over the sighting. I had written down every detail I'd noticed, but I was filled with uncertainty. Fortunately, the bird came back, accompanied by another bird of identical size and shape: a perfect adult Ross's Gull! Graceful and buoyant in flight, colored in indescribable shades of the softest pink and pearly gray, it was one of the most beautiful birds imaginable.

This, I told myself, had to be the single most impressive bird at Gambell. But I was to see another that would rival it for magical impact.

On the fourth day of my visit, as I trudged along the north side of the lake, an ATV came roaring up behind me and stopped. Turning around, I saw that the driver was an older Eskimo, beaming a gap-toothed smile. "You the birdwatcher!" he said.

I nodded.

"You seen the Rosy gulls? The red ones?"

I told him I had seen a couple. He nodded sagely. "Plenty this year," he observed. "Lot of ice. Lot of red gulls. Never see them like this." He paused for a minute and looked out across the gravel. "You seen the white gulls?"

"Which white gulls?" I asked. Could he possibly be talking about Ivory Gulls? "All of these gulls are white."

He waved his hand as if to dismiss the Glaucous Gulls, kitti-wakes, and other commonplace types. "The real white ones. Ice birds. They come around here in winter. You seen those?"

I admitted that I had not, and he chuckled with glee. "My boy saw one yesterday! Just down the beach there. It was eating on a dead seal. Could've shot him easy, but he didn't."

"How far down the beach? Could I walk there?"

The old Eskimo started up his three-wheeler again and laughed. "Walk there easy! Maybe a mile, maybe two." He stopped, as if trying to remember something to add. "If you see him, you see him good! Can walk right up to him. That bird not afraid of anything." And lurching into gear, he sped away.

So there might be an Ivory Gull around! I had hardly dared to hope such a thing. But I had read that these phantoms of the shifting ice were curiously unafraid of men. And I had read that their food habits belied the purity of their white plumage: oppor-tunists, they would feed on scraps left by the polar bears, or rotten carrion washed up on shore. If the remains of the dead seal were still on the beach, the Ivory Gull might still be coming to feed on it.

I never found the seal carcass. Perhaps it had washed away. But having started down the shoreline I continued walking, trudging slowly through the gravel, listening to the silence.

A low bank of clouds from offshore had moved in, and now fog closed around me. It seemed I was on an island — not St. Lawrence Island but a much smaller one, measured in yards, measured in the distance I could see. There was the crunching of gravel underfoot, and wavelets lapping nearby, and beyond that the world ended in gray. Every so often a kittiwake would come by, but when it dissolved in the fog I would be alone again.

The sun, low in the northwestern sky, must have caught the edge of the cloud bank, because the mist around me was gradually pervaded with a yellow glow that grew brighter as I walked. Where minutes before everything had been a study in blue-gray, now it seemed I was walking in a golden cloud. In this eerie setting, it seemed, anything could happen. And it did.

Out of the golden mist behind me came a bird the color of deep snow, the color of distant icebergs, a bird of shocking white. It was right beside me before I realized it, and then I was beside myself — staring open-mouthed, forgetting even to reach for the binoculars. The bird was looking at me, and in its big dark eyes I saw no sign of fear. But no sign of interest, either; it continued down the shoreline. Just at the point where it would have melted into the cloud, it circled once, as if to return, and I heard myself saying aloud "Come back, come back," but the bird resumed its course and vanished forever.

Late the next afternoon, after another search for birds on the slopes of Sevuokuk Mountain, I found a comfortable spot to sit and write. After working on my bird notes for a while, I wrote a brief letter, wanting to try to communicate with someone about the magic of this place. I licked the flap to seal the envelope, and then I addressed it to Elaine, the girl I had met at the convention in North Dakota — only two weeks earlier, but a world and a lifetime away from this place. Then I paused over the space for the return address on the envelope.

Return address? I had none. As far as postal service was concerned, I might as well have been in outer space. But this place demanded something. Instead of a return address, I wrote

> Birds of white and sky of gold
> All that shivers is not cold

Then I stuffed the envelope into my backpack, to mail when I reached the mainland again, and leaned back to survey my surroundings.

I was sitting among boulders high on the side of Sevuokuk Mountain. Even though big patches of snow still lay on all sides, this place was clearly into the full swing of the short northern summer. I could tell by the songs of the Snow Buntings, by the swarms of auklets coming and going from the highest rockpiles. As the ground mist cleared away, I could see the brave little village of Gambell facing the sea. Away on the northwestern horizon, the low sun gleamed on the snow-covered ranges of the Siberian mainland.

Tomorrow, if the plane came through, I would be flying back to Nome — the first stage in my return to familiar surroundings. Tonight, I sat on this mountain at the edge of the world and looked toward the shining peaks of Siberia.

Full Summer

"No, just like I told you, there's nothing here." The postal clerk, irritated at my suggestion that he should look a second time, was emphatic that there was nothing for Kaufman in the general delivery box at the Anchorage post office. *Well, I shouldn't be surprised,* I told myself. *She was obviously just kidding when I dared her to write to me here and she said that she would.*

It was no reason to feel let down. Still, in the weeks after my visit to St. Lawrence Island, it was hard to avoid developing a feeling of letdown. When you have gone out to the outer edge of the world, whatever follows is likely to feel like an anticlimax.

There was no letdown while I was still in Alaska. Returning to Denali National Park, which I had visited the summer before, I marveled once again at the wildlife in the land dominated by the great mountain: caribou and grizzly bears, marmots and wolves, eagles and owls. Hitching down to Homer, on Alaska's southern coast, I enjoyed the mysterious little Kittlitz's Murrelets and the smart-looking Red-faced Cormorants. Everywhere I went in Alaska there were towering peaks, pristine lakes, wonderful birds.

But then it was time to go south — down the hard road of the Alaska Highway, on such a slow trip as to compensate for the fast rides I'd had going the other direction. Down out of Canada, through the Mountain West, shuttling back and forth between stops in Montana, Wyoming, and Colorado, rattling south like a pinball through the maze of roads near the Rockies. Spending an entire day, now, to find just one new bird: just this Black Swift, just this Brown-capped Rosy-Finch, then a long hitchhike to the next new one.

As I left the mountains and headed for the Atlantic Coast, I was also heading into the downhill half of the year. I had broken the year-list record in late July, and now I was up to 630. Hardly forty species remained that I could reasonably hope to find before the year ended. But the five months ahead might not be enough time to find them all; those forty species were scattered all over the continent, mostly uncommon birds in out-of-the-way places. Each new bird would take hours or days of thumbing. The prospect was not inviting.

As long as I'd stayed in the North, I'd had so much high adventure, seen so many unbelievable sights, encountered so many new places and people and birds, that I had not given a damn what anyone *else* was doing that summer. But now that I was back in the mundane States there was a snide little demon looking over my shoulder, looking at my year-list tally and saying: Okay, you saw some neat birds in Alaska — but did you see *enough* of them? How well did your competition do there?

And I didn't want to think about how the competition had fared in Alaska. I had a feeling that he must have done quite well indeed.

Talking to birders as I traveled, I was gradually picking up rumors from Alaska. It seemed that everyone who had journeyed there in early to mid-June of 1973 had seen rare birds galore. They had seen every interesting bird that I had, and more: things like Mongolian Plover, Eurasian Dotterel, Great Knot, Bristle-thighed Curlew, and a host of others. No one specifically told me that Floyd Murdoch had seen all these things. But he had been there at the right time, earlier in the season than me. If he had seen all of those rare birds, there was no way I could catch up to him.

Which gave me a new sense of kinship with Tom Thomson: maybe we both would turn out to be also-rans. I thought of calling Thomson on my way east, but since I passed through his home territory of Ohio in the middle of the night I figured he would not appreciate that.

I was to meet the Lancaster County Bird Club for a field trip to New Jersey the weekend of August 11 and 12. Arriving on the Atlantic seaboard with time to spare, I spent a day birding the Delaware coast on my own — walking, in sweltering heat, all the way around the impoundment at the Little Creek Wildlife Area — and then hitched on up to Pennsylvania.

Arriving at Lancaster on Friday, I had to go around to pay my respects to the ancient Christmas Tree, desiccated but still decorated, reigning over Charlie Mellinger's living room. Friday night I rode down to New Jersey with Charlie, Harold Morrin, Andy Mack, and Ted Parker. We reached the salt marshes of Tuckerton about ten at night and decided to camp right there on the beach. Most of the field trip participants would be joining us in the morning, but Harold mentioned that the Cooks, from Baltimore, were coming down tonight as well. (The guys had been razzing me about Elaine Cook, but I didn't know why. *I* hadn't said anything about her. The only way these characters could have picked up rumors, I guessed, was from Eric Witmer, who had been around at the ABA Convention when I had been getting acquainted with Elaine. I made a mental note to punch Eric when he came down with his folks in the morning.)

We all lay around in Harold's camper, talking birds. Eventually Andy suggested that we ought to close the door of the van: he had noticed a few mosquitoes. With the cool sea breeze cut off it was a little muggy inside the camper, but not uncomfortable enough to interrupt our conversations.

Around midnight, a set of headlights came bobbing down the uneven road to the beach. The headlights were attached to Doug Cook's big red-and-white camper. (This was about the time that Andy was digging out the insect repellent — he'd noticed a few more mosquitoes.) The Cooks must have assumed we were already asleep; they parked quietly a few yards away.

Around one in the morning, we were drifting off to sleep when we were jolted by a loud voice from the other camper: muffled, but with an unmistakable Scottish accent. "That's Doug Cook," said Harold, sitting up. "I wonder what's wrong?"

"I'll give you three guesses!" said Andy. He leaped up, brandishing a flashlight, and aimed it at the screen window. "Look at this!"

The window was *swarming* with mosquitoes. Many more were drifting about inside the camper; and I suddenly realized that the bites I was scratching were not all left over from Delaware. When we had arrived at Tuckerton earlier in the evening, the strong sea breeze evidently had been keeping the insects down — but now the breeze had died, and the mosquitoes were attacking en masse. "What's wrong with us?" said Andy. "We ought to know better than to camp out in the salt marsh in summer!"

After a brief council-of-war with Doug Cook, it was decided that we would relocate away from the shore. Tough Charlie Mellinger had already sacked out on the beach in his sleeping bag, and he laughed at us for giving up so easily. But the rest of us rolled back up the road into the town of Tuckerton.

Harold and Doug parked the campers on the first available street corner in town. While everyone else went back to sleep, Ted Parker and I walked up the street a few blocks to an all-night diner, where we drank coffee and talked about tropical birds until five in the morning.

So I was not in great condition for meeting a mob of birders — the trip of the Lancaster club, as usual, was going to be drawing quite a crowd. As it turned out, the *first* birder I ran into on our way back to the campers was Elaine Cook. She had awakened early and slipped out of her parents' camper to come join Ted and me.

The night sky faded to dawn over Tuckerton. Sporadic late-summer chants of Whip-poor-wills gave way to tentative late-summer songs of Wood Thrushes. Harold and Andy and the Cooks woke up and hailed us as Ted and Elaine and I wandered by the campers. Other birders began arriving. We went out to the beach to pick up Charlie and look for shorebirds, and then we started down the coast toward the legendary Brigantine wildlife refuge.

Brigantine was famous. In the summer of 1971, Ted Parker's Big Year, all four of the world's species of godwits had been there at once: not only the two American species, uncommon enough in New Jersey, but also single Black-tailed and Bar-tailed godwits from Europe. The following winter there had been two Gyrfalcons on the refuge at the same time. Brigantine was also noted as a good place to find Ruff and Curlew Sandpiper, and sometimes other rarities. I was curious to see a place with such a strong birding tradition.

On an August Saturday at the height of the shorebird migration, birders, serious and casual, had flocked to Brigantine. There was a steady stream of cars on the dike roads through the refuge.

Eric Witmer and his father Jan were the official leaders of the Lancaster field trip; but Harold Morrin, as club president, was trying to make sure that everyone had a good time and got to see every bird. He also wanted to make sure that everyone knew about Ted's record Big Year in 1971, and about my similar attempt for 1973. Every time the group's telescopes zeroed in on a particular bird, Harold would call Ted and me over to "confirm" the identification.

We all hoped for rarities. Ted, being pragmatic, was looking for Curlew Sandpiper, a reasonably good possibility at this season. I was holding out for a Spotted Redshank — it was far less likely, but I knew I could identify one if I saw it. However, we saw no such strays. There was minor excitement over a Parasitic Jaeger and a Red-necked Phalarope, which we would have expected offshore instead, but the group was going to be taking a boat out to sea the next day anyway. So a little past noon, we abandoned the marshes of Brigantine and moved south along the coast.

We stopped for a while at Somers Point, where thousands of Red Knots crowded the beach. At Stone Harbor, we visited a heron nesting colony in a grove of trees right in the middle of town. Finally, in the evening, we arrived at Cape May, the southernmost tip of New Jersey.

I had been feeling sluggish all afternoon, and I should have hit the sack early. Instead, I stayed up until midnight, talking with Elaine.

She surprised me with one piece of news: she *had* written to me in care of General Delivery in Alaska. As proof, Elaine showed me the envelope, stamped "Return to sender" by the Anchorage post office. But when I asked to read the letter, she refused. "I wrote things for you to think about from a distance," she said. "If you read it now, it would be like me telling you in person. You don't expect that to happen, do you?"

I didn't want to press it, so we talked of other things. When I finally left, it took me a long time to hitch back to the campground where Harold's van was parked. Once again I caught only a couple of hours of sleep.

Up before the sun the next morning, I felt pretty rocky. As Harold's van rolled down the deserted road toward Cape May Point, I said, "I may not be much good at identifying seabirds today."

Harold smiled sympathetically. "Don't worry. We probably won't see many species anyway."

Parker spoke up immediately: "That's right. You never see good birds on an East Coast pelagic trip. We'll be lucky if we even see any gulls." Charlie took it up: "Don't get your hopes up. If we're lucky, maybe we'll see a few sparrows hopping around on the dock after we get back." Andy chimed in: "Just my luck. I never see any good birds." They were razzing Harold. A year earlier, Andy Mack had taken his first pelagic trip, and all the way to the boat Harold had been warning him not to expect much. The advice had been based on experience; but as it turned out, *that* was the trip on which they saw a White-faced Storm-Petrel, only the third or fourth record for U.S. waters.

Harold laughed, now, with the rest of us, but he added, "Seriously, Kenn, this is nothing like boat trips off California. On this part of the East Coast, you can be offshore for hours without seeing a single bird. We might get lucky, of course, but I really wouldn't expect too much."

On this day, Harold's conservative prediction proved correct. We saw few birds — few seabirds, anyway. The day before, we had seen a jaeger and a phalarope onshore at Brigantine; today, we saw several migrating landbirds out at sea. There were swallows, and Chimney Swifts, and a Red-winged Blackbird. A Yellow Warbler landed atop the pilothouse, and one Common Yellowthroat flew around the boat for ten minutes before flying away to the south. We also had a remarkable list of seagoing insects, including cabbage butterflies, monarchs, moths, dragonflies, and a lone cucumber beetle.

But these misplaced landlubbers were minor interruptions in a day of general boredom. For hours, our eyes scanned the empty waters in vain. Sunlight danced on the surface, and a few Wilson's Storm-Petrels danced and fluttered against the glare, but they were the only seabirds that we encountered.

Everyone had a different take on the day. Harold was apologetic, as if the lackluster showing were his fault. Ted talked strategy: "You've got to go out a lot of times to make sure you'll be along on that one good trip." Charlie Mellinger was having a great time; he wasn't about to let a few birds — or the lack of them — spoil his day.

I was stoical about it, but Elaine was concerned that this unproductive day might hurt my list for the year. I told her not to worry; I expected to have the regular eastern seabirds wrapped up in three days anyway. I had a reservation for the approaching Wednesday to make a round-trip crossing on the *Bluenose* ferry, across the Bay of Fundy between Bar Harbor, Maine, and Yarmouth, Nova Scotia. Everyone had told me that the *Bluenose* offered the best pelagic birding in the East.

By the following Saturday, six days from now, I planned to be back down in Lancaster. Ted Parker was going to be delivering a friend's car to Tucson, and I'd arranged to ride out with him, saving myself a couple of thousand miles of thumbing. It looked like I had just enough time to hitch up to Maine, make the round trip on the *Bluenose,* and get back to Pennsylvania by Saturday.

Elaine seemed disappointed that I wouldn't have time to come visit her in Baltimore. She and I had talked a lot, but with so many other people around, it was hard to communicate, hard to sort out confused thoughts and reactions. Now we were going separate ways. It seemed unlikely we would ever really get acquainted.

I got a ride with one of the birders from the trip, a man who had to be in northern New England the next day for a scientific conference. He was going to be driving overnight, and he may have hoped I'd be able to help out. But after two nearly sleepless nights, there was no way I could fill that role. I dozed off in the middle of New Jersey; the next thing I knew, it was daylight (still? No: again) and the man was saying, Come on, wake up — we're in Vermont. He had to drive on north from where we were; I got out, took a right turn, and hitched toward Maine.

Central Vermont and New Hampshire were quiet and green, peaceful in that lull between the birdsong of early summer and the leaf-color of autumn. The coast was not so quiet; roads there were packed with tourists, but somehow I didn't mind. I spent Monday afternoon and evening at Popham Beach, Maine, watching a colony of Roseate Terns, and hitched on north the next day to arrive at Bar Harbor on Tuesday afternoon.

I slept in the woods not far from the *Bluenose* terminal and awoke with a start at first light, apprehensive about missing the 7:30 ferry. Shouldering my backpack, I trudged down to the terminal.

As I walked in the front door, with the glare of early morning sun still in my eyes, I had the illusion that I saw someone I recognized. She was sitting in a chair near the door, reading a magazine, and she looked for all the world like —

But it couldn't really be her, of course. She would have had to talk her protective father into giving her permission. She would have had to drive all night from Baltimore, taking the freeways and turnpikes north through New Jersey and New York and New England. That was the only way she could be here now, putting down her magazine and rising and coming toward me with a smile on her face.

If I could have looked down the years then and seen everything from beginning to end — the good times, the best times, the bad times, the bad decisions, the indecision, and then finally the divorce — I still would not have traded anything for that moment.

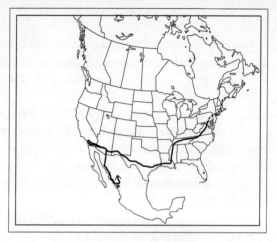

Birdman's Holiday

THOSE FEW days were the kind that should last forever, but
they passed all too quickly. I had to leave, to go back west, catching a ride to Tucson with Ted Parker. So Elaine dropped me off at
the Parker house in Lancaster and drove back to Baltimore; Ted
and I jumped in the car and headed for Arizona.

In a way, it was ironic to travel across North America with
Parker. This continent was not his place anymore. He showed
some interest when I talked about Alaska, but his intensity multiplied when the topic shifted to the tropics. Ted had worked up
a thorough grasp of Mexican birdlife quickly, and by now he
seemed to have memorized the names of all three thousand South
American birds, even though he had never been there. He could
talk with passion about what was known of tropical birds, and
about the much larger amount that was not yet known. In North
America, he implied, not enough challenges remained.

The Tucson Five did not reconvene that fall. We knew Dave was not coming back — he was transferring to Evergreen State College in Washington. Joel Greenberg we expected imminently, but he never showed up. Later we learned that he had transferred at the last moment. He would start at the end of September up at Humboldt State, where, back in May, he had been so impressed by the birding youth culture of northern California.

But Mark Robbins was back for another year. And about the time that Ted and I arrived from the East, Paul Lehman came in from the opposite direction. I'd last seen Paul in June in North Dakota; he had spent the summer birding all over the West. Mark and Paul and I compared notes. In southern California, within easy range for the upcoming weekend, were several birds that I still needed for my year list and that would be new life-listers for the other two guys; so as soon as Mark was registered for classes, we were off. We took his trusty station wagon and headed west for a quick blitz. Elegant Terns on the coast, Mountain Quail and the famous California Condor at Mount Pinos, and various other birds appeared right on cue. Successful in our searches, we rode back in triumph to Tucson.

Then I had to decide what to do next.

My year list was over 640, but it was still missing a few species at every point of the compass: on the West Coast, on the plains, in Florida. Even here in the Southwest, my list was still short a few birds. It was hard to decide which way to go first.

"Take a break," Ted Parker advised. "You need to get out of this AOU listing area, take a vacation. Come to Mexico with us."

Parker had a particular Mexican bird on his mind: Eared Trogon. Most birders then had never even heard of it. If you said "trogon" to us we would think only of the Elegant Trogon, a creature of metallic red-and-green plumage and croaking voice, an uncommon denizen of Arizona canyons. It was the only trogon we could ever imagine seeing in the United States. Most of us were only vaguely aware that there were other kinds in the tropics.

"Look, it's unique among trogons." Ted was expounding on the bird one night in Sambo's restaurant, gesturing across a table-ful of coffee cups, raising his voice, heedless of the strange looks we were getting from surrounding tables. "There are a lot of trogons in the Neotropics — more than a dozen in the genus *Trogon*, and four or five quetzals. But there's only one *Euptilotis*. And nobody knows anything about it! It's right here in the Sierra Madre . . . all the Eared Trogons in the world are between here and Mexico City. But hardly anything has been written about it. I'm not sure its nest has even been described."

If we couldn't learn about the bird by reading, Ted said, we should go and learn about it through personal observation. What was more, we had directions. Friends of Rose Ann Rowlett's had seen Eared Trogons in Durango; Ted had gotten exact directions to the site. So we were going to Mexico.

Although the birds south of the border would not count for my Big Year, the trip was too tempting to resist. In November of the preceding year I had gone into western Mexico with the Tucson Five, and it had been an eye-opening trip — so much to see, so much to know. Going on this trogon expedition with Parker would do nothing for my listing game of the moment, but it fit right in with my long-term goal of learning about birds.

The prospect of the trip convinced Paul Lehman to postpone his return to New York, to hang around until the coming Labor Day weekend and go with us. A local birder, Steve Hanselmann, was intrigued by the idea as well, and he had a car (Mark temporarily lacked the necessary papers to take his station wagon into Mexico). The trip was on.

We left at midnight Friday, crossing the border at two in the morning, and drove on through the black night of Sonora, slowing only for the scattered small villages. At dawn the sky paled behind arid hills, while Lesser Nighthawks coursed over the desert floor.

This was Paul Lehman's first visit to Mexico, and as the sky grew lighter he was getting keyed up. At this point, only 250 miles below the border, we had not reached the zone where he could expect life birds. All the species here also occurred in the United States. White-winged Doves crossed the sky, Crested Caracaras patrolled the roadside, and from the moving car we could hear Botteri's Sparrows occasionally. In Arizona, we would have regarded all of these as part of the Mexican element — but here these were old familiar birds, American birds to us.

At Guaymas the highway met the coast. The desert stretched to the edge of the Gulf of California, with frigatebirds hanging in the air above hillside regiments of tall cactus. Among the water-birds on the bay there were few that we could not have seen in San Diego, and shorebirds in the roadside pools (this was the rainy season) did not include any tropical species either. "Give it another hundred miles," said Ted. "Then we'll start to see real Mexican birds."

Of course Parker was right. We had been on the road another hour and a half when suddenly Paul Lehman hit the roof. "Hey!" he shouted. "Did you see that?" We stopped, backed up to look: three White-fronted Parrots were calmly perched on roadside wires. As we were watching them, squealing calls behind us announced a flock of Sinaloa Crows. A short distance beyond, at the edge of Navojoa, we stopped at the Rio Mayo. Among the thickets and sandbars and cottonwoods, we found many birds — along with many people swimming and doing their laundry and wandering aimlessly. Our path was crossed repeatedly by two small boys herding a large gang of goats. But the birds did not seem to mind. Distinctly Mexican birds here (which by now we had designated as "Lehman Lifers" or "Paul Bearers") were two with quaint names, Social Flycatcher and Happy Wren. Varied Buntings flashed through the thickets, Groove-billed Anis flopped about near the water, and numerous Broad-billed Hummingbirds added to the tropical element of the place.

What felt most tropical, though, was the incredible, oppressive heat. We'd thought we were used to birding in the sun, but half an hour on that blazing riverside left us exhausted. Proceeding into

Navojoa we found a restaurant, miraculously air-conditioned, where we tanked up on refrescos before driving south.

The heat pervaded the car, riding along like a sixth passenger, as if we would have had room for one. In the cramped quarters of Steve's little Ambassador, the heat and humidity were magnified. The wind blowing through the open windows was like a blast from a furnace, and it filled our eyes with the dust of endless road repairs. Dulled by the heat, we dozed; only two of us were awake when, at noon, we crossed from Sonora into Sinaloa.

As we moved south in Sinaloa in the glare of midday, the plant life on the roadsides and hillsides was changing. Tall columnar cacti, like those in the deserts farther north, still figured — but here the cacti were crowded in among a forest of short trees, all a uniform fifteen to twenty feet tall. This was a new habitat type, Thorn Forest. Aside from flocks of Western Kingbirds and Cassin's Kingbirds we saw few birds, but that was probably because of the time of day. Butterflies were abundant. Swallowtails and Gulf fritillaries sailed across the highway, and there were

Gulf Fritillaries

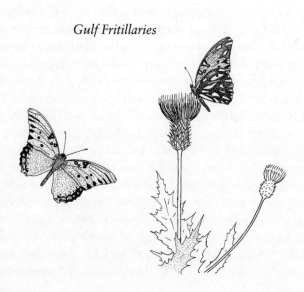

sulphurs of all sizes, from giant *Phoebis* and *Anteos* to small *Eurema;* little white pierid butterflies swarmed around magenta blossoms on the road shoulder.

By about four in the afternoon, just past Culiacan, we were all awake again, though the heat had hardly diminished. Birds were becoming active again as well, flitting in and above the roadside trees. In the car, arguments broke out: how many of these birds should we stop for? Paul wanted to see every bird, naturally, but Ted shot back, "If we stopped to look at *everything*, we'd never get out of Tucson."

Each of them had a point. In the morning we'd be up in the mountains, with no more chance at the distinctive birds of this coastal zone. On the other hand, we were running this trip on a tight schedule. So we compromised. The best thorn forest birding was still ahead, just north of Mazatlán. If we bombed straight south for a couple of hours, we'd arrive at the best habitat with some daylight left.

In theory, the plan sounded good. In practice, the plan was ignored when a flock of Yellow-winged Caciques crossed the road, forgotten when a Lineated Woodpecker flashed into nearby branches, abandoned when the first gang of Magpie-Jays raised their raucous shrieks from hilltop trees. We stopped for all of them. A Streak-backed Oriole glowed in treetop twigs, Blue-black Grassquits performed funny little up-down display hops from the fence wires, and we stopped to watch. The clock ran down on the remaining daylight, while we all got a kaleidoscopic eyeful of tropical birds.

Past nightfall we rolled into Mazatlán, into traffic and confusion. The long night and hot day had left our nerves frayed. Finally out of Mazatlán, moving up the Durango Highway, we ran into rain. The deluge began at the foothills and went on before us into the mountains. It was a torrential, slashing rain, numbing in its intensity. The highway vanished — in the darkness, and occasionally under water; Mark, at the wheel, had to pick his way along by the feel of the road. The switchbacks and blind curves went on for hours. Then, as abruptly as it had begun, the rain stopped. Half an hour later, Mark exclaimed: "Hey, we're here!" — in an incredulous tone, as if he had not expected to make it — and we turned into the rough pullout below the trail to the Rancho Liebre fire lookout.

After a much-needed half night of sleep we were up at daybreak. The dawn was overcast and chilly, but after our broiling of the previous day this came as a welcome change.

We had an active morning with the birds of the Sierra Madre. There were Mountain Trogons, and Rufous-capped Brush-Finches, and we occasionally heard Brown-backed Solitaires singing from the pines. Loose flocks of warblers moved through the trees: familiar migrants from the north, like Townsend's and Hermit warblers, and distinctive Mexican species like Golden-browed Warblers and Slate-throated Redstarts. The Red Warblers, as usual, stole the show. They were a shock to the eye and mind: tiny flaming-red birds with silver ear patches, glowing in the dark evergreens, the reddest birds imaginable.

But we were still conscious of our mission to seek the Eared Trogon. At one point an oddly plumaged young Mountain Trogon flew across the trail, and three of us nearly went into orbit. This made it clear where our main interest lay. So late in the morning we crammed ourselves back into Steve's car and headed on up the highway toward El Salto.

The sky had been overcast all morning, with high thin clouds. But as we were leaving Rancho Liebre to move into unfamiliar regions, the sky began to darken. Clouds rolled lower across the slopes. The brooding mountains loomed nearer the road, closing us in. Under this mysterious half-light the road we traveled was as strange to us as the invisible highway of the night before; and although we had been in good spirits when we had left the barranca, we became vaguely troubled, touched by an illogical sense of unease, as we drove up the road.

Trying to shake the depression, we made too many stops during the afternoon. We stopped on the rim of a ravine that turned out to be a yawning canyon; small birds on the far wall called once or twice, and then flew away. In the aftermath of rain there was water seeping and running down all the exposed faces of rock, and we passed one tall cliff with a single plume of white waterfall hanging in space. White-naped Swifts came across the road: huge dark swifts, flying like bats, maintaining an eerie silence. As the afternoon wore on, we were mostly silent as well.

It was evening by the time we reached the highway edge of El Salto. Under that baleful sky, darkness was going to arrive early. We passed a big Pemex station, its electric lights garish and sickly in the dusk, and next to it a cafe with big trucks rumbling in the parking lot, and then we turned off onto the tooth-rattling, narrow dirt streets of the town. Everyone in El Salto seemed to be out walking in the streets, and we could hardly drive faster than a crawl. After a few wrong turns and false starts down canyoned alleys, we located the town square and headed out on a route leading toward the southwest.

It was almost dark; carefully we watched the narrow dirt road before us, and as carefully we watched the tenths-of-a-mile ticking off on the car's odometer. To reach the trogon stakeout, we were supposed to start by going exactly two miles from the town square and then turning right on a side road. But there seemed to be an inordinate number of side roads here. Half a mile from town we passed one that led to the right, and then three in succession that angled uphill to the left. "Ignore them," said Ted. "These side roads look recent . . . probably some kind of construction or logging going on up here."

Two miles from the square, there was no sign of a road going to the right; we stopped to reconsider. Should we try one of the left-hand roads behind us, or go on looking for a right turn? We were arguing about it when Paul suddenly said: "Hey! What in the world is that?!" An odd grinding roar, a glare of light, growing out of the darkness ahead of us. Around the next bend came a huge truck, groaning and swaying under a stack of massive pine logs . . . a truck as wide as the road itself, and coming right at us.

Hastily Steve drove the Ambassador up onto the road shoulder, and the truck rumbled past.

We were all silent for a minute. Then Steve said, "Let's go on ahead and try to find that right turn," and no one offered any objections.

Half a mile on we were confronted again by the bobbing headlights of another monstrous truck, weighted down with pine trunks. Here the road was too narrow for us to get out of the way, and Steve had to jam the car into reverse for a hundred yards to a spot where he could edge off. The truck rolled on by, closely followed by another one.

Mark stared after the trucks. "God," he said, in a quiet voice. "Did you see the size of those logs? There must be some huge trees in here — some fantastic forest."

"Must *have been,* you mean," growled Parker, in a black mood. "When did those people see the Eared Trogons here, anyway? The forest is *gone,* by now; it has to be! Look at this! — They're even working on a Sunday evening; they can't wait to get the last big trees cut down and hauled away!"

After another mile we met another logging truck. This one was going a little faster than the others, and it almost ran us down. By this time our argument over what to do next had reached an antagonistic pitch. "Look," I said, "we are *completely* lost. It's ridiculous to even think about finding the trogon stakeout tonight. The best we can hope for tonight is to find someplace to *park* this dumb thing out of the way." About that time we came to a wide spot in the road, the first really wide place since the town limits of El Salto; so we pulled over and parked there.

We would have to wait for morning, go back to the town square and try once again to unravel the directions . . . and even if we could find the exact spot, we suspected, the trees would be gone, and the trogons with them. And we had come a thousand miles for this.

Murky filtering of light, of dawn; and I am hearing a Whip-poor-will call, once or twice, from a long distance away. Where in the world am I?

Lying on the hard and stony ground . . . from somewhere down to the right, below these shadowy trees, the sound of a rushing stream. (Oh, yeah: this is Mexico, and the mountains.) From nearby, a few yards away, a rustling sound — this is Mark, sitting up and looking around. He wears a confused expression, probably a match for mine, not quite recognizing this place. Okay, right: this is the place where chance dropped us, where bad luck left us stranded, in the confusion of the night before.

With an effort I forced myself to sit up. All of us were awake now . . . talking in quiet tones, subdued by the surroundings. It was still only half light, and the ground-mist drifting among the trees gave the whole scene an air of mystery.

Parker stood looking down through the shadows toward the stream below us and Look at this, he said, intrigued; there are still trees here. Good-sized ones. Down in this ravine. The slope here must be too steep for easy lumbering; the loggers have gone beyond here, to more convenient trees. We should spend a minute checking out the birds here, he said, before we try again to decipher the directions to the trogon spot.

We picked up our sleeping bags, still damp with dew, and tossed them in the car. By now it was almost light enough to see all right. Parker, impatient, turned around and started up the road. He had gone only a few paces when an odd noise came out of the ravine to our right.

The sound seemed to come from some distance away. But it was loud — a strange, ventriloquial voice, querulous but strong. *It must be a bird,* I said to myself, *because it couldn't be anything else.* Yet no bird that I could think of would make these whining squeals and cackles that rose at intervals from the far wall of the ravine:

Quwhhheeeeeeeaah?

. . . and then a pause.

Quwhhheeeeeeah? . . . Chack!
. . . another pause.
Chac-chac-chac-chac-chack!
We were frozen where we stood, listening. The voice did not fit with any group of birds I knew. Parker's face was a mask: not identifying the sound, not even trying to; simply listening.

Quwhhheeeeeeah? . . . Chack!
Cautiously, the five of us started down toward the stream. Halfway down the ravine a huge boulder stood out among the pines; we climbed it to scan the far side. The light was now improving by the minute. We could see the pines below us descending the slope for another twenty or thirty yards to the stream, and then marching up the far side for fifty yards to where they ended abruptly at a series of rock bluffs.

The strange calls rang out again, seemingly no nearer or farther away than before. While the other three stood atop the rock, wielding their binoculars, Ted and I continued down the slope. We had just reached the stream when a wild, bizarre noise came from the hillside behind us. Not the mystery creature, though; this time it was Mark — yelling at the top of his lungs, drowning out the shouts from Paul and Steve.

The one word we could make out was: "*. . . TROGON!!*"
We scrambled back up the hill. Mark was literally jumping with excitement: "Over there!!"

It was all the way across the canyon, fluttering right up against the rock wall on the far side. Even at that distance it was obvious this was a big trogon, much larger and chunkier than the Mountain Trogons or Elegant Trogons. Its head and back were a deep dark green, its lower belly a deep geranium red, and the white in its tail flashed in flight — as the bird flew down to perch on an exposed branch in front of the rock face.

And at that moment the Eared Trogon called again:
Quwhhheeeeeeeaah? — raising its long tail almost to the horizontal.

Chack! — dropping the tail again. The raucous call echoed off the rock wall of the ravine. We five birders were whooping with jubilation now, figuring we were too far away to scare the bird. After half a minute the trogon took off and fluttered among the pine branches, appearing to catch an insect. Then a long, swooping flight carried the bird down out of sight.

All of us scrambled down the hill now, splashed across the stream. On the far side, up the steep slope, we cast about for bearings; the trogon was not calling now, so we were uncertain where to look. We climbed a bit farther, angled to the left, looked at each other with uncertainty: shouldn't this be about the right spot?

Then the trogon flushed from trees directly above us. Momentarily we were stunned, dazzled, because the bird was so near, so large, so striking — and so *loud:* calling now with a new intensity, its harsh chatter ringing in our ears as the bird circled behind us, came up again on the right, still calling . . .

But Ted Parker, quick on the draw, had noticed something else. "Look," he said. "Look where that bird came from."

Up on the nearest pine trunk, a scant twenty feet above our heads, was a smooth round hole about three inches across — an old woodpecker digging. As we focused our binoculars on the empty opening, there was a movement in the interior, something moving up to the edge of the hole to peer out. It was a *baby* Eared Trogon, and it was looking down at us from its nest!

We left, late, after studying the trogons and their nest from a respectful distance for several hours. We dropped down eastward through the city of Durango and then took the long road north across the plateau toward El Paso, driving fast, knowing that the guys were going to be late for class Tuesday morning anyway. But they said it was worth it. We had had a remarkable encounter with one of the least-known birds in Mexico.

Amazingly, just four years later, this mystery bird would show up in the United States — in the Chiricahua Mountains of Arizona. It would show up again, and eventually it would prove to be a rare nesting bird in the Arizona border ranges. Birders who had never even heard of an Eared Trogon would suddenly develop a keen interest, once it appeared north of the border: now it represented a checkmark for their North American lists.

So the tropical birds were moving north, it seemed. And Ted Parker was headed south.

Ted's mind was focused on the American tropics, the region of the richest bird diversity anywhere. If Mexico was great, South America was the ultimate. In South America, amazing discoveries were waiting around every bend, and species unknown to science were still being found. Ted would be going to South America before that school year was over. Noting that Ted's sharp mind was almost never focused on classwork, an Arizona professor would pull strings to get him sent along on an expedition to Peru — thus unleashing the brilliance and pent-up energy of Ted Parker on the green continent.

We did not know it then, but it would not have surprised us to learn that Ted would soon become a leading expert on the birds

Eared Trogon

of the Neotropics. We did not know that within twenty years Ted would be recognized as one of the greatest field ornithologists of all time, the ultimate authority on the ultimate bird continent. Mercifully, we did not know that those twenty years would be all the time he had. His career would end abruptly against a mountainside in Ecuador while he was flying surveys for bird habitats, working to protect the birdlife he loved. We did not know any of those things; we were just kids, we thought we would live forever.

But 1973 was not going to last forever. Time was still ticking away toward the end of the year. Running up a list in North America, north of that artificial boundary, seemed less interesting to me now; having started, however, I intended to finish. Just four more months of this list-chasing, and then I could forget checkmarks and focus on real birds again.

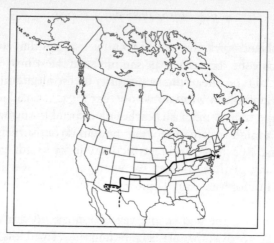

Spots Before the Eyes

FOLLOWING our Mexican trip I had gone to the Chiricahua Mountains, where I had picked up White-eared Hummingbird and Spotted Owl for my year list. After that I had planned to head up the Pacific coast toward Washington. But my plans were overturned when I stopped by Ted Parker's dorm at the University of Arizona.

Ted was on the phone, keyed up, firing questions, grinning at the answers. Finally hanging up, he told me, "You're not going to like this. There's a Spotted Redshank at Brigantine!"

"Right," I said. "And I saw a flock of Rowlett's Owlets tunneling into the science library, too."

"No, I'm serious," he persisted. "It was found yesterday. Dozens of birders went over there today and saw it. Too bad it didn't show up a month ago, when we were there, hey?"

So he was not joking. A Spotted Redshank! This Old World sandpiper had turned up only a very few times in North America; there were just a couple of confirmed records then, from the Northeast and from Alaska.

Spotted Redshank was one of those fine species that combined rarity with good looks. A large sandpiper of the genus *Tringa,* it resembled our Greater Yellowlegs, but it had red legs and a touch of red on the bill. In winter it was silvery gray; in breeding plumage it was a velvety purplish black with a sprinkle of small white spots. In a family of creatures that were subtle or downright dull, the Spotted Redshank stood out as that true rarity, an unmistakable bird.

I was mulling this over, damning the two thousand-plus miles that lay between me and the Brigantine refuge in New Jersey, when Mark Robbins walked in. When he heard the news, he collapsed into a chair. "Oh, man," he said. "I've looked at the picture of that in the European guide so many times . . . Is it still in breeding plumage, this late in the season?"

"Partly," said Ted. "They said it was changing now — still black on the underparts, and still with some black around the head and neck. Maybe halfway through the molt."

"Me, I wouldn't care what plumage it was in," said Mark. "If I didn't have classes . . ." He looked up at me. "Guess you're off for New Jersey now, right?"

Up to that moment I had not really considered it. But why shouldn't I go to Seattle by way of Atlantic City? I got up and started pacing the room. "Wonder how long the bird's going to stay around?"

Parker laughed. "There's *no* way to predict that. But Brigantine's sometimes a good 'holding' spot. Some rarities have stayed for months. Most of them don't, obviously. But if you decide not to go, you'll find out later that it stayed a couple of weeks, and was seen by everyone who went for it."

"Including Floyd Murdoch," Mark put in.

I continued pacing. "That's a lot of time, a lot of thumbing for one bird. Or for no bird. No logical basis for a decision." Then something occurred to me. "Hey! Ted! Do you recall — last month at Brigantine, you remember how I was talking about Spotted Redshank, predicting that we'd see one?"

"How could I forget? We were all sick of it."

"All right. You know how I just fantasize about one incredible rarity at a time. That day at Brig, there were all kinds of rare waterbirds I could have been babbling about, but the Spotted Redshank was the one I picked. Don't you see, man? It's a sign!"

"If that's your idea of logic, I'm glad you're not the president," said Mark.

Ted grinned wickedly. "If you talk yourself into going east . . . Cornell University's no more than a few hundred miles from Brigantine, right? And a certain young female student should be back in class."

"Come on. That hadn't even entered my mind." But I was already digging into my backpack for the right road maps. "It can be done," I announced. "I can be in New Jersey in two or three days . . . then, on my way from there to Washington State, I can stop through South Dakota and pick up the White-winged Junco. It'll work out fine. I'll leave tonight."

It was near midnight Sunday when Mark and Ted drove me out to the freeway. In a way, the scene was a replay of another night eight months earlier: back in January, when I'd started out to go for the Loggerhead Kingbird in Florida. Once again, the guys were dropping me off at the freeway interchange on South Stone. Once again, I was in a hurry, going for a staked-out rarity that might not stay long. Once again, I was going all the way across the continent to seek a single bird.

As I soon discovered, this was to be a replay of the Loggerhead Kingbird trip in another way. Once again, right when I wanted all possible speed, my luck turned bad. Just as it had in January. The song came back to mind: *You'll go back, Jack, and do it again.*

Luck on the road could be defined in several ways. For the recreational thumbers, good luck would mean good times, parties on the road. For others, the derelicts who were going away rather than going to anyplace, good luck would mean a level of comfort, so as not to disrupt their hazy dreams. For me, good luck simply meant getting there fast. That September trek from Tucson to Brigantine would have been considered, by any criterion, a bad trip: I didn't have a good time, I didn't maintain any level of comfort, and altogether it took me far too long to get to New Jersey.

When sunrise Monday found me standing a scant twenty miles east of Tucson, I told myself that I was just getting spoiled. This was the first long-distance hitching I'd had to do in a month. Starting in August I'd had rides with other birders and friends from Cape May to New England, from Maine back to Lancaster, from Lancaster to Tucson, and then to California and Mexico. Between these trips, my sorties by thumb had been short. Now, back on the long haul, I reaffirmed what I already knew: thumbing across the continent was vastly different from driving across.

About the time I was moving, finally, into the Texas panhandle, I ran into a scatter of rain showers. I might have known: it was mid-September, and the first fall weather was advancing across the continent. The weather got worse as I continued east. Lines of thundershowers, one after another, intersected my route across the midwestern states; and as I approached the Pennsylvania border, weather reports on the car radios would tell me that rain blanketed the mid-Atlantic states, solid rain from the Appalachians east.

Fall weather fronts were bringing cooler temperatures as well, so I had to watch out for getting soaked. Pneumonia would slow me down. Besides, most drivers seemed disinclined to pick up sopping wet hitchhikers. So from Texas on, I was watching the sky as warily as I watched for the police.

For a while, I was lucky. A pattern developed: I would be let off on a roadside still wet from rain, under skies that foretold more rain any moment, but after a long wait I would get another ride just before the shower began. The ride — whether for five miles or for a hundred — would take me through the downpour to another spot where it was, at that moment, not raining. Then the sequence would repeat. I won every round of this rainfall roulette across Oklahoma, but I knew the weather must take the lead eventually. It did. A short distance into Missouri rain caught me

out, soaking me to the skin before I could reach the shelter of the
nearest overpass.

From there east it was raining nearly every time I was let off —
and I was let off far too often. Usually, hitching on Interstate 70, I
would eventually catch a long ride, but on that trip to New Jersey
the long ride never materialized. It was nearly all short hops —
ten, twenty, maybe fifty miles in which to dry out and warm up a
little, and then I'd be out on the rainy roadside again.

In the long Indiana night I stood for five hours beneath an
overpass where the trucks pounded through, one after another,
trailing plumes of mist from the wet pavement, so that I remained
thoroughly wet even though I was out of the falling rain itself.
Tired, I was tempted to crawl up to a high dry corner under the
bridge and fall asleep. But I had to keep thumbing; I was still in a
hurry, even though my quest was beginning to seem more and
more absurd. Asked where I was going, where I was coming
from, I'd mumble, "Atlantic City. Sure, it's fun. Got friends there.
No, not far; just coming from St. Louis. From Indianapolis. Left a

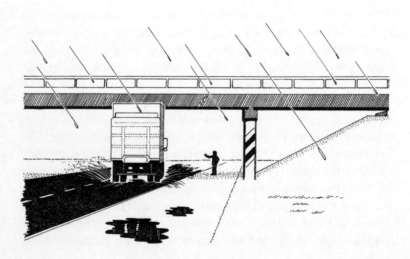

week ago. Nah, I haven't done much hitchhiking. Not in any hurry . . ." Anything was easier than trying to explain where I was really going and why.

Well into Pennsylvania I finally got a decent ride, a couple of hundred miles' worth, with a casual longhair from Seattle. He was smoking a pipe of some illegal substance and listening to tapes by Blue Oyster Cult, and we talked about theories of education, and about why modern poetry might have abandoned the strict meter of former days. After a while, in this context, my trip almost began to make sense. So I told him about it.

The guy listened, intrigued. He had never heard of any such thing — but as with most children of the sixties, he had no trouble handling the idea. There were many paths in life, after all. If some character wanted to thumb 2,500 miles to look at one individual bird, this was a pursuit that did no harm to anyone. Far out, he said.

So I kept talking about how this European shorebird had come like some messenger from across the water . . . no telling what winds had driven it, what path had brought it to the Jersey shore. Then by another coincidence, some watcher had chanced upon this Spotted Redshank. I could picture it: the discovery. The image coming into focus, the birder's hands beginning to shake because he knows there is only one big sandpiper that could show so much black in the plumage. Then the dash to the nearest telephone: No kidding — a Spotted Redshank at Brigantine. More telephones ringing, in New York, Philadelphia, Washington, the unofficial birding grapevine swinging into action. The next day, the first wave of cognoscenti descending on the refuge, to locate the bird and agree: No question — a Spotted Redshank at Brigantine. The message would have been put on the local Rare Bird Alerts, from which the news would reach a wider circle of birders. During the week, a second wave of observers would come, those who could get away on weekdays. And then on the weekend following the initial discovery — which was tomorrow, damn it, because it had taken me all week to get across the country and it was now Friday — tomorrow, I told the guy, there should be a real crowd at Brigantine, all looking for this one bird.

"Heavy," said the dude. The whole thing was obviously crazy enough to appeal to him. "Must be one fine-looking bird, huh?"

"Well, yeah," I said. "Pretty striking. Plus the fact that it's European. Usually can't see it around here at all."

"Do the birds in Europe just *look* better than the ones in Arizona?" He was stuck on the idea that the bird's visual appeal was the root of all the excitement, as if we would ignore all drab birds and travel miles to see those that pleased the eye.

"You can't make that much of a distinction," I told him. "Once you get into it, any bird looks good. I even like to look at sparrows. But say I'm an American birder who's probably never going to *go* to Europe — if I *ever* want to see a Spotted Redshank, I've gotta get down to Brigantine right now. Because there may not be another one within range during my lifetime. And when you see something that you know is a once-in-a-lifetime bird, that makes it beautiful, no matter *what* the hell it actually *looks* like."

And now the guy was starting to smile, a look of understanding lighting his face. "I get it, man," he said. "I really *do* get it. It's like that line from the Beatles, right?" He started tapping out a slow drum solo on the edge of the steering wheel. "Like what John Lennon wrote in 'Come Together': this bird, he's 'got to be good-looking cuz he's so hard to see!' Am I right?"

Right. Exactly.

That night I got into New Jersey, got to within a hundred miles of Brigantine — but I was so tired. Little lightning flashes were going off inside my eyelids, and the rain came down like thunder, as if it would smash everything into the muddy ground. Finding a bridge at a highway interchange, I crawled under it and curled up into a catatonic cocoon, thinking, This is it: the deluge. The European birds are heading to New Jersey to gather for the second voyage of Noah's Ark, because the great flood is coming again.

Isn't there some city around here called New Ark? The sound of rain drummed me off to sleep.

When I awoke, the rain had stopped. Crawling from beneath the bridge, I saw that dawn was breaking, and the sky was completely clear. Of course: weather fronts move from west to east across the continent. I had been traveling right along with a rainy system, which I could have escaped any time by waiting a day for the front to move on. Live and learn. Feeling reprieved, I thumbed on down toward Brigantine. After a few quiet rides and a fair amount of walking, I arrived at the Brigantine refuge headquarters about nine in the morning.

. . . Arrived on foot, asking myself, Where are all the cars? Very few were there. On our August visit a month earlier we had seen throngs of vehicles crowding the dike roads, and that had been just a normal weekend. Today, with the added lure of the Spotted Redshank, the place should have been packed.

Perhaps the bird had flown. Even so, many die-hard birders would have hung around, searching the refuge, hoping it would reappear. I took off my backpack and walked into the visitor information booth.

The guest book for the past few days read like a Who's Who of birding. Knowing where many of these people lived, I could almost see the circle widening as the news spread — local birders on Saturday, a mid-Atlantic crowd on Sunday, and then on into the week with observers arriving from farther and farther away. Harold Axtell had even come down from Ontario. Of course, Dr. Axtell enjoyed new life birds just as much as any of us; he would have rushed down here along with the crowd, hoping for a glimpse of the Spotted Redshank.

No, I corrected myself, *not just hoping for a glimpse.* Not if I knew Axtell. He would have come to examine the bird carefully, to study it at length before he decided to enter it on his life list. Sure enough — checking the dates in the guest book, I saw that Axtell had arrived Monday and stayed four days. It was reassuring that someone so careful was following along behind the pack, applying the final stamp of approval, even when the bird was so unmistakable as this one.

Turning from the guest register to the Recent Sightings clipboard, I found one of the most amazing documents of 1973.

An entire page was filled — crammed — with Harold Axtell's neat, precise handwriting. Everything he said he stated clearly. But the point he made was so startling that I had to read the page twice to understand completely.

He had arrived on Monday and soon encountered that which he sought: a large, blackish shorebird, the focus of attention for a line of telescopes and a gaggle of excited birders. So Axtell had settled in to study it. The situation was made more complicated because the bird would not stay in one place — it kept moving around the extensive marshes and mudflats of Brigantine, so that it was necessary to seek and relocate the bird repeatedly. But after a couple of days, Axtell had seen enough to be convinced.

Convinced that the bird was *not* a Spotted Redshank.

Diplomatically worded, clearly intended not to offend anyone, Dr. Axtell's written explanation still left no room for doubt. A Spotted Redshank, he said, should exhibit a touch of red at the base of the bill; on this Brigantine bird, the bill showed no trace of such red. This bird's legs were a nonconclusive color — they only looked red in the low-angled rays of the evening sun; under normal daylight, they appeared a stained yellow. The molt did not seem to be proceeding in the right sequence; this bird was still blackish underneath, but not elsewhere. Bill shape was not quite right, and flight pattern was all wrong, looking more like that of a Greater Yellowlegs. In size and shape the bird was disturbingly identical to the yellowlegs with which it sometimes associated.

True, wrote Axtell, its behavior was not quite typical for a yellowlegs. But its actions reminded him of something he had seen before: other waterbirds, suffering from encounters with petroleum products. In short, Axtell's conclusion was that this mystery shorebird, with its blackish feathers, odd-colored legs, and strange behavior, was merely a yellowlegs that had gotten into some oil.

Standing there reading and rereading this bombshell, I was in shock. So the "unmistakable bird" had been a mistake.

No wonder there are no birders here today, I thought. Axtell's declaration had been written Thursday. The news would have gone out immediately, I supposed, probably spreading faster than had the news of the bird's initial discovery. All over the East, birders would have begun hotly defending their original identification, or grimly erasing the Spotted Redshank from their life lists. On this Saturday morning, I imagined, many of these birders had decided to wash the car, or catch up on yardwork, or go birding anywhere at all except Brigantine.

No one was ever able to make a strong case that Axtell was wrong. One countertheory claimed that both an oiled yellowlegs and a genuine Spotted Redshank had been on the refuge at the same time; and given the great size and great potential of Brigantine, this was not impossible. But the general conclusion was that Harold Axtell had been right and that all the dozens of other birders had been wrong.

This episode had a profound impact on me — partly because I'd spent five days hitching in the rain, 2,500 miles out of my way. But there was more than that.

In past conversations with Harold Axtell I had always been a little amused by his obsession with fine points that had seemed unnecessary, even trivial. But now I saw their practical application. Not every bird could be named by simple field marks. Sometimes one had to know the birds extremely well to be able to name them.

What about those birders who had checked off the Brigantine bird as a Spotted Redshank? Many of them were good birders, and every one of them, no doubt, had already had Greater Yellowlegs on their lists. Sure, they knew the yellowlegs. But they didn't *really know it,* not in fine detail and inside out and up and down, as Axtell did. Certainly I did not know the bird at that level either.

Looking back, it seemed I had been lucky not to arrive in New Jersey earlier. With really good luck crossing the continent, I might have made it in three days — it had happened before. I might have arrived Wednesday evening, seen the bird and missed Axtell, and gone away with the super-rare redshank written on my list . . . because I would never have identified this bird correctly. My approach, my knowledge were just too superficial.

It was late September, and three-quarters of my Big Year had passed already. In the three months that remained, I would be criss-crossing the continent yet again, in search of only a handful of new species. But I resolved to look at birds more carefully from now on, look at them all, common or rare, to see if I could really get to know them. It was the beginning of the end of my interest in listing.

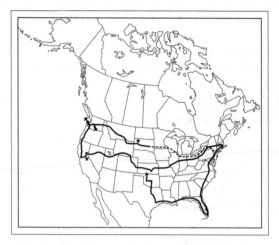

Exhausting the Possibilities

"YOU DON'T belong on the road, kid."

A couple of older hitchhikers had told me that early in my travels, when I was only sixteen or seventeen. Later on, I would come to wish that they had been right.

You don't belong on the road, they said. But apparently I did; and the hard part was to come back off the road when it was over, to stop myself from endless and aimless wandering. Even years later, I would sometimes wake at night with a radical desire to be out on some nameless road, with no money, no identity, no destination, just going somewhere or nowhere.

Short-distance hitching, especially going to out-of-the-way birding spots, took concentration. Long-distance hitching, just following the interstates on and on, was hypnotically mindless. By the latter part of 1973, so few birds were left for my list, and those birds were so widely scattered, that I spent most of the fall covering long distances rather than actually birding. I was worn down by the pace of the year, and the period from late September through November went by in a haze. Only a few bright spots of experience stood out as images later.

The garish-purple roadster had been souped up for drag-racing on county roads. But they were taking it west — because, as all-American kids from rural Tennessee, they felt the need to acknowledge the American West, to go and take part in it. So they had walked out of school one day in the second week of classes and now they were on the road, taking in that larger education of Experience.

South Dakota to these three kids might have been an endlessly repeating loop from a western movie, and they might not like it. While the inhuman landscape of the Badlands rolled past the car windows, they might listen to the radio or reread that month's *National Lampoon*. Yet beneath their flippant facade lay the sense that this was a significant event, that later in life it would be important to them to have experienced the West.

They picked me up out in the middle of South Dakota, and I rode with them from Rapid City down into the Black Hills, to the official vantage point from which the public was meant to view Mount Rushmore. The visitors' center was strategically located across a valley, with patios and huge windows aimed at the monument, and displays commemorating the four presidents and the carving of them. Even though this was late September there were still distracting numbers of tourists here, including girls in tight jeans, bickering elderly couples, and tots running around throwing gum wrappers on the floor. Far away from all this, across the valley, the four stone presidents gazed blankly into the past and the future.

"When I was a little kid," said one of the Tennessee dudes, "my old uncle told me that this mountain was like that naturally. That it just looked like those four guys by accident. I believed him for years." And he laughed, approvingly.

Out around the edges of the parking lot I found the only specialty bird of the Black Hills, the White-winged Junco. Four of them were flitting along under the pines, making little ticking notes like other juncos anywhere. In appearance they were much like the abundant Slate-colored Junco of the East, but they were a little larger, paler gray, with more white in the tail and two prominent white bars across their wings.

The American Ornithologists' Union, in a decision published earlier that year, had decreed that the White-winged was just a local variety, not a full species. So much for the Black Hills' only claim to birding fame. The juncos themselves, of course, did not seem to care; watching them, neither did I.

From the Black Hills I went on west across the northern route, taking Interstate 90 across the high plateau of Montana and Idaho, where a chill in the air and intermittent cold rain gave an early hint that winter was on the way. I was headed for the coast of Washington. Rich Stallcup had told me I should try to take an October pelagic trip offshore from Westport, Washington, and that his friend Gene Hunn would be able to help get me on such a trip.

I reached Seattle on a Friday night and called Gene, who greeted me like an old friend, even though we'd never met. "I'm sure there's still room on the Westport trip," he said. "I'll just call Terry Wahl — he runs the trip — and ask him to save you a spot. Are there any birds you need around here besides the seabirds?"

There was one northwestern specialty that I was keen to see: Sharp-tailed Sandpiper. This was actually an Asian bird, but every fall a few young ones would go south on the wrong side of the Pacific, turning up in British Columbia and Washington.

The preceding autumn, when I had left Arizona and gone north up the coast, I had searched unsuccessfully for Sharp-tailed Sandpipers. While I was away, Bob Witzeman had discovered one at Phoenix: the first record ever for Arizona. That bird had stayed for several days; by the time I got back, I was the only member of the Tucson Five, maybe the only birder in Arizona, who had *not* seen a Sharp-tailed Sandpiper. This fall, I was hoping for less irony and more luck.

Gene suggested I try Washington's Leadbetter Point, where one or two Sharp-tails had been turning up almost every fall recently. But meanwhile, Saturday morning I went birding with Gene and two other local aces, Bill Tweit and Mike Perrone. As we took the ferry across to Whidbey Island, watching for alcids on the gray waters, I was reminded of my earlier trip to the San Juan Islands. Now, six months and tens of thousands of miles later, my list for the year was up to 650 species, but the larger it grew the less important or even interesting it seemed. I was more concerned with getting to know more about these birds I had already checked off.

In that regard, it was good to go afield with Gene, Bill, and Mike, who had plenty to tell me about the local birds. Since no species new for my year list were likely, I could relax and focus on whatever birds we saw. White-winged Scoters and Surf Scoters, big sea ducks, were offshore in rafts of hundreds, and at coastal vantage points we saw Rhinoceros Auklets, Common Murres, and Parasitic Jaegers. At a pond on the island we found a Franklin's Gull — a common migrant around my boyhood home in Kansas, but only a rare straggler here.

Early in the afternoon we were working along the edge of the lagoon at Crockett Lake when a callnote came from behind us, a soft *wirrritt* with a musical, liquid quality. My reaction, as I turned, was that it sounded like some unfamiliar shorebird, but the local guys were quicker: "Sharp-tailed Sandpiper!" The bird swept past with quick, buoyant wingbeats, then circled back to land at the edge of the marsh nearby. It was an exquisitely marked young Sharp-tail, rich golden-buff with a bright chestnut-red cap, one of the most beautiful sandpipers I had ever seen.

Gene Hunn had seen Sharp-tailed Sandpipers before, but he thought this one was probably a first for Island County. "Guess now you won't have to hitchhike to Leadbetter Point," he told me. Several months later I learned that no one, despite much searching, had been able to find a Sharp-tail at Leadbetter Point during the fall of 1973.

With a week until the Westport pelagic trip (and with my wallet virtually empty), I hitched back to central Washington to find work picking apples, as I had done the autumn before. At the employment office in Yakima I sat with other would-be pickers while the growers looked us over. Before long I was in the back of a pickup truck, riding out to the orchard where I would spend the next four days.

Mr. Allen's orchard was fairly small, so he had only a small crew. I worked along with three guys from western Mexico, who told me that they slipped across the border and came up here every year. They were much faster than I, but each person was being paid by the amount he picked, not by the hour; I did the best I could, and my three Mexican friends laughed good-naturedly and tried to show me how I could speed up my work.

It was easy to slip into the routine of physical labor, letting the mind rest. Early in the morning the air would be chilly, the grass under the trees wet with frost as I carried the unwieldy twelve-foot ladder out to the next tree. Studying the tree, I would seek the best spot to place the ladder so that I could reach as many apples as possible before having to move again. Then up the ladder to twist off apples one by one, filling the kangaroo-pouch of the picker's bag until the bag was full and the straps burned my shoulders; down the ladder to dump the apples carefully into the bin I was filling. Then up the ladder again. It was physically tiring but it was useful work, and I was getting paid for it.

Occasionally I would rest, perching on a rung of the ladder and munching on a Golden Delicious. From high on the ladder I had a good view of the valley. It was peaceful in the orchard, despite the distant hum of busy tractors and trucks, and I could hear the occasional squawking of a pheasant or piping of California

Quail from the surrounding grassland. Looking westward, beyond the green orderly rows of fruit trees, I could see hills clothed in sagebrush and golden grass, with big gray boulders where ground squirrels played, and beyond them more hills rising up to the west. Above them all, on clear mornings, the great peak of Mount Rainier floated like a dream.

The Westport boat trip on October 7 was like a reunion. My friend Dave Hayward was there — formerly of the Tucson Five, now a student near here at Evergreen State College. Gene Hunn was there, and most of the other active Washington birders were there. And so was my friendly competitor, Floyd Murdoch, whom I hadn't seen since April.

Floyd admitted that he was getting a little tired of the whole Big Year business, too. At that point he was several species ahead of me, but he said, "I'm almost out of possibilities. I could see several new ones on today's trip — but after that, there's hardly anything I can chase, except Bohemian Waxwing. Now in your case, Kenn, you've got several more birds to look for, and almost three months to spend searching."

"Well, consider this," I said. "We could send a powerful message, suggest that competition is not the best approach for birding, if we just declared a tie right now. And then we could stop this idiotic running around, and just *enjoy* the birds."

Floyd gave me a big smile. "I would consider that very seriously," he said, "if I didn't happen to be ahead of you! Anyway, regardless of the competition, I think we'll both enjoy the birds today."

He was right about that. The offshore waters teemed with birds. Most abundant were the omnipresent Sooty Shearwaters, but most impressive to me were the Buller's Shearwaters. Gliding low over the waves, tilting so sharply that one wingtip pointed at the sky and the other almost brushed the surface, they seemed more graceful than the Sooties, effortless in their control of the air currents just above the water. Pale gray with crisp black markings above, they were bright white on the underside. As they tilted one direction and then the other in flight, the effect was striking. I had seen Buller's Shearwaters the previous autumn off California, but not in numbers like this; we estimated more than seven hundred for the day.

Many other seabirds added to the show. There were numbers of big Black-footed Albatrosses, little silvery Fork-tailed Storm-Petrels, sharply patterned Sabine's Gulls, and one bird I had never seen before, Flesh-footed Shearwater. In color it was much like a Sooty Shearwater, dark sooty-brown all over, but it was bigger with a different flight. Coming past the boat with a flock of Sooties, the Flesh-foot would easily outdistance its smaller cousins with its deceptively slow, loping wingbeats; it made me think of a greyhound running with a pack of beagles.

Rich Stallcup obviously loved the Great Gray Owl. It was big, wild, mysterious, unpredictable — just like he was. Rich had given me detailed advice about where and when to seek the owl in Yosemite National Park. "This should be a fabulous time of year to go to Yosemite," he had said. "Summer can be crowded. There aren't nearly as many people there in October."

He was right about the park not being crowded. Hitching to the entrance was easy enough, but within the park itself it took me a long time to get rides into the higher country. On Rich's advice I headed for the Bridalveil Campground, arriving about midday, and began my search.

Hiding my backpack under a jumbled pile of logs back in the woods, I began methodically walking the edges of all the meadows in the area. Birdlife seemed sparse. At this high elevation the autumn was well advanced, and many of the summer birds had departed already. For hours I prowled the borders of the woods, checking every branch, every stump. As evening shadows stretched across the meadows I was alert, watching for a sign that the big owl might be stirring, coming out in the open. But finally it was getting dark, and I concluded that I would have to camp here and spend another day searching the area.

As night settled in I laid out my waterproof poncho as a groundcloth and rolled out my sleeping bag. I was almost asleep when the light caught my attention.

Light? Yes, a sliver of light, unnaturally bright, spreading slowly across the meadow just beyond the trees. Of course: I had forgotten that this was just past the night of the full moon. *You don't have to stop birding now,* I told myself. *You are looking for a nocturnal bird. It will be active at night, and with this moonlight, you might be able to see it.*

Suddenly wide awake again, I got up, got dressed, laced up my beat-up hiking boots. The moon was climbing in the east, flooding the valley with light. Again I began to walk the edges of the meadows, slowly, watching on all sides, listening intently. But listening was pointless. A couple of hours later, when the owl appeared, it sailed right over my head without even a whisper of sound.

It was like a shadow come to life. Gliding silently across the clearing, the Great Gray Owl swept up sharply at the last moment to alight on top of a small tree a hundred yards away. Even in silhouette, it was unmistakable: huge, with broad wings, longish tail, big rounded head. After it landed I thought it turned to look my direction, although I could not see the details of its face; it was bobbing its head up and down in a peculiar motion, no doubt seeing *me* perfectly well. The owl remained there for only a minute or so, and throughout that time, there was not a sound except the pounding of my pulse. The frost on the grass was catching the moonlight now, so that the meadow glowed like silver. I felt uniquely privileged to encounter the owl in its own element of the night.

By late November, I felt cut off from both the past and the future. My hometown of Wichita seemed like some alien planet now;

aside from immediate family, I never heard anything from anyone there after I went out on the road. All my classmates in the honors classes at South High would be into their second year of college now, taking the approved route toward careers and steady paychecks. But I had gone careening off onto a divergent path. Now I was standing by a deserted road in western Oklahoma, trying to pursue a bird that not even most birders would consider very interesting.

The range of the Lesser Prairie-Chicken extended into five states, but it was peripheral to all of them: scattered sites in the Texas panhandle, and nearby edges of New Mexico, Colorado, Kansas, and Oklahoma. No state would be eager to claim the species anyway. It was like a smaller, paler, duller version of the Greater Prairie-Chicken. The Greater had a much more extensive range — north to Minnesota, south to coastal Texas, east to Illinois and Michigan. A traveling birder had a good chance of intercepting a Greater Prairie-Chicken somewhere, without too much of a detour. No one ever saw a Lesser Prairie-Chicken unless they made a long, inconvenient side trip.

Doing research some months earlier, I had looked at the results of the latest Christmas Bird Count; the highest tally of Lessers (and practically the only count reporting them) had been at Arnett, Oklahoma. Writing to the compiler of the count, Kenneth

Great Gray Owl

Seyffert from Amarillo, I had received directions to the best area for the prairie-chickens. "It can take a while to find them if you go in fall," Seyffert had told me. "But they're always there, so you'll see them if you spend enough time."

Now it was taking time just to get to the area. I knew that plenty of thumbers came across Oklahoma on I-40, but apparently few ever ventured up the sixty miles of U.S. 283 north to Arnett from the interstate. This was farm and ranch country, and the drivers of the passing pickup trucks gave me odd looks. Via a series of short rides interspersed with long walks, it took me half a day to get to Arnett.

The location that Kenneth Seyffert had recommended was east and a little south of Arnett, an area with fields of sorghum and winter wheat. Flocks of the prairie-chickens were supposed to forage in that area part of the time, especially in early morning and late afternoon.

It was a mild day — mercifully warm for late November; I knew the plains could be much colder at that season. After I had wandered up and down dirt roads for a while, I decided to stash my backpack, to be able to walk without the weight of it. Wrapping it up in my waterproof poncho, I leaned it against a fence-post away from the road and continued exploring.

Late in the afternoon, after more than four hours of walking the roads and scanning the fields, I still had not seen a Lesser Prairie-Chicken. But as I walked back to get my pack, I saw trouble brewing.

A pickup truck, cruising slowly along the road, had come to a stop next to my backpack. Looking through binoculars, I could see that the driver — a man with a big cowboy hat — was peering suspiciously at the formless blob of the pack wrapped in the poncho. Then he took a shotgun down from the rack in the back window of the pickup, climbed out of the truck, and began stalking slowly toward the pack.

This IS the West, I said to myself. Whatever was going to happen here, it seemed better to confront it, so I began walking more rapidly in that direction. Just then another truck pulled up behind me. This one had official lettering on the door — it was from the state game department — and the driver looked more friendly than the rancher ahead. "Son, can I help you with something?" the man asked.

"Maybe," I said. "I think that guy up there is about to shoot my backpack."

"Why don't you hop in," the game warden said, "and we'll go talk to him." As we drove up to confront the rancher, I hurriedly explained that I was birding, and that this area had been recommended for the elusive prairie-chicken. The warden seemed amused, but not skeptical.

The man with the shotgun was now standing over my backpack, looking mystified. "Hey, Verne," the warden called to him, cheerfully. "You don't want to shoot that thing. It's out of season."

"Hello, Mosely," the rancher replied. "What's going on here?"

"Nothing to be concerned about. This young man is a birdwatcher. He's looking for prairie-chickens."

The rancher looked incredulous. "A *birdwatcher?!*"

"Yep. Like those boys from Amarillo that come over here around Christmas, do that bird count."

"Those boys from Amarillo don't look like long-haired hippies."

"You know kids, Verne," said the warden. "He looks pretty scruffy, but he's not breaking any laws. Soon as he sees his prairie-chickens, he'll move on." So I was able to retrieve my pack, and put it in the back of the warden's truck, and we drove on down the road.

The game warden — he introduced himself as Haskell Mosely — told me that people had called the sheriff to report my suspicious behavior. The deputy had been busy, so as a favor, Mosely had offered to check things out. "Lucky for you," he said. "I can tell you all about your prairie-chickens."

He dropped me off about three miles to the east, where the

cultivated land gave way to rolling grassland, cattle country. The landowner, a friend of Mosely's, showed me a couple of bare patches at the tops of low hills. These were the "booming grounds" where the male prairie-chickens would gather to perform their odd display dances in spring. One of these grounds had been used for at least forty years. Although this was the off-season, the man said, if I camped here overnight I undoubtedly could find a few prairie-chickens nearby in the morning.

Just before daylight I awoke with a start. In my sleep I had thought I heard the little foot-stamping sounds and gurgling moans of prairie-chickens performing their "booming" display. By the time I was fully awake I heard the sounds no more, so I assumed it had been a dream (only later did I learn that prairie-chickens sometimes will display in fall, as well as in spring). When it was light, though, I found four of the birds very close to the north booming ground.

Seeing them this morning, after the trials of the previous day, I was inclined to regard the Lesser Prairie-Chicken as interesting after all. It was not just a drab copy of its Greater relative, stuck off in a corner of the map; rather, it was perfectly adapted to its surroundings. Here the land was arid, the grass was short and often dry, so the prairie-chicken was accordingly smaller and paler for better camouflage. It would not have been a good fit for the tall-grass prairie, but here it was right at home.

As I started walking back toward the highway, a familiar truck came along the road: the game warden, Mosely, was coming to see whether I'd found my birds. He even took me to a diner in Arnett for breakfast, where local farmers and ranch hands insisted on hearing the full story of my hitchhiking travel and my Big Year. These men all had firm ideas of what was normal, and this wasn't. "You're a pretty odd bird yourself, son," one said. "But I guess your bird-watching is better than smoking LSD, or whatever it is that the *other* hippies are doing."

So for a brief moment I had an identity among the good people of Arnett. Then I went back out on the road, to become an anonymous stranger again.

I still had no vision of the future. The road ahead was veiled in mystery, just as it had been nearly eleven months earlier, when I had begun my quest. With November drawing to a close, only a little time remained before the calendar would run out — and I still had no idea what I would do afterwards, in 1974, without this quest to spur me on. All I knew was that I should spend the remaining month of this year seeking the few new birds that were still possible. If I remained true to my quest for now, the future would be here soon enough.

Border Patrol

DURING December 1973 I stayed close to the Mexican border, crossing it a couple of times, and finding surprises on both sides. Early in the month I went to Mexico for a reason that would have seemed inexplicable just a few years later: to build up my list for North America.

It was a matter of definitions. For many years, birders had accepted the American Ornithologists' Union definition of "North America" as consisting of Canada, the United States, and three other nearby areas with similar birdlife: Greenland, Bermuda, and the peninsula of Baja California.

Greenland and Bermuda were far beyond the limits of my budget, but Baja was not. I could hitch rides to the Mexican border and then take cheap buses on south. When Stuart Keith had been working on a Big Year, way back in 1956, he had visited Bermuda, adding two birds to his tally. Why should I not take advantage of the additional birds available in Baja?

Although the southern tip of Baja pushed across the Tropic of Cancer, the peninsula shared almost none of the tropical birds found on the Mexican mainland. Right to the tip, almost all the birds were the same species that occurred in Arizona and California. (That was why the AOU considered this region to be, ornithologically, part of North America.) But a few seabirds were much easier to find off Baja than off California, including some I had missed north of the border, like Craveri's Murrelet and Least Storm-Petrel. And Baja had a few birds found nowhere else in the world — birds like Gray Thrasher and Xantus's Hummingbird. With a quick Baja trip, I calculated, I might pick up five new birds for my "North American" year list.

After tracking down the Lesser Prairie-Chicken in Oklahoma at the end of November, I hitched back to Arizona. I wanted to tell Ted Parker and Mark Robbins about my adventures of the fall and ask their advice about Baja.

"If you go over to California and head south from there, like you're planning," Ted told me, "you'll spend a lot of time just staring offshore, hoping to pick up seabirds. There are ferries across the Gulf of California. Why don't you go south from here, take a ferry across from Guaymas or Mazatlán, and watch for seabirds on the way?"

The plan sounded good, and I adopted it immediately. "Your only problem," Mark said, "will be getting *into* Mexico. If you go strolling up to the border with your backpack — no offense, pal, but you don't exactly look like Mister Businessman. Better try to disguise yourself as a respectable person before the border officials see you." So I borrowed a pair of scissors and hacked my hair a little shorter and spent a few precious quarters at a laundromat. Thinking that my backpack might mark me as an impoverished traveler, I asked if either of the guys had a small suitcase I could borrow. The best they could come up with was Ted's typewriter case. It looked sort of like a small hard-sided suitcase, so I stuffed a few essentials into that, left my backpack in a corner of Ted's dorm room, and headed south toward Nogales. (This strategy almost backfired once during my trip, when police in La Paz stopped me to ask why I was walking around with a typewriter!)

At the big railroad terminal in Nogales, Sonora, the Mexican

Customs officials hardly gave me a second glance. I bought a ticket south to Guaymas. Mexican train rides, as I was to learn over the next few years, were not only very cheap, but also generally fast, punctual, and clean. The same was true of the Mexican buses, which appeared to provide frequent service along every conceivable road in that country. Public transportation in general seemed much better in Mexico than in the United States.

In Guaymas I learned that the big auto ferry that ran across the Gulf of California to Santa Rosalia on the Baja peninsula would be leaving a day and a half later. I spent the time exploring the area. Even though I was three hundred miles below the border, almost all the birds were of species common around San Diego or Tucson. But the ferry ride, a long afternoon trip, was more rewarding. On the latter part of the crossing, well within Baja waters, I saw those long-winged tropical fishers, the Blue-footed Boobies. More exciting to me were a couple of pairs of Craveri's Murrelets. These little divers were the southernmost of the alcid family, like outcasts from the alcid stronghold in the cold Bering Sea.

The ferry reached Santa Rosalia after dark, and I caught the next bus south early the following morning. The ride to the southern end of the peninsula lasted the entire day and most of the night. All day, watching out the bus windows, I saw mile after mile of arid plains, rocky slopes, jagged hills; an ever-changing panoply of cactus gardens, with bristling little cholla, tall columnar cardón, and a plethora of bizarre spiny plants whose names I could not guess. This had to be the most magnificent desert in the world. When darkness fell and the full moon rose in the east, a partial eclipse whittled away the edge of the moon's disk for an hour or two. Even though the cause of the eclipse was, of course, out in space, I was inclined to link it to the strange surroundings through which we were traveling.

Joe Taylor had recommended a birding spot in far southern Baja, south of La Paz, along a minor dirt road running northeast from the town of San Antonio. After a local bus dropped me off at San Antonio, late morning on December 10, I spent the next twenty-four hours carefully birding along a stretch of about three or four miles. The "road" followed the course of a stream that mostly ran underground through arid hills. Here and there, where the water came to the surface, plant growth was lush and birds were abundant.

To judge by the birdlife, this could have been an exceptionally rich desert wash in southwestern Arizona in late fall. Ash-throated Flycatchers and cardinals and mockingbirds were common on the dry hillsides, and I saw a couple of Black-chinned Sparrows. An occasional flock of White-winged Doves raced by overhead. Where water broke the surface of the streambed and palm trees lined the banks, there were Scott's Orioles and noisy Gila Woodpeckers. At dusk on the tenth, as I tried to find a good place to sleep on the stony ground, I was sure I heard Elf Owls calling a few times from the desert slopes.

Everywhere in brushy places there were migrant birds, down from the north, evidently here to spend the winter. Green-tailed Towhees mewed like kittens from the dense undergrowth. Gray Flycatchers perched in the open, scanning for gnats. Flocks of Brewer's Sparrows ranged the hills. Where green growth was thick, near open water, there were Wilson's Warblers, Lincoln's Sparrows, Lazuli Buntings, and others.

It could have been just another great Arizona birding spot — except for the abundant Xantus's Hummingbirds. These were Baja specialties that I had hoped to see. Colorful, noisy, they proved to be among the most conspicuous birds along the stream. Often I saw them sparring in midair, chasing away smaller hummingbirds that I guessed to be Costa's, or feeding at the yellow blooms of the tree-tobacco plants. When they hovered overhead, their chestnut-orange tail feathers glowed in the sun.

How unfortunate, I thought as I watched them, that so few birders were likely to come here in the future. Rumor had it that the rulemakers in the American Birding Association were soon going to delete Greenland, Bermuda, and Baja from the North

American listing area. If that were true, then in future account-ings of my 1973 list, these Baja birds would not "count." That was all right. But it was sad to think of the thousands of birders in the future who might not have the incentive to bird the peninsula.

It did not matter to me what country I was in. Bird-list regions, like political regions, were just human inventions. The birds were wonderful, regardless of where you saw them. It was silly, I told myself, to be preoccupied with how a bird's location was related to some artificial boundary.

Ironically, though, just a week later, I would be wildly excited about a specific bird, just because it happened to be a quarter-mile beyond a significant border.

By the time I came back from Baja in mid-December, only one bird remained as a likely addition to my year list: that elusive gnome of the marshes, the Black Rail.

And I knew just where to find it. A year earlier, Bob Witzeman had told me that Black Rails had been discovered recently along the lower Colorado River, near Yuma, on the Arizona-California border. "They're present all year," Bob had told me. "If you're still missing Black Rail by December, you can get it on the river."

This confident prediction had been true enough when it was

Xantus's Hummingbird at tree tobacco

made, but in the intervening twelve months Bob had spent much of his time fighting the government agencies that had suddenly proposed draining and/or spraying the marshes. (It was one of his first skirmishes: birding was leading Bob Witzeman into the role of environmentalist. Protecting the Black Rail was his first concern, but it evolved into a determination to protect the entire marsh system, and then other southwestern habitats.) So far, Bob had prevailed; the rails were still there.

So after crossing the border back into Arizona, after participating in the Phoenix Christmas Bird Count again, I rode over to the Colorado River with Bob and Janet Witzeman. They were going to take part in the Yuma Christmas Count, which straddled the river, half in Arizona and half in California. My first plan was to just pick up the Black Rail and backtrack immediately for Texas, but the Witzemans talked me into agreeing that I would stay another day and take part in the Yuma count. I think Janet steadfastly believed that, having seen so many birds, I was under a moral obligation to help on as many counts as possible.

So on count day, I wound up birding the California side with the compiler, Dr. Steve Liston. As usual, the Colorado River marshes and brushlands were productive. The Black Rail at West Pond was one of the first birds of the day, just before sunrise: in response to my borrowed tape recorder, the rail gave its curious little "growl" call and even approached closely enough for me to glimpse it through the marsh grass. From West Pond we worked our way slowly north along the river.

As usual on the lower Colorado, the heat was oppressive, the sun a little too fierce to look natural over the river marshes. We birded one area after another, thoroughly, methodically. Around noon we drove down to a little park at the west end of Imperial Dam, Phil Swing Park, and sat in the car eating lunch.

On the park's palm-lined triangle of lawn, a hundred yards away, three White-crowned Sparrows and a robin were drinking from a puddle. Steve commented that it was an exceptional year for American Robins; we had been seeing them all day.

Suddenly, something about the park bothered me, a feeling I could not quite place. Something was wrong here — but what? I looked around the park again. The three sparrows and the robin were still at the puddle, and I put my binocs on them. The sparrows? They were distant, and the light was bad, but it was obvious they were all White-crowns. The robin? Well . . .

If this were Arizona, it would be almost worthwhile to walk over and check on the robin, to see if it might be the Mexican species, Rufous-backed Robin. From a distance, Rufous-backs could look a lot like American Robins. I had seen one in Tucson in January, my first really rare bird of the year. In Arizona, one or two individuals of the species were being seen every winter now. But this was California. Rufous-backed Robin had never been recorded in California.

I got out of the car, feeling a little dizzy. *Must be the sun,* I told myself.

An elderly couple, strolling across the park, put the birds to flight. The robin flashed up into a palm tree. And I could not help myself — I had to go take a closer look at that bird. It was sure to be just my imagination, or the bad angle of light, but something was making that robin look odd. I think I mumbled at Steve: "Hey, come on, man, I want to look at something . . ." and set off at a rapid trudge across the park.

Standing under the palm tree, looking up among the fronds, I could not even find the bird at first. Had it flown? Circling the tree, I tried for a better angle. Then a movement caught my eye . . .

We were only ten miles north of Mexico, and only a quarter of a mile west of Arizona. But because of that coincidence of artificial boundaries, the phones were going to ring and the birders were going to converge on this spot. The bird peering down at me from among the palm fronds was the first Rufous-backed Robin ever for the state of California.

Close to the End

"Now you can die happy," Janet Witzeman told me.

I couldn't resist teasing. "Thanks a lot," I said. "Trying to get rid of me, now that your Christmas Count is over?"

"You know what I mean. You've done something now, something to be proud of. Your Big Year — and finding a first for California. It's an accomplishment."

But was it? Had I accomplished anything? I wondered about that during the next two days, as I took to the road one more time, heading for the upper Texas coast.

I must have been a disappointing rider for the drivers who picked me up in those last days, near the end of the year: lost in thought, I probably failed to make much conversation. But I was tired of hitchhiking — tired of the small talk that was repeated, with minor variations, on virtually every ride. By my rough calculations I had thumbed my way some 69,000 miles that year, on top of many thousands over the preceding three years, riding with many hundreds of drivers. I was grateful to them all. But I was tired of being grateful. Now I never wanted to get a free ride, or a free anything else, ever again. I wanted to work for every inch, pay for every mile.

Had I accomplished anything? That was a good question. Maybe I had set a record — if it meant anything to set a record in a sport that had few fans, no professionals, and no referees.

Or maybe I was an also-ran. There was no way to know. Somewhere out there, Floyd Murdoch was still seeking Bohemian Waxwing, which I had seen in Alaska in July; he might also get word of some fantastic rarity someplace, and jump a plane to go see it. Floyd still had potential new birds to list. I did not. Black Rail had been my last serious possibility for the year in North America.

Now Mexico beckoned, with the promise of dazzling tropical birdlife, a world of birds that I could enjoy without having to focus on list-keeping. I would heed the call before December ended and start the new year in the teeming birdland of southern Veracruz. But first I had an appointment with birding tradition.

A few years earlier, as an energetic teenager, Victor Emanuel had started a Christmas Bird Count at Freeport, Texas. With his organizing, planning, and recruiting, he had made it one of the top counts in the nation. In 1971, close to the end of his Big Year, Ted Parker had taken part in the count; that year, naturally, Freeport had set an all-time national high, with 226 species. Although I could not expect any additions to my year list there, I would go to Freeport for tradition, and for fun.

So it was back across Interstate 10 one more time, and then angling down a series of state highways toward the coast, to avoid the Houston-to-Galveston traffic. As we approached Freeport and the coast, the horizon was filled with tall oil tanks, chemical tanks, steel towers for powerlines, factory buildings, dozens of smokestacks, and derricks and cranes for ongoing construction. It looked like some bad dream of a science-fiction future. I was just as amazed as when I had passed this way the preceding April: amazed that Victor Emanuel had been able to see past this surface ugliness, to see that the surrounding habitats would add up to the most diverse Christmas Bird Count circle in North America.

Past this techno-scape, over the high bridge across the Intra-coastal Waterway, the highway came down to the beach at Surf-side. Victor had reserved an A-frame house on the beach as a rendezvous point and accommodations for the counters. When I arrived, late in the afternoon, hardly anyone was there: the earlier arrivals were out scouting the count circle. As daylight faded they drifted in, dozens of birders, from all over Texas and from farther afield.

Victor Emanuel was radiating energy as he orbited around the room, welcoming all the counters, discussing the prospects for the morrow, planning where to position the available observers. Jim Tucker arrived, and we talked about our Big Day exploits from the preceding April, the Kenmare convention in June, and things that had happened since. Rose Ann and Pelican came in, all smiles and good cheer as usual, brightening the A-frame with their presence. They had failed to drag the hard-working Edgar Kincaid away from his desk to take part in the count, but to demonstrate his support he had sent along his best wishes and his good telescope.

We ate that night in a seafood diner just down the beach from the A-frame, a place called the Shrimp Hut, where the waitresses wore little mock sailor suits. Dozens of birders were there. An air of cheerful confusion reigned. In the midst of it all, Victor was still debating, planning, organizing, trying to find the perfect al-lotment of birders to birding areas. This count circle contained so many patches of different habitats, each with a different poten-tial. Counters had to be assigned to the old groves of live oak, to the willow-saltcedar thickets, to the marshes, to the open fields, to the suburbs with their feeders, and so on. I could hear Victor giving out final assignments, mentioning some of the key birds to watch for, telling each person how important his or her par-ticular area was. When Victor got to me, he had an inspired look in his eye.

"Western Kingbird!" he said, greeting me by my Texas bird name. "We have an excellent assignment for you, if you're willing. This is a Noble Task. There are certain seabirds that are probably present offshore every year; but we rarely record them. We need someone with stamina and skill to stand out at the end of the Freeport jetty all day, watching for pelagics."

Sure, I thought, kids from Kansas are always good at seabirds. But I was complimented. "Yeah, I'll do it."

"You'll need a telescope," Peli told me. "Why don't you take Edgar Kincaid's scope? Rosie and I will be in the woods, so we won't need it."

"Just make sure you don't drop it in the water," Rose Ann added. We all laughed.

Morning came to the A-frame as a chorus of rustlings and shufflings, as people crawled out of their sleeping bags in the dark and started off to reach their birding areas by first light. I lingered in the warm blankets a while — there was no point in looking for seabirds in the dark — but as soon as gray dawn lit the windows, I shoved my backpack into a corner and started off alone down the beach.

A gusty cold wind was blowing under a dark and restless sky. The pale sand beach was deserted except for a few Sanderlings, nervously skittering ahead of me. Behind the dunes the tawny beach grass whipped in the wind, and the wooden houses on stilts looked shuttered up and empty.

In the mile between the A-frame and the base of the jetty, as I was waking up more thoroughly, I began to notice just how loud the ocean was. The jumbled gray peaks of the waves turned to brown as they roiled up silt in the shallows, and then to white as they smashed on the beach. Big waves were visible as far out as I could see, all the way to where the gray ocean blended into gray sky; the lack of any stable horizon gave an unsettled feeling to the scene.

The Freeport jetty was a massive pile of stone blocks, incredibly long, extending perhaps half a mile out to sea. A similar jetty paralleled it a few hundred yards away; between the two ran the ship channel that led to the inner harbor. No boats seemed to be traversing the channel today.

Looking out along the jetty, I could see waves breaking violently out near the end. *Hot rats*, I thought; *it's no wonder they can't usually get anyone to go out there*. I was too unfamiliar with the area to realize just how much the weather had worsened since the afternoon before. *Well, this is the West*, I said to myself; *I'm not going to chicken out on my assignment*. There was no point in hesitating. The big gray slabs of stone that formed the center of the jetty were almost level, and I started out toward the end, leaping from rock to rock, in a hurry now to get out there and man my post.

Out at the very tip of the jetty, I found a solid place to station myself, a huge level block of stone. Planting the tripod firmly on the rock, I aimed Edgar Kincaid's telescope out to sea. I was determined that no seabird would slip past me unnoticed. Alternating between scanning with binoculars and sweeping the distant waves with the telescope, I began my day's vigil.

It was good to be just birding, just looking to see what was there, not trying to build any personal list. At the precount gathering the night before, so many people had been asking, "Could you get any new year birds tomorrow?" "Do you think you'll win the Big Year competition?" It was impossible to explain to them that I really did not care anymore.

The Big Year had been a great excuse to go birding. To both Floyd Murdoch and me, that had mattered more than the numerical outcome. All along, Floyd had been more interested in the protection of birds and their habitats than in the accumulation of checkmarks. As for me, my own passion for list-chasing was dwindling fast, while my interest in the birds themselves was becoming stronger than ever. So the contest was coming to matter least of all to the contestants.

The whistling wind that flapped my poncho around also drove each breaker against the base of the jetty at my feet. The waves seemed to be getting bigger. I was being misted with spray from every wave now, and some of them broke high enough that water washed around the soles of my beat-up hiking boots. As a whimsical precaution, I tied the drawstring of my poncho to the tripod that held the borrowed telescope.

Gulls were tacking into the wind, hanging on updrafts where the gusts were deflected by the jetty, streaking downwind on backswept wings like errant boomerangs. They were wonderful to watch, but did I really know them? All the North American species of gulls were on my list, so I should have recognized each one here with confidence. But I didn't. Not really. In the past I had always checked them off by finding the adults in their distinctive plumages, ignoring most of the motley younger birds. So, what were all these young gulls flying past now? I thought they were probably all Ring-bills and Herring Gulls; but if something rare had been among them, I would not have recognized it. I still had a lot to learn.

One thing was becoming obvious to me now: list-chasing was not the best way to learn birds. It had been a good way to start, an incentive for getting to a lot of places and seeing a lot of species. But the lure of running up a big list made it all too tempting to simply check off a bird and run on to the next, without taking time to really get to know them. And there was so much that I did not know.

So much left to learn . . . And one other lesson was sinking in, near the end of 1973, as I ran into the expectations of other birders. Just because I had broken listing records, they expected me to be a top-notch birder — and I was not. They were comparing me to Ted Parker, who had set the record just two years before — but there was really no comparison. None of us realized then just how fast the world of bird listing had been changing. Indeed, the entire approach to doing a Big Year had been undergoing a radical change.

Ted Parker had set his record in 1971 on the strength of sheer skill and knowledge and energy. For me, as for Floyd Murdoch, the mix had involved less skill and a lot more information: just two years had made that much difference, as the fledgling American Birding Association had broadcast the directions to dozens of good sites for scarce birds. The totals amassed by Murdoch and me would be edged out in 1976, as a young ornithology student named Scott Robinson made a low-budget, high-knowledge run around the continent. But that would be the last time that any record could be set by a birder who focused on the normally occurring birds.

The information explosion, in birding as in everything else, was bringing us more and more data, faster and faster. The new bird-finding booklets let us know about good birding spots that had been productive within the last five or ten years. The notes and inserts in *Birding* gave us specific sites that had been productive within the last year or so, even within the last few months. But before long, the burgeoning communication among birders would bring news of rarities that were *really* current: found today, even found within the last few hours.

A couple of times in 1973 I had heard about rare visitors in time to go and look for them, like the Loggerhead Kingbird that had spent the whole winter in Florida. But before the end of the 1970s, the growth of birding "hotlines" would make it possible for birders to find out about such strays almost instantly. A birder with money could then jump on the next flight, rent a car, and check off a bird that he had never even heard of just a few hours earlier. It was inevitable that Big Year listing would come to focus more and more on such rarities. Listing would shift away from knowledge and planning and experience, toward contacts and hotlines and money.

And, no doubt, it would continue to be a tremendous amount of fun for those who could afford it, the greatest of games. But list-chasing had lost most of its appeal for me. What I needed to do now was to go back and look at all those birds again, taking more time.

By now the sea was in a frenzy all around my perch near the

end of the jetty. The waves were still coming from ahead and to my right. I could not see them approaching as individual waves, only as a dance of whitecaps, but I could tell each time one arrived, running *wham!* into the massive rocks and sending up a curtain of spray. If I looked quickly back along the jetty I could see how the angle of the breaker would run itself out against the line of rocks, and at the same time I would feel the water from the spent wave washing over my feet. Gradually it was coming to me that this must be unusual weather, and that perhaps I should move back a little from the end of the jetty. But I would take one more scan out over the ocean first.

Gulls had been flying past the jetty and out over the whitecaps, but scanning farther out I suddenly picked up one that looked different. With a start, I realized it was a species I could recognize with certainty, one I'd seen by the thousands in Alaska: a Black-legged Kittiwake, a rare bird in Texas, the kind of prize that Victor had hoped would come out of my vigil on the jetty. I strained to follow it in the telescope as the wind rocked me and spray stung my eyes.

Seeing the kittiwake brought back sudden images of Gambell, Alaska, the magical place that I had visited half a year and most of a continent earlier. Perhaps my Big Year attempt had no value in itself, but it had led me to incredible places, a whole series of extraordinary destinations. It had taken me through life-changing experiences. Regardless of final list totals, it had been worthwhile.

Listing, at its best, could be a wonderful quest, I reflected. We list-chasing birders, at our best, could be like knights seeking the Holy Grail — except that the birds were real, and we birders were rewarded at every turn. If we made an honest effort, the birds would come. This kittiwake, appearing out of the storm like a winged messenger, seemed to confirm that. Inspired, I began another scan of the ocean.

Just then I felt another wave washing over my feet, tugging at my ankles. The breakers were obviously getting higher. Despite all my macho intentions, common sense was insisting that I really should move back a little. But at that moment, I picked up something flying far out over the horizon. A dark gull, flapping hard — No! it was a jaeger, another bird that would be a great addition to the count. But which kind? With difficulty I found it in the telescope and struggled to see field marks. White flashes at the bend of the wing, dark chest band; could be either Pomarine or Parasitic. Salt stung my eyes and I lost the bird, still undecided about which it was. But maybe I could find it again. I would take one more scan —

The next wave rumbled up onto the jetty, and I could feel that this would be a big one. Instinctively I flexed my knees to brace against the current, but it was futile. With a sense of unreality I felt my feet slipping, and then I was sliding sideways, flailing for the telescope, tumbling off the top of the jetty. My shoulder hit a rock with a tooth-rattling crunch, and then I was gulping salt water and thrashing in the cold green darkness.

When I came to the surface I was looking up at the jetty, now seeming to tower above me, several yards away. My tattered jeans and boots were heavy as lead, and my poncho wrapped around my arms like a shroud, but when I reached for the poncho drawstring that had been tied to the tripod and scope I felt nothing — the cord had pulled free, and the telescope was gone.

Another wave crashed over the top of the jetty, and I was underwater again. Floundering toward the boulders at the jetty's base, I grabbed them and pulled myself up. The rocks were covered with barnacles, and their razor edges sliced my palms. Surprised, I loosened my grip, and another wave knocked me off again.

Treading water heavily, I tried to think rationally about what to do. The sharp little cones of barnacles appeared to cover every inch of the jetty rocks near water level. For a moment I considered trying to swim to shore, but the beach was so far away; I doubted I could swim that far in my sodden clothes. I had to go up the rocks to survive.

Twice more I tried to climb the rough boulders. Twice more, waves coming over the top of the jetty knocked me loose, sending me sliding down, barnacles ripping my palms and the knees of my jeans. But finally I was able to clamber up to the top of the jetty, above the level of the barnacles. Slowly, half crouching and half crawling, clinging to the rough rocks when each wave broke, I made my way back toward shore. It seemed like an eternity before I was finally standing on the beach again.

My hands were bleeding and stinging so badly that I could not even hold my binoculars. There was no point in looking for assistance at the deserted houses behind the line of dunes. Then I remembered the Shrimp Hut, up the beach near the A-frame, where the group had had dinner the night before. Maybe it was open today. Shivering now in the cold wind, I walked back in that direction.

The waitresses in the Shrimp Hut were shocked by my appearance — and no wonder. As unkempt as I usually looked, I was now also sopping wet, bleeding, and probably wild-eyed. But when they saw my hands, their expressions changed. Although the waitresses were no older than I, their maternal instincts seemed to take over. They sat me down, washed and soaked and bandaged my hands, and even spoon-fed me some warm soup. Silently I rebuked myself for having laughed at their mock sailor uniforms the night before; regardless of their uniforms, they looked like angels to me now.

I tried to pay for the bandages and the soup, but they refused the wet dollar bills I fished out of my wallet. So I thanked them again and turned to leave.

"You're not going back out on the jetty, are you?"

"I have to," I said. "This is our big bird count."

Trudging back up the beach, I hardly noticed that the waves still pounded the sand, the wind still gusted and cried; I was inured to the weather. Once again I picked my way out onto the jetty, jumping from rock to rock, gauging how far I could go in safety. A little more than halfway out, just before the first stretch where the waves began to get bad, I took my stand.

You're not going back out there, are you? But of course I was. It was the only thing to do. The certainty of that decision gave me a sense of calm. In the midst of the turbulent sea and sky, I was overcome by a great feeling of peace: I was doing exactly what I was meant to do today. *Any day could be a special day, and you just had to get outside, and see what the birds were doing . . .* Birding is what I came here for; this is how I spend this day and my days and my life.

The borrowed telescope was gone, my hands were bandaged, and my cheap binoculars were clouded with salt water, but I was keeping my vigil. I could still see rare seabirds if they came in close. As the afternoon waned, the sun might find a break in the clouds, and then it would be low in the western sky behind me — flooding everything in front of me with perfect light.

Somewhere out there, maybe not too far away, jaegers were coursing over the waves. They might come this way again. I was sure they would. Experience had shown me that jaegers and other seabirds might come in closer to shore early in the morning and then again late in the afternoon and evening. Surely in this stormy weather they would come in close. I would be here, ready, when they came.

The Freeport jetty

Now, when I look back many years later, as though from a great distance, I can still see that young man standing out on the jetty. And at least on my better days, I can see myself standing there with him: shaken by experience, perhaps, but still confident that the light will be better, that the birds will come in closer, that we will see everything more clearly at last, before the day is over.

Notes on List Totals

SOME BIRDERS, I know, will consider this book incomplete if I omit the results of the 1973 year-list "contest." One simple answer would be to say that Floyd Murdoch won: in the region that would become the official checklist area of the American Birding Association, he tallied 669 species, three more than I. However, many birders in 1973 were still using the old checklist area of the American Ornithologists' Union, which included Baja California; my five Baja birds brought my list up to 671.

These totals were calculated according to how species were classified at the beginning of 1973. By the end of the year (as I described in the chapter "The Fall of a Sparrow"), scientists had "lumped" certain species together. More lumping followed later in the 1970s, and our list totals dropped each time. However, by the 1980s, changes in scientific opinion led to several rounds of "splitting," with more local forms being recognized as full species. If we had cared, Floyd Murdoch and I could have gone back to recalculate our lists each time. Fortunately, by then the point was moot.

In 1979, a Mississippi businessman proved once and for all that a big list does not make a top birder. Freely admitting that he was a novice, he hired experts to plan his trips and show him the birds, and he ended the year with a list of 699 species. Since then, several birders have had Big Year totals over 700. They report that year listing is still a lot of fun, but that it has become very expensive.

I did set one record in 1973 that may never be broken — in the category of "birds per buck." My *total* living and traveling expenses for the year came to less than a thousand dollars, and nearly half of that amount went for a couple of plane flights in Alaska; most of the time I was getting by on less than a dollar per day. I know of some others who have practiced similarly draconian levels of economy while birding a particular region (such as Rich Stallcup in California, and various dedicated "twitchers" in Britain), but few have been crazy enough to even attempt it on a continent-wide scale.

Acknowledgments

I WROTE the first draft of this book in 1974 and 1975, while the experience was fresh in my mind. That first draft was dismally bad; I tossed it in a box and essentially forgot about it for fifteen years, while I worked on other bird-related projects. When I finally pulled out the draft and started working on it again, I received tremendous help from Harry Foster's wise and perceptive editing, which improved all aspects of the text and taught me some new things about the craft of writing. Shannon Davies also provided some improvements, and Suzanne Winckler gave me some good suggestions and historical corrections. The manuscript benefited from final polishing by Lisa White, an editor of consummate intelligence and skill. Thanks also to ace designer Anne Chalmers, who created this book's interior design.

In writing about an experience spanning more than a year, one cannot include every event or every person involved. For example, it would not be possible for me to acknowledge all the people who gave me rides during my vagabond years. I have to be slightly amazed that they picked me up, considering how disreputable I looked during that period: besides the effect of my unkempt long hair and scruffy clothes, I always had funny-looking binoculars hanging around my neck. (They *did* look funny. One night early in my travels I had had a dream about a birder who rode through the West, identifying everything in sight, and his binoculars were made of gold. The next day I had bought some cheap gold enamel and painted mine. The gold soon faded to a sickly greenish yellow.) Certainly I owe my thanks to all these drivers.

In addition, the following people all helped me in important ways during or just before the time described here, even if they did not make it into the book: J. R. and Sara Bader, Nancy Benninger, D'Anna Briggs, Wally Champeny, Jeff Cox, Ben Feltner, Larry Gray, George E. ("Terry") Hall, Dan Hardy, Isobel Hicks, Dan Kilby, Leslie Kinder, Gene and Eulalia Lewis, Lee Nellis, Fred Newman, Betty Phinney, Carol Pohl, Paul Pratt, Terry Pratt, John Rowlett, Fritz Scheider, Wayne Shifflett, Bob Smart, Donna Smith, Sally and Walter Spofford, Sheri Stiles, Chason Sundberg, Dixie Swanson, Clem Tillion, Ralph Wiley, Jan and Pat Witmer, Julie Wren, and probably some others that I have neglected to mention. I appreciate them all.

I can never say enough to thank my parents, John Yates Kaufman and Joan Bader Kaufman, who had the faith to let me go and follow my own dream. With their words and their deeds, they taught me the strong values that sustained me in my early travels and through all the years since. I can only hope that someday I will live up to the examples they set.

Finally, heartfelt thanks to Lynn, who came along several years after the events described in this book had ended. She had to be exceptionally patient while I was revising my old original manuscript; in order to keep the story authentic, I had to put myself back into a mental state from my past, so that I was thinking like a nineteen-year-old for weeks at a time. When I apologized to her for that, she gave me a bemused look and said, "But what's different about that? You *usually* think like a teenager." I'm not sure exactly what she meant, but I've decided to take it as a compliment.